Jobs and Careers With Nonprofit Organizations
Profitable Opportunities With Nonprofits

Ronald L. Krannich, Ph.D.
Caryl Rae Krannich, Ph.D.

Second Edition

IMPACT PUBLICATIONS
Manassas Park, VA

Jobs & Careers With Nonprofit Organizations

Copyright © 1999, 1996 by Ronald L. Krannich and Caryl Rae Krannich. All rights reserved. Printed in the United States of America. No part of this book may be used or reproduced in any manner whatsoever without written permission of the publisher: IMPACT PUBLICATIONS, 9104-N Manassas Drive, Manassas Park, VA 20111-5211, Tel. 703/361-7300.

Library of Congress Cataloguing-in-Publication Data

Krannich, Ronald L.
    Jobs and careers with nonprofit organizations: profitable opportunities with nonprofits / Ronald L. Krannich, Caryl Rae Krannich.—2nd ed.
        p. cm.
    Includes bibliographical references and index.
    ISBN 1-57023-084-6
        1. Nonprofit organizations–Vocational guidance–United States.
    2. Associations, institutions, etc.–Vocational guidance–United States.
    3. Nonprofit organizations–United States–Employees. 4. Associations, institutions, etc.–United States–Employees. I. Krannich, Caryl Rae.
    II. Title.
    HD2769.2.U6K7   1999   98-48609
    361.7'02—dc21   CIP

Publisher: For information on Impact Publications, including current and forthcoming publications, authors, press kits, online bookstore, and submission requirements, visit Impact's Web site: *www.impactpublications.com*

Publicity/Rights: For information on publicity, author interviews, and subsidiary rights, contact the Public Relations Department: Tel. 703/361-7300.

Sales/Distribution: All bookstore sales are handled through Impact's trade distributor: National Book Network, 15200 NBN Way, Blue Ridge Summit, PA 17214, Tel. 1-800-462-6420. All other sales and distribution inquiries should be directed to the publisher: Sales Department, IMPACT PUBLICATIONS, 9104-N Manassas Drive, Manassas Park, VA 20111-5211, Tel. 703/361-7300, Fax 703/335-9486, or Email *nonprofit@impactpublications.com*

JOBS AND CAREERS WITH NONPROFIT ORGANIZATIONS

Books and CD-ROMs by Drs. Ron and Caryl Krannich

101 Dynamite Answers to Interview Questions
101 Secrets of Highly Effective Speakers
201 Dynamite Job Search Letters
Best Jobs For the 21st Century
Change Your Job, Change Your Life
The Complete Guide to International Jobs and Careers
The Complete Guide to Public Employment
The Directory of Federal Jobs and Employers
Discover the Best Jobs For You!
Dynamite Cover Letters
Dynamite Networking For Dynamite Jobs
Dynamite Résumés
Dynamite Salary Negotiations
Dynamite Tele-Search
The Educator's Guide to Alternative Jobs and Careers
Find a Federal Job Fast
From Air Force Blue to Corporate Gray
From Army Green to Corporate Gray
From Navy Blue to Corporate Gray
Get a Raise in 7 Days
High Impact Résumés and Letters
International Jobs Directory
Interview For Success
Job-Power Source CD-ROM
Jobs and Careers With Nonprofit Organizations
Jobs For People Who Love Travel
Mayors and Managers
Moving Out of Education
Moving Out of Government
The Politics of Family Planning Policy
Re-Careering in Turbulent Times
Résumés and Job Search Letters For Transitioning Military Personnel
Shopping and Traveling in Exotic Asia
Shopping in Exciting Australia and Papua New Guinea
Shopping in Exotic Places
Shopping the Exotic South Pacific
Treasures and Pleasures of Australia
Treasures and Pleasures of China
Treasures and Pleasures of Hong Kong
Treasures and Pleasures of India
Treasures and Pleasures of Indonesia
Treasures and Pleasures of Italy
Treasures and Pleasures of Paris and the French Riviera
Treasures and Pleasures of Singapore and Malaysia
Treasures and Pleasures of Thailand
Ultimate Job Source CD-ROM

Contents

- The Nonprofit Sector 1
- Going Nonprofit 2
- Neither Public Nor Private 3
- Opportunities Closer Than You Think 3
- What Is a Nonprofit? 5
- Positions and Skills Sought 15
- Choose the Right Resources 16
- Empower Yourself in the Nonprofit World 17

- Myths and Realities 19
- Positives and Negatives 25
- Current Trends 28

Responsibilities and Context

While we have attempted to provide accurate information in this book, please be advised that names, addresses, and phone and fax numbers do change and that organizations do move and go out of business. This is especially true for organizations located in the New York City and Washington, DC metropolitan areas. Service and program orientations may also change. We regret any inconvenience such changes may cause to your job search.

If you have difficulty contacting a particular organization included in this book, please do one or all of the following:

- Check several Internet gateway sites to nonprofit organizations which are identified in Chapter 5 as well as use various Internet search engines or directories to locate the organization.

- Consult the latest edition of the *Business Phone Book USA* or call Information for current phone numbers.

- Contact the Information section of your local library for online services or directories with the latest contact information.

Inclusion of organizations in this book in no way implies endorsements by the authors or Impact Publications. The recommendations are provided solely for your reference. It is the reader's responsibility to contact, evaluate, and follow-through with employers.

The names, addresses, phone numbers, and services appearing here provide one important component for conducting a successful job search amongst nonprofit organizations. Placed within the larger context of an effective job search, this component should be carefully linked to your self-assessment, research, networking, and resume writing and distribution activities. Such contact information should never be used for mass mailing resumes—the most ineffective way to find a job!

Preface

Get ready for a new nonprofit world in the decade ahead. It's likely to be more active, responsive, and effective than ever before. Indeed, the coming decade should be one of the most challenging and exciting periods for nonprofit organizations. As governments at all levels "reinvent" themselves through downsizing and decentralization, many of the social welfare, education, environmental, consumer protection, and entitlement programs that evolved since the 1930s will be significantly modified, if not eliminated altogether. While governments may contract-out some downsized programs to nonprofit organizations, many programs will simply disappear.

Nonprofit organizations play very significant roles at the local, state, regional, and national levels. They represent well defined interests, conduct research, provide direct services, and lobby for legislation. Representing thousands of employers, these organizations especially appeal to individuals who are passionately committed to a cause, enjoy pursuing public issues, and love their work. While you may not get rich working for a nonprofit organization, your life most likely will be forever enriched by the experience.

As both governments and businesses continue to downsize their personnel and programs, nonprofit organizations will most likely grow. Providing new and expanded services, nonprofits will need to hire more competent personnel as well as better mobilize and manage their limited financial resources. Nonprofit jobs that once served as stepping-stones to jobs in government and business will increasingly become important career tracks within the nonprofit world. We expect more and more individuals to pursue long-term and profitable careers with nonprofit organizations.

If many of our predictions come true, we expect nonprofits will increasingly become important employment arenas for job seekers who would normally turn to government or business for career opportunities. Individuals first entering the job market will look to nonprofit organizations for their first job and then advance or change their careers by moving on to other organizations within the nonprofit world. Others who work for government and business will turn to the nonprofit world for new job opportunities or to change careers.

The following pages provide a glimpse into one of today's least understood but most important employment arenas. Standing between government and business, nonprofit organizations offer millions of job opportunities for individuals interested in the type of work performed by these organizations. The first six chapters examine the structure of the nonprofit world as well as outline job search strategies appropriate for these types of organizations. The remaining three chapters provide brief descriptions and contact information on more than 300 nonprofit organizations, including several major nonprofits that primarily operate in the international arena.

Our organizations by no means represent the larger nonprofit world. Instead, we've included organizations as **examples** of the types of employers and information you will likely encounter once you launch your own job search within the nonprofit world.

Throughout this book we recommend several key resources for conducting your own research on nonprofit organizations. We cannot over-emphasize the importance of familiarizing yourself with these resources early in your job search. Indeed, we strongly urge you to use the Internet and visit your local library immediately—within hours of examining this book—to acquaint yourself with many of these resources, especially several key Web sites and recommended directories. Only if you use this book in conjunction with these other resources will you put yourself in the best position to find a nonprofit job that is right for you.

We wish you well as you navigate your job search through the fascinating world of nonprofits. If you follow our tips and use our recommended resources properly, you should be well on your way to finding a job that may lead to a long-term career with nonprofits.

Ron and Caryl Krannich

Jobs And Careers With Nonprofit Organizations

The Nonprofit Job World

H ave you ever had a job you felt passionate about, one that really made a significant difference in the lives of others? If you've had such a job, you know it feels much different from many run-of-the-mill, profit-driven jobs that take you back and forth to an office to do the bosses' work, collect paychecks, and perhaps get promoted to other positions with greater responsibilities for pushing the bottomline.

If you've never had such a job, perhaps you'll want to join millions of others who have discovered a unique world of jobs that combines passion with purpose—the nonprofit arena. That's the central purpose of this book—put you in touch with an exciting and profitable job world driven by both passion and purpose.

The Nonprofit Sector

Where can you find over 1,000,000 organizations that spend more than $500 billion a year and employ nearly 10 million Americans? Closer to you than you may think. You'll probably find them just down the street or across town. They seem to be everywhere you turn.

Largely neglected by job seekers, nonprofit organizations comprise a kind of "hidden job market" with low visibility and questionable reputation. Indeed, many job seekers are either unaware of these organizations or they avoid them altogether because of their "tin cup" image—beggar organizations in constant need of funding and offering meager salaries.

But nonprofits are found everywhere—in neighborhoods and communities across the country as well as abroad. They comprise a huge complex of organizations focusing on some of today's most exciting issues, dealing with many of today's most passionate problems, and representing some of the nation's most powerful interests. Collectively known as the "nonprofit sector," these organizations offer some of today's most rewarding job opportunities. Best of all, they hire hundreds of people each day. Many require basic skills and little experience while others seek individuals with high level skills and experience. Chances are you qualify for a profitable job in nonprofits.

> **Many job seekers are either unaware of these organizations or they avoid them because of their "tin cup" image–beggars in constant need of funding and offering meager salaries.**

Going Nonprofit

So you think you might want to work in the nonprofit world. But what exactly is a nonprofit organization? How do they differ from government agencies or business firms? What type of work do they do? What skills and experience do they require? What motivational patterns are best suited for these types of organizations? What types of positions do they offer? What are some of the positives and negatives of working for these organizations? Do jobs with nonprofits lead to career advancement? How much do they pay? How secure are nonprofit jobs? Where can I find vacancies? Whom do I contact? How can I best land a job with a nonprofit? Are there really profitable careers with nonprofits?

These and many other questions provide a basis for examining the nonprofit employment arena. Straddling both the public and private sectors, this complex of organizations offers thousands of exciting and rewarding job opportunities for those who know the who, what, where, and how of navigating the nonprofit sector. Since nonprofits mean different things to different people, let's take a brief look at what comprises the nonprofit sector.

Neither Public Nor Private

Most people have a distorted and dichotomous view of the world of work. At the simplest level, jobs appear to be found in *either* the public or private sector. Working in the public sector usually means being employed with federal, state, or local government agencies; private sector work is normally considered to be employment in business. And business is usually equated with large Fortune 500 corporations—despite the fact that 85 percent of the population is employed by businesses having fewer than 100 employees and nearly 30 million people are self-employed. Conclusions about the state of the economy and the world of work are often shaped by these simplistic "public/private" and "large corporation" views of employment.

The public/private sector distinction misses a great deal of what really goes on in the world of work. The public sector, for example, includes many government corporations that operate like businesses. It also includes political parties and lobbying groups that primarily focus on influencing the conduct of government but which appear to be neither public nor private organizations.

Worst of all, the public/private sector distinction neglects thousands of organizations that employ over 10 million people or nearly seven percent of the population—nonprofit organizations. Being both non-governmental and non-business organizations, nonprofit organizations fall outside the purview of most job seekers' lists of potential employers. Except for an occasional scandal (the United Way and the New Era Foundation in the mid-1990s) or a major fundraising campaign (your local United Way, Red Cross, Salvation Army, or police benevolent organization), most nonprofits tend to have low public profiles. Understandably, organizations with little visibility are not well-known among job seekers. Ironically, you are probably acquainted with many nonprofits but you may not think of them as such organizations.

Opportunities Closer Than You Think

While nonprofit organizations may have a low profile amongst job seekers, most people are acquainted with these organizations by means of membership or direct contacts. Indeed, you probably belong to two or three such organizations already, or you regularly come into contact with them during the year. You may even be a card-carrying member.

If you belong to a church, it is most likely operated as a nonprofit organization. If it's a very large church, it will have full-time employees, from custodians and receptionists to word processors, accountants, and computer specialists. It may also be affiliated with a large religious service organization, such as the Catholic Relief Services or Lutheran World Relief, which spend millions of dollars each year on overseas relief, social development, and technical assistance operations.

If you belong to a labor union or a professional association, you participate in a nonprofit organization. If you're a member of the American Chemical Society or the American Bar Association, you're affiliated with two of the largest professional associations that employ hundreds of individuals.

If you donate money to the United Way, Red Cross, or the Salvation Army, you've made contact with three of the largest and most respected nonprofit organizations that provide full-time employment for thousands of individuals. The Salvation Army in particular is considered by many seasoned observers to be America's best nonprofit organization, a great model for other nonprofits.

And if you sponsor a child through Childreach or the Christian Children's Fund, help the housing poor through Habitat For Humanity, enroll your child in the Girl or Boy Scouts of America, or join the American Automobile Association (AAA), the American Association of Retired Persons (AARP), or the National Rifle Association (NRA), you participate in some of the largest and most effective organizations that define the nonprofit world.

> **During the past three years nonprofits have begun to embrace technology and get wired via the Internet.**

Most people think of nonprofit organizations as volunteer and charitable advocacy groups, but savvy job seekers know better. The nonprofit world offers numerous job opportunities for enterprising job seekers. While many such organizations do have volunteer programs, engage in charitable activities, and advocate for a particular cause, they do much more. Many of these organizations operate with large full-time staffs that handle annual budgets in excess of $25 million. Because it is a well-defined employment arena, the nonprofit world has its own employment publications and services. Best of all, during the past five years, nonprofits have begun to embrace technology and get wired via the Internet (start with these sites:

www.idealist.org, *www.nonprofitjobs.org*, *www.nonprofitcareer.com*, *www.philanthropy.com*, or *www.pj.org*). By using the Internet, you can quickly identify hundreds of nonprofits offering thousands of job opportunities. In just a few minutes of cyber-sleuthing, you may discover the perfect job that leads to a rewarding long-term career in the nonprofit sector.

Whatever you do, don't overlook nonprofit organizations as potential employers. While they may have a low public profile amongst job seekers, they offer thousands of exciting and rewarding opportunities for individuals interested in the type of work performed by nonprofits.

What Is a Nonprofit?

In strictly legal terms, a nonprofit organization is any organization that has been granted tax exempt status by the Internal Revenue Service. Under Section 501 of the Federal Tax Code, these organizations are granted tax exempt status. According to government regulations, nonprofits do not engage in profit-making commercial activities.

However, such a simple, legalistic definition has little to do with day-to-day realities of nonprofits, especially those that need to be increasingly entrepreneurial in raising funds in today's new economy. Some nonprofit organizations do indeed fit this legal definition, but many others engage in profitable commercial activities in order to fund their operations. The U.S. Committee for UNICEF, for example, sells greeting cards. The American Association of Retired Persons (AARP) and National Education Association (NEA) both sponsor profitable travel programs. Similar to major businesses, many nonprofits pay their top administrators generous salaries, extend nice corporate perks, and house their operations in attractive high-rent commercial buildings. The National Wildlife Foundation, American Automobile Association, and the American Association of Retired Persons, for example, operate very lucrative direct-mail operations, offer special health and life insurance rates, and sponsor profitable educational programs. Subsidized by the U.S. Postal Service—which permits them to use inexpensive nonprofit postal rates for running lucrative direct-mail operations and for mobilizing members to political action—many of these groups ostensibly compete with businesses.

In reality, over 1,000,000 nonprofit organizations employ more than 10 million people or approximately seven percent of the total workforce.

While many of these organizations consist of only one or two-person volunteers or part-time employees, at least 35,000 nonprofit organizations offer full-time job and career opportunities; more than 5,000 organizations have full-time staffs of ten or more people and operate large volunteer programs. Engaging in a variety of interesting activities, these organizations tackle popular public policy and social welfare issues that make them so appealing to millions of job seekers. Whether they are strictly "nonprofit" is less important than what they actually do on a day-to-day basis.

At the most general level, nonprofit organizations are neither public nor private organizations. Falling between these two groups, nonprofits are non-governmental and non-business organizations that at times behave like government and business organizations. They perform a bewildering array of functions and engage in an amazing range of public activities. Many of these organizations are at the forefront of getting major issues, such as health, education, child labor, auto safety, homelessness, AIDS, civil rights, housing, cancer, and environmental degradation, on governments' policy agendas. Many function as educational groups, foundations, charities, and trade and professional associations.

Perhaps the best way to define nonprofit organizations is to examine their specific activities, primary missions, or public passions. While nonprofit organizations come in many different forms, shapes, sizes, and orientations, most fall into these twelve categories:

1. **Private educational organizations:** Consist of private nonprofit elementary, secondary, and postsecondary educational institutions. Primarily local groups with affiliated national and international alumni.

2. **Religious organizations:** Include a wide range of religious groups, such as churches, synagogues, mosques, and evangelical organizations with small to large membership bases. Comprised of local groups which may be affiliated with larger national and international groups.

3. **Arts, cultural, historical, and community-educational organizations:** Encompass museums, opera companies, symphony orchestras, nonprofit theaters, and libraries. Primarily consist of community-based groups.

4. **Health organizations:** Include hospitals, clinics, nursing homes, and allied health care organizations involved in delivering a variety of health care services. Primarily local groups controlled by local boards of notables.

5. **Social service organizations:** This category encompass the largest number of nonprofits. These groups provide a wide range of assistance to different population groups, from the homeless, orphans, and battered spouses to the handicapped, elderly, and refugees. Primarily local groups, but many of these organizations also are affiliated with national and international parent organizations. These groups are the stereotypical charitable organizations that define the non-profit world in many peoples' minds.

6. **Advocacy and political groups:** Include such noted groups as Greenpeace, Common Cause, NAACP, and the Sierra Club. Many are national and international in scope. Focus on influencing the content of public policy through public education and political action.

7. **Business, professional, and trade/labor organizations:** Promote educational and political support activities for members. Many of these groups or associations border on being for-profit organizations. Some of the best-known such groups include the American Bar Association, American Medical Association, AFL-CIO, National Rifle Association, National Manufacturers Association, and the U.S. Chamber of Commerce. Many are national in scope and include regional, state, and local chapters. Offer excellent job opportunities for individuals skilled in communication and meeting planning.

8. **Scientific and research organizations:** Conduct research and experiments used by government agencies and businesses. Include research and development organizations and think tanks, such as RAND Corporation, American Enterprise Institute, Brookings Institution, CATO Institute, and the Urban Institute.

9. **Community development organizations:** Focus on ways of strengthening communities in the areas of employment, economic development, housing, education, and health care. Primarily local grassroots organizations.

10. **Foundations:** Engage in philanthropic activities that fund many other nonprofit organizations, especially education, art, health, and social service groups. While most are community-based, others such as the Lilly Endowment, Ford Foundation, Rockefeller Foundation, and Johnson Foundation are national and international in scope.

11. **Youth leadership and development organizations:** Consist of groups such as the Cub Scouts, Boy Scouts, Girl Scouts, and Camp Fire Girls and Boys.

12. **Utility companies:** Include cooperative electrical generation and irrigation organizations primarily operating in rural areas and small towns.

While this is a useful classification encompassing nearly 90 percent of all nonprofit organizations, some groups tend to fall into more than one or two categories. For example, many religious organizations also operate educational, social service, and health organizations. Business and professional groups also may sponsor educational and research organizations.

These twelve types of organizations further break out into several major activity categories with corresponding examples of nonprofit organizations:

Aid to the Handicapped

- American Foundation For the Blind
- Federation of the Handicapped
- Goodwill Industries
- National Industries For the Blind
- Paralyzed Veterans of America

Alumni Associations

- Associated Students UCLA
- Princeton University Alumni Organization
- Stanford Alumni Association
- University of Virginia Alumni Association

Blood Banks

- American Red Cross
- Blood Systems, Inc.
- Oklahoma Blood Institute

Business Associations

- American Bankers Association
- American Petroleum Institute
- National Association of Home Builders
- U.S. Chamber of Commerce

Care and Housing For the Aged

- Council For Jewish Elderly
- National Lutheran Home For the Aged
- Methodist Home For the Aged, Inc.

Care and Housing of Children

- Childreach
- Father Flanagans Boys Home
- James Barry-Robinson Home For Boys
- Save the Children Federation

Church Groups

- Catholic Relief Services
- Lutheran Church Missouri Synod Foundation
- Seventh Day Adventists
- United Methodist Church

Civil Rights

- NAACP
- National Urban League
- Southern Christian Leadership Conference

Community Chest, United Fund, etc.

- Heart of America United Fund
- Salvation Army
- United Way of America

Community Foundations and Trusts

- Chicago Community Trust
- The Columbus Foundation
- Kalamazoo Foundation
- New York Community Trust

Conservation and Environmental Groups

- Greenpeace U.S.A., Inc.
- National Audubon Society
- National Geographic Society
- National Wildlife Federation
- Sierra Club

Credit Unions

- Commonwealth Credit Union
- Credit Union National Association, Inc.
- Metropolitan Credit Union
- Telephone Workers Credit Union

Cultural and Arts

- The Asia Society
- American Film Institute
- Wolf Trap Foundation For the Performing Arts

Emergency and Disaster Aid

- American National Red Cross
- Food For the Hungry, Inc.
- World Relief

Evangelism

- Billy Graham Evangelistic Association
- Robert Schuller Ministries, Inc.
- Jimmy Swaggart Ministries

Family Planning

- Pathfinder International
- Planned Parenthood Federation of America
- Population Council

Gifts and Grants

- American Institute For Cancer Research
- Amnesty International of U.S.A., Inc.
- Ford Foundation
- RJR Nabisco Foundation

Health Insurance and Services

- American Academy of Family Physicians
- American Lung Association
- Dr. Martin Luther King Health Center
- Health Insurance Association of America
- Total Health Care

Hospitals

- Good Samaritan Hospital Association, Inc.
- Holy Cross Hospital
- Presbyterian Hospital
- University Hospitals of Cleveland

Housing

- Habitat For Humanity

Housing For the Aged

- Episcopal Retirement Homes, Inc.
- Hebrew Home For the Aged
- United Methodist Memorial Home

Libraries

- Brooklyn Public Library
- Online Computer Library Center, Inc.
- Enoch Pratt Free Library of Baltimore City

Museums, Zoos, Planetariums

- American Museum of Natural History
- Cleveland Museum of Art
- Zoological Society of San Diego

Nursing or Convalescent Homes

- Mega Care, Inc.
- Peninsula General Nursing Home
- Scripps Home

Prepaid Group Health Plans

- Blue Cross and Blue Shield
- Group Health Service Plan
- Kaiser Foundation Health Plan, Inc.

Private Schools

- Harvard School
- Menninger Foundation
- Phillips Academy

Professional Associations

- American Bar Association
- American Medical Association
- National Association of Manufacturers
- National Rifle Association

Radio or Television Broadcasting

- Christian Broadcasting Network
- National Public Radio
- Trans World Radio

Religious Activities

- Aid Association For Lutherans
- Catholic Aid Association
- United Jewish Appeal
- Womens Christian Association

Scholarships

- Culver Education Foundation
- Ford Motor Company Fund
- National Merit Scholarship Corporation
- The Rotary Foundation of Rotary International

School Related Activities

- African-American Institute
- Close Up Foundation
- Up With People, Inc.

Schools, Colleges, Trade Schools

- Adelphi University
- Bard College
- Colorado College
- Roosevelt University

Scientific Research

- American Cancer Society
- Hudson Institute, Inc.
- Salk Institute For Biological Studies
- Wortham Foundation

Special Schools

- Braille Institute of America
- Landmark Foundation
- Perkins School For the Blind

Sponsored Research Groups

- Brookings Institution
- Petroleum Research Fund
- Rand Corporation
- SRI International
- Urban Institute

Student Loans

- College Foundation, Inc.
- Dartmouth Educational Loan Corporation
- Student Finance Corporation

Utility Companies

- Cooke County Electric Cooperative Association
- Mountain Electric Cooperative, Inc.
- Tri-County Electric Cooperative

YMCA and YWCA

- Armed Services YMCA of the U.S.A.
- Young Mens Christian Association of Metropolitan Chicago
- Young Womens Christian Association of Los Angeles

Youth Organizations

- American Youth Soccer Organization
- Boy Scouts of America National Council
- Boys Clubs of America
- Girl Scouts of the United States of America
- Little League

Most nonprofits function at the state and local levels. However, many nonprofits also are organized at the international and national levels. Some, such as the United Way and the International Red Cross, have affiliated state and local organizations that operate at the grassroots level.

Positions and Skills Sought

Like any organization that operates in a public arena with both money and a mission, nonprofit organizations need public relations specialists, marketing managers, comptrollers, program officers, meeting planners, accountants, bookkeepers, librarians, office managers, computer specialists, community organizers, education and communication specialists, publicists, researchers, writers, editors, lobbyists, word processors, and mail room personnel along with front-line specialists in particular subject areas.

> Nonprofit organizations hire for all types of positions, from chief executive officer to receptionist.

Because nonprofits are heavily dependent upon membership dues, contributions, grants, and direct-mail sells to fund their operations, they highly prize individuals who demonstrate strong communication, public relations, and fundraising skills. If you have strong communication skills, enjoy working with the public, and feel comfortable recruiting members and asking strangers for contributions, you may be an ideal candidate for working with a non-profit organization!

The types of jobs and skills required for nonprofit organizations will vary with the type and size of nonprofit organization. **Private educational organizations**, for example, disproportionately hire elementary, secondary, and postsecondary teachers and administrators, similar to those in the public sector. On the other hand, **museums, opera companies, symphony orchestras, and theaters** hire talented curators, artists, production personnel, actors, and stage hands as well as both full-time and part-time administrative staff disproportionately engaged in communication and fundraising activities. **Social service organizations** hire numerous professionals who provide counseling and development services. **Advocacy and political groups** hire a disproportionate number of public policy specialists, researchers, writers, and community activists. **Business and professional organizations** seek communication specialists, researchers, writers, meeting planners, publicists, and lobbyists. **Scientific and research organizations** disproportionately hire subject specialists with demonstrated research and writing skills as well as librarians. **Foundations** need program officers, researchers, and librarians.

> Most nonprofits need individuals with strong communication and fundraising skills.

Regardless of the type and size of organization, most nonprofits need individuals with strong communication and fundraising skills, because they must constantly mobilize public support for their activities. Indeed, individuals with limited work experience, but who can demonstrate strong communication skills, can organize and manage well, show a willingness to engage in critical fundraising activities, and are enthusiastic and eager to get things done are in a strong position to land an entry-level position with a nonprofit organization.

Choose the Right Resources

We wish you well as you pursue a job or career in the nonprofit sector. In the following chapters we primarily survey major nonprofit employers. Many other job search issues, especially key job search steps we allude to in Chapter 4, are outlined in several of our job search books: *Change Your Job Change Your Life, Discover the Best Jobs For You, High Impact Resumes and Letters, Dynamite Resumes, Dynamite Cover Letters, Dynamite Tele-Search, 201 Dynamite Job Search Letters, Interview For Success, 101 Dynamite Answers to Interview Questions, Dynamite Networking For Dynamite Jobs, Get a Raise in 7 Days*, and *Dynamite Salary Negotiations*. We also address particular jobs and career fields in the following books: *Best Jobs For the 21st Century, Complete Guide to Public Employment, Directory of Federal Jobs and Employers, Find a Federal Job Fast, Complete Guide to International Jobs and Careers, International Jobs Directory, Educator's Guide to*

Alternative Jobs and Careers, and *Jobs For People Who Love to Travel.* Many of these books are available in your local library and bookstore or they can be ordered directly from Impact Publications (see the "Career Resources" sections at the end of this book). Most of these resources, along with hundreds of others, are available through Impact's comprehensive online "Career Superstore":

www.impactpublications.com

Impact's site also includes new titles, specials, and job search tips for keeping you in touch with the latest in career information and resources. If you don't have access to the Internet, you can request a free copy of their career brochure by sending a self-addressed stamped envelope (#10 business size) and it will be mailed to you:

IMPACT PUBLICATIONS
ATTN: Free Career Brochure
9104-N Manassas Drive
Manassas Park, VA 20111-5211

Empower Yourself in the Nonprofit World

The chapters that follow should help empower you for the wonderful world of nonprofit organizations. If you follow our tips and are persistent in making key contacts and following-up, you'll discover a large complex of organizations involved with all types of interesting and challenging issues and representing important interests. In many respects the nonprofit world is an organizational jungle, but it's one you should be able to easily untangle. You must take a great deal of initiative to make sense of that portion of the nonprofit world that most appeals to your interests, values, and skills.

We wish you well as you put this book into practical use. The remaining chapters are designed to introduce you to the nonprofit employment world. Take the time to explore some of our many recommended resources which are readily available at your local library. Better still, during the next week, introduce yourself to some nonprofit organizations by making a few phone calls for information, advice, and referrals. You may be surprised what you learn. You'll discover the nonprofit world is much closer than you think. And it may just have the perfect job for you. If you do this, you'll understand why so many other people love what they are doing in the nonprofit sector. They have a job that's "fit" for them!

2

Myths, Motivations, & the Future

If you're not familiar with nonprofit organizations, you may try to approach them like you would any other type of organization. But non-profits differ from government and business organizations in many ways. They have their own particular financial and support structures as well as employment and work cultures which you should attempt to understand before approaching them for job opportunities.

Let's look at these organizations by way of some popular myths, realities, and trends. In so doing, we should better understand these groups.

Myths and Realities

Numerous myths relate to the nonprofit sector. Unfortunately, many of these myths dissuade job seekers from exploring opportunities with nonprofit organizations. Ten myths in particular discourage individuals from seeking job and career opportunities with nonprofits:

MYTH 1: Nonprofits offer few job opportunities.

REALITY: Employing nearly 10 million people, nonprofits serve as employers for nearly eight percent of the American workforce. While many nonprofits are very small and only employ one or two full-time people, many other nonprofits employ over 100 individuals. Many job seekers overlook nonprofits as sources for employment not because they offer few job opportunities but simply because they know little about these organizations and thus do not automatically come up on their radar screens. One of the major reasons they don't know much about nonprofits is because they don't fit neatly into standard thinking about a job market being divided into business (private) or government (public) organizations. Nonprofits are neither but sometimes they may be both.

MYTH 2:   **It's difficult to find information on opportunities with nonprofit organizations.**

REALITY: In addition to this book, you will find many useful printed resources on opportunities with nonprofit organizations published by Barricade Books, Gale Research, Macmillan, Planning/Communications, and The Taft Group. You'll also find a wealth of information on the Internet about individual nonprofit organizations (*www.guidestar.org*) as well as job vacancies with nonprofits (*www.nonprofitjobs.org*). Within the past three years, most nonprofits, including small ones in rural areas, have created their own Web sites which include information on their operations as well as job listings. With the help of a few key books and Web sites, the whole nonprofit world will unfold before you in a matter of hours. The biggest problem you will probably face is the fact that you have too much information on nonprofits!

MYTH 3:   **Nonprofits are primarily volunteer organizations involved in charitable activities.**

REALITY: Many nonprofit organizations depend on volunteers, but many of these same organizations have large full-time paid staffs. It is inappropriate to stereotype nonprofit organizations as charitable organizations made up of volunteers. Nonprofits consist of a wide range of different types of organizations, from educational groups to foundations. Volunteers play important roles in only some types of nonprofit organizations.

MYTH 4: **Nonprofits lack good entrepreneurial skills and a sense of productivity and accountability. Like government employees, they are used to drawing salaries unrelated to performance.**

REALITY: By definition, nonprofits must be entrepreneurial, productive, and accountable. Their funding operations require recruiting members, acquiring donations, receiving grants, and operating profitable commercial enterprises. Indeed, they must be entrepreneurial in order to raise sufficient funds to survive and grow. Like most government and business operations, they work within annual budgets. Similar to thriving businesses, nonprofits must increasingly advertise their activities and vigorously market their products and services. However, nonprofit entrepreneurism differs from private sector entrepreneurism. Nonprofit entrepreneurism disproportionately centers on raising funds and recruiting members. Nonprofits also must be productive and accountable in relation to board members who set policies, approve budgets, and oversee operations. Nonprofit productivity is measured differently from business productivity. Similar to government productivity, nonprofit productivity is measured in reference to organizational goals. Nonprofits are increasingly under pressure to clearly state their missions in terms

> **Similar to thriving businesses, nonprofits must increasingly advertise their activities and vigorously market their services.**

of measurable goals as well as be more and more
accountable to their boards.

MYTH 5:   **Nonprofit organizations are primarily located in
            the metropolitan areas of Washington, DC, New
            York, Chicago, and Atlanta.**

REALITY: Many of the large nonprofits, which are national and
            international in scope, are headquartered in these
            major metropolitan areas. The organizations have
            large full-time staffs which offer excellent job oppor-
            tunities leading to career advancement within the
            nonprofit sector. However, more than 90 percent of
            all nonprofits operate at the local level as community-
            based organizations. While these groups have smaller
            staffs and fewer positions than the large nonprofits
            headquartered in major metropolitan areas, nonethe-
            less, the local nonprofits generate millions of job
            opportunities.

MYTH 6:   **It's difficult to break into the nonprofit world.**

REALITY: It is usually easier to enter this employment arena
            than to find jobs in government or business. Many
            nonprofits offer entry-level volunteer and internship
            positions through which individuals can acquire
            experience and skills with nonprofit organizations.

MYTH 7:   **Most nonprofits are liberal groups that hire do-
            gooder, social-action types.**

REALITY: While many nonprofits attract individuals with such
            political and social orientations—especially liberal
            social advocacy groups—many other nonprofit organ-
            izations attract conservatives and those who do not
            have social action agendas. Nonprofits fall all along
            the ideological spectrum, from liberal environmental
            and abortion rights groups to conservative religious
            right and pro-life groups. Both types of groups attract

individuals who have a passion for taking action related to a particular social issue. Other groups, such as professional associations, are relatively apolitical as they seek to promote the collective interests of their members. Nonprofits need public relations specialists, marketing managers, accountants, fundraisers, researchers, writers, communication specialists, administrators, and managers who have the necessary skills to develop organizations and maintain day-to-day operations.

MYTH 8:   **Nonprofit jobs tend to be deadend jobs.**

REALITY: This is a huge employment arena where many individuals develop long-term careers and report high levels of satisfaction. Career advancement often takes the track of moving from small to larger nonprofit organizations that offer increasing responsibilities, larger operating budgets, and better salaries and benefits.

MYTH 9:   **Nonprofit organizations offer low salaries and few benefits.**

REALITY: The level of pay and benefits can vary widely, depending on the nature of the nonprofit organization. It's true that many nonprofit organizations, especially charitable and social service organizations, offer low-paying jobs because of the volunteer nature of the work and their shoestring budgets. But many nonprofits, especially health groups, research organizations, foundations, and business and professional associations, offer excellent salaries and benefits.

MYTH 10:   **The best way to find a job with a nonprofit organization is to respond to vacancy announcements in local newspapers and to jobs listed on various Internet employment sites and on the home pages.**

REALITY: Many positions are advertised in local newspapers and professional journals, such as Access's *Community Jobs* and the *Journal of Philanthropy*, as well as on the Internet. Since more and more nonprofits advertise jobs on the Internet, you are well advised to visit their home pages or regularly check several key employment Web sites:

> *www.ajb.dni.us*
> *www.careermosaic.com*
> *www.careerpath.com*
> *www.careerweb.com*
> *www.espan.com*
> *www.monster.com*
> *www.occ.com*

Better still, visit several Web sites that specialize in nonprofit job listings. The major such sites include:

> *www.clark.net/pub/pwalker*
> *www.communityjobs.org*
> *www.essential.org/goodworks*
> *www.idealist.org*
> *www.nonprofitjobs.org*
> *www.nonprofitcareer.com*
> *www.nonprofits.org*
> *www.nptimes.com*
> *www.pj.org*
> *www.philanthropy.com*
> *www.opnocs.org*
> *www.tmcenter.org*

Many of these sites have search engines that enable you to select your specialty field and desired work location. However, not all jobs appear through these print or electronic sources. Many jobs also are found through direct application or by networking through friends and acquaintances. For a comprehensive review of hundreds of international, national, state, and local job vacancy resources, see the latest edition of Dan Lauber's *The Nonprofits and Education Job Finder* (Planning/Communications).

Positives and Negatives

What's it really like working in the nonprofit sector? Most people either know little or nothing about nonprofit work, or they have certain stereotypes about what it's really like working in this employment arena. Reality depends on the type of organization, where you work, and whom you work with. In general, however, the following positives and negatives are normally associated with nonprofit organizations. Some are two-edged swords—they function as both positives and negatives.

Positives

1. **Rewarding work:** Many nonprofit organizations have a positive impact on the health and welfare of people. They do "good works" that are compatible with the religious and social values of individuals who want to help others and become involved in improving their communities. People who seek meaningful work find nonprofits provide an excellent job "fit". They enable many people to pursue their passions in well-focused work environments.

> Nonprofits enable many people to pursue their passions in well-focused work environments.

2. **Interesting and exciting work:** Much of the work of nonprofits is very interesting and exciting. Arts, cultural, historical, community-educational, social service, advocacy, political, and business and professional organizations engage in some of today's most important work. Many of their missions center on pressing social and political issues. If you want to change the attitudes and behaviors of individuals, groups, and communities, you'll find many nonprofits to be ideal employers.

3. **Positive work environments:** Some of the nicest, most caring, and selfless people you will ever meet work for

nonprofit organizations. Many of these organizations also hire very bright and well-educated individuals who contribute to an intelligent and stimulating work environment. If you like working with such people—and especially those who share your values and are very likable—a nonprofit organization may be the right type of work environment for you.

4. **Easy entry and valuable experience:** Nonprofits offer excellent opportunities for acquiring work experience. Indeed, it is often easier to acquire entry-level positions with nonprofit organizations than with government agencies and businesses. Indeed, nonprofits offer a large number of volunteer and internship experiences for acquiring work experience. Recent college graduates and women re-entering the workforce often find nonprofit organizations to be more responsive to their job search initiatives than government agencies and businesses.

5. **Career advancement:** Many nonprofit jobs lead to career advancement within the nonprofit sector. This often involves moving from small to larger nonprofit organizations. Nonprofits also are excellent stepping stones for acquiring jobs in government and business. Indeed, many people working in government and business today first acquired work experience with nonprofit organizations.

Negatives

1. **Low pay:** Constrained by limited financial resources, many nonprofit organizations offer below average to low salaries. Comparable jobs paying $40,000 a year in government or business may only pay $25,000 to $30,000 with a nonprofit organization. A 25 percent salary differential is quite common. Consequently, don't expect to make as much money working for a nonprofit organization as you might with other types of organizations. The rewards are elsewhere, and primarily non-monetary, with nonprofits.

2. **Limited career advancement:** Since many nonprofits are small organizations, your career within such an organization

may quickly plateau. Career advancement requires leaving a small nonprofit organization for a higher level job in a larger nonprofit organization. However, many of the larger nonprofits are found in only a few major metropolitan areas such as Washington, DC, New York, Philadelphia, Boston, Atlanta, Chicago, Minneapolis, Denver, San Francisco, and Los Angeles. If you are unwilling to seek employment with larger nonprofits headquartered in these cities, don't expect to advance your career much in the nonprofit sector.

3. **Stressful and frustrating work environments:** Work environments of many nonprofit organizations leave much to be desired. While many problems relate to the financing of nonprofits, other problems are endemic to the traditional voluntary structure and organization of nonprofits. Many nonprofits are stressful places to work because of the chaotic nature of their organizations and decision-making. Some are highly political and bureaucratic. Boards of directors often work against their best interests. Some nonprofits have

> **Many problems are endemic to the traditional voluntary structure and organization of nonprofits.**

notorious reputations for administrative incompetence and disorganization; lack quality personnel and staff development; operate with antiquated equipment and from cramped quarters; and have attitude problems. Relationships between the CEO, board members, staff, and volunteers can become a nightmare. If you prize strong leadership, clear decision points, high levels of efficiency, and the latest in office technology, many nonprofit organizations will disappoint, frustrate, and discourage you. If you can tolerate ambiguity, inefficiency, and chaos and function well in make-shift work environments, you may do well in such work environments.

4. **Lack of concrete results and accountability:** While many nonprofits promote positive social values, many of these same organizations are hard-pressed to point to concrete measurable results to justify their operations. Unlike a business that

measures its performance by its bottomline profits, few non-profits have similar types of performance indicators. They operate *processes* which may or may not be directly related to specific performance and outcomes. Many of these processes involve frequent meetings, reports, and other related activities —but few measurable outcomes. Like government agencies, nonprofit organizations have annual budgets which they must expend. The closest they may come to performance is a clear *mission statement* of what they hope to accomplish. Only a few nonprofits have clear mission statements that guide their performance and hold them accountable.

5. **Uncertain financial future:** By definition most nonprofits depend on a variety of unstable fundraising activities, from membership fees, public donations, and corporate sponsor-ships to foundation grants, government contracts, and com-mercial activities. Fluctuating from year to year, such unpre-dictable revenue streams can create anxiety amongst employ-ees, generate job insecurity, and affect motivation. Many nonprofit organizations operate as if they were in a permanent downsizing mode.

Current Trends

Recent trends appear to be supportive of a greater role for nonprofit organizations. Indeed, we see the continuing increase, expansion, and strengthening of nonprofits in the decade ahead. However, their long-term financial viability will remain in question unless they undergo radical transformation in how they operate in today's new public and private economies. Eight trends in particular lead us to this conclusion:

1. **Nonprofits are taking on more "public" responsibilities as governments continue to downsize and divest themselves of certain social welfare and community development functions.** The watershed congressional elections of Novem-ber 1994 signaled a significant shift in how government would do business in the future. Numerous programs which used to receive generous federal, state, and local government support —from education and social welfare to museums, libraries,

and public radio and television—have experienced major cuts in their annual government-supported budgets. Nonprofits that depended on government grants for a large portion of their funding have had to find alternative private funding sources due to government cutbacks on grants. As a result, more and more of these organizations have had to both "reinvent" and "realign" themselves in order to survive and prosper. Much of this reinvention and realignment will take the form of new "partnerships" with corporations, citizen groups, and other nonprofits. Successful nonprofits must conduct very aggressive public relations, fundraising, and sponsorship campaigns which will require the hiring of more talented personnel skilled in these organizational development and marketing functions. As governments continue to downsize and divest themselves of traditional social welfare functions, more and more nonprofit organizations, especially charities, will play an increasingly important role in providing welfare assistance.

> **Nonprofits will reinvent themselves by developing new "partnerships" with corporations, citizen groups, and other nonprofits.**

Functioning as new and expanded service delivery organizations, they will increase their professional staffs to provide such services as well as secure increased funding through government contracts and grants. In the international arena, NGOs (non-governmental organizations) will play a more important role in international development and relief efforts as the U.S. Agency for International Development and the UN undergo further budgetary cuts.

2. **Funding activities continue to increase despite occasional recessions and scandals.** Americans continue to support and use nonprofits at unprecedented levels, especially during boom economic times. They view nonprofits as more responsive and accountable than government bureaucracies. Since many nonprofits are community-based, they also seem to be more democratic and participatory than government. As the federal government continues to divest itself of certain edu-

cational, cultural, health, and welfare functions as well as downsize many entitlement programs, nonprofit organizations must source new and innovative revenue sources. While occasional scandals, such as the United Way and New Era Foundation episodes in the mid-1990s, will likely continue in the future, they will not substantially affect public commitment to supporting nonprofit organizations. At the same time, nonprofits operate in a highly competitive environment of limited resources. With both government and corporate funding down, nonprofits increasingly need to seek out revenue sources, from operating "nonprofit businesses" to developing innovative community-based funding activities.

3. **Nonprofits will become more entrepreneurial and innovative.** Whether they like it or not, nonprofits must think and behave like businesses. They require sound technical, managerial, communication, marketing, and sales talent in order to survive and prosper in today's highly competitive "sink or swim" environment. Being nonprofit is no longer considered an excuse for being inefficient and ineffective. The old "tin cup" image of nonprofits must give way to that of a "productive business." Nonprofits must increasingly behave like businesses by having clear mission statements, demonstrating productivity, being accountable, subjecting themselves to regular evaluations, and lowering their overhead. Often underfunded and lacking strong administrative capabilities, many of these organizations need creative self-starters who can move these organizations into the 21st century on sound financial, technical, and managerial bases.

> Being nonprofit is no longer considered an excuse for being inefficient and ineffective.

4. **Nonprofits will continue to offer excellent employment opportunities in the decade ahead.** As nonprofits grow and become more visible to job seekers, they will continue to expand as attractive employment arenas. Best of all, they are major players in the revolving door of government and

business. Many people who work for government and enjoy public arenas will choose new careers with nonprofit organizations. Many who work in business also leave to work for nonprofits, especially those who seek a different and more personally rewarding organizational culture. It's not unusual to find individual career paths beginning in government, moving on to nonprofit organizations, and then going on to corporations. Experience with nonprofit organizations can be an important stepping-stone to exciting career opportunities in both government and business. We expect more and more individuals who work in business to turn to nonprofits. Their experience and skills will be increasingly attractive to nonprofits that need to operate more like businesses.

5. **Nonprofits will continue to include numerous types of organizations, many of which will be controversial.** While most nonprofits are stereotyped as charitable organizations, in reality they represent a very diverse set of organizations. Expect to see more and more nonprofit organizations, especially advocacy groups, come under closer government scrutiny because of their political and commercial activities. Some of these organizations may lose their nonprofit status.

6. **Jobs with nonprofit organizations will increasingly become more technical in nature.** Today's fast-paced and highly competitive nonprofit world requires individuals who have adequate technical skills to operate effective high-tech organizations. As nonprofits increasingly embrace the latest technology, use the Internet, and transform themselves into sound businesses, they need to recruit individuals who are proficient in using the latest computer technology and communicating via the Internet.

7. **The nonprofit job market increasingly will be centered on the Internet.** As more and more nonprofits get wired and embrace the Internet, they will recruit many of their employees via the Internet. The nonprofit job market will be easily accessible through several key Web sites that specialize in nonprofit jobs as well as through the home pages of individual

nonprofit organizations. Job seekers increasingly need to incorporate the Internet into their nonprofit job search.

8. **Jobs and careers with nonprofits will continue to expand in the decade ahead.** We expect the continuing expansion of nonprofit operations and the further growth of nonprofit organizations. Organized like efficient businesses, many of today's large nonprofits will continue to grow and prosper in the decade ahead. Like many start-up businesses in the private sector, we expect the continuing emergence of hundreds of new nonprofits each year which will organize around single issues or causes. We also expect many small nonprofits will cease operations or transform their missions in the future.

These and other trends continue to change the complexion of this fascinating employment arena. Taken together, these trends pose new challenges for nonprofit organizations as they enter the 21st century. Like the talent-driven economy within which businesses and governments now function, nonprofit organizations need new talent in order to survive and prosper in the decade ahead. Much of this talent needs to be savvy in business and technology. Just being a "do-gooder" with good motivations and attitudes is not enough. You need solid business and technology skills that will contribute to the productivity of nonprofits. Like your counterparts in the private sector, you need to "add value" to your employer's operations.

> Just being a "do-gooder" with good motivations and attitudes is not enough. You need solid business and technology skills for success in the nonprofit sector.

Neither public nor private, nonprofit organizations offer some terrific job and career opportunities for those who understand where they are coming from and where they are going in the decade ahead. If you plan to join the nonprofit sector, do so with skills that will prove profitable for nonprofits. If you seek employment with nonprofits because you lack skills appropriate for business and government, you may do both you and nonprofits a disservice. Ironically, the skills for success in the nonprofit sector tend to be similar to those required for success in business and government.

3

What's Your Nonprofit I.Q.?

D o you have the right skills, motivations, and attitudes to do well in today's nonprofit job market? Maybe you do, maybe you don't, or perhaps you need to take certain actions that will enhance your ability to do well in the nonprofit sector.
Not everyone is a good candidate for the work of nonprofit organizations. Take a look at your potential level of success in the nonprofit sector by completing the exercise on pages 33-36.

Your NSL (Nonprofit Success Level) Quotient

Respond to each of the following statements by circling which number at the right best represents your situation.

SCALE: 1 = strongly disagree   4 = agree
        2 = disagree   5 = strongly agree
        3 = maybe, not certain

1. I enjoy working with people who
   need assistance.   1   2   3   4   5

2. I work well with different types of
   people and in diverse work settings.   1   2   3   4   5

3. I'm a self-starter who takes initiative
   in pursuing new ideas and solving
   problems.   1   2   3   4   5

4. I work well without close supervision.   1   2   3   4   5

5. I'm enthusiastic about my work.   1   2   3   4   5

6. I can influence others to do things
   my way.   1   2   3   4   5

7. I'm more interested in the type of
   work I'm doing and the people I'm
   working with than in the amount of
   money I'm making.   1   2   3   4   5

8. I'm tolerant of other peoples' views
   and generally empathize with others.   1   2   3   4   5

9. I'm more interested in providing
   public services and helping others
   than in making money.   1   2   3   4   5

10. I can handle ambiguity and
    complexity in my daily work.   1   2   3   4   5

11. I'm tolerant of most organizational
    politics.   1   2   3   4   5

12. I can work well in loosely structured
    environments and can tolerate a certain
    degree of on-going disorganization.   1   2   3   4   5

13. I'm flexible in the way I deal with
    people, processes, and problems.   1   2   3   4   5

14. I enjoy working in environments
    where consensus building is important
    to decision making.   1   2   3   4   5

15. I'm tolerant of relatively chaotic work
    environments that may lack leadership,
    quick and decisive decision-making, and
    strong administrative processes.   1   2   3   4   5

16. I'm a team player who does not require
    strong leadership for direction.   1   2   3   4   5

17. I'm not interested in having a big
    office and acquiring organizational
    perks normally associated with large
    businesses.   1   2   3   4   5

18. I'm willing to accept a lower salary
    for a job I really love.   1   2   3   4   5

19. I enjoy working in small organizations. 1   2   3   4   5

20. I'm willing to engage in fundraising
    activities.   1   2   3   4   5

21. I'm a committed advocate who is
    interested in persuading others to
    support my views.   1   2   3   4   5

22. I'm looking for meaningful work that
    involves associating with people who
    have similar interests and goals.   1   2   3   4   5

23. I'm not a "get rich quick" type of
    person; I'm more interested in the
    work I'm doing than in making money.   1   2   3   4   5

24. I'm willing to accept a job that
    offers limited career advancement.   1   2   3   4   5

25. I'm willing to learn and grow a
    career in the nonprofit sector.   1   2   3   4   5

26. I have strong written and oral
    communication skills.   1   2   3   4   5

27. I don't mind making cold calls and
    asking strangers for information and
    assistance.   1   2   3   4   5

28. I know where to find vacancy
    information on jobs with nonprofit
    organizations.   1   2   3   4   5

29. I have a resume designed specifically
for nonprofit organizations.   1 2 3 4 5

30. I know at least three people who work
with nonprofit organizations, who are
willing to talk to me about their work,
and who will provide me with information, advice, and referrals.   1 2 3 4 5

31. I can present myself well at a job
interview.   1 2 3 4 5

32. I know the types of questions an
interviewer is likely to ask me
at an interview for a nonprofit job. 1 2 3 4 5

33. I know how to find information on
specific nonprofit organizations,
including the salaries and benefits
they offer.   1 2 3 4 5

34. I know at least five nonprofit organizations that hire individuals with
my interests, skills, and abilities. 1 2 3 4 5

35. I'm Internet and computer savvy.   1 2 3 4 5

TOTAL

Interpret Your Score

Although there is no scientific validation to correlate one's responses on this NSL questionnaire to one's success working for a nonprofit, you can get an indication of your *potential for success* by adding the numbers you circled to get an overall composite score. If your total is under 70, you may not be a good candidate at present for a job with many nonprofit organizations. You may need to work on improving your knowledge, skills, and abilities and reassessing your attitudes in relation to each item for which you circled a 3, 4, or 5. If your overall score is over 100, congratulations; you are probably a good candidate for success in the nonprofit sector!

4

Skills and Habits For Success

inding a job with a nonprofit organization is similar to finding a job with many other types of organizations. You first need to understand how the nonprofit job market is structured and then focus on where to find job vacancies, how to uncover job leads, and how to best communicate your qualifications to employers. To be most effective, you need to develop job search strategies and techniques that are particularly responsive to nonprofit organizations. Above all, you need to acquire certain skills and habits for successfully navigating the nonprofit job market.

10 Steps to Job Search Success

Conducting an effective job search with a nonprofit organization should include the following steps:

1. **Decide what it is you do well and enjoy doing in reference to nonprofit organizations.** It's always best to begin any job search by conducting a thorough self-assessment of your interests, skills, and abilities. In addition to completing our exercise in Chapter 3, you should take different tests, such as the popular *Myers-Briggs Type Indicator* or the *Strong Interest*

Inventory, which are readily available through professional career counselors, testing centers, or counseling centers of community colleges. Alternatively, you may want to complete a variety of self-directed exercises which can also yield valuable information on your interests, skills, and abilities. We've included many of these exercises in our other book, ***Discover the Best Jobs For You.***

The real value in doing this up-front self-assessment work is knowing how suitable you will be for particular positions with nonprofit organizations. These tests and exercises will help you identify your pattern of motivated abilities—those things you really do well and enjoy doing. Once you identify a potential employer and a specific position, you want to know if you have the right combination of interests, skills, and abilities to do the job. In other words, will the position be a good "fit" for you or might it be "unfit" for your particular mix of interests, skills, and abilities? If you fail to do this, you could well end up with a job that is not fit for you, one which leads to unhappiness and disappointments for both you and the employer. This self-assessment will also help you identify an appropriate language with which to write your resumes and letters as well as talk about your interests, skills, and abilities with employers.

> **Will the position be a good "fit" for you or might it be "unfit" for your particular mix of interests, skills, and abilities?**

2. **State a clear objective of what it is you really want to do if and when you become employed by a nonprofit organization.** Employers are especially receptive toward hiring individuals who have a clear idea of what they want to do. They especially like individuals whose goals coincide with their specific needs. Job applicants with clear objectives tend to write well-crafted resumes and letters as well as communicate confidence and enthusiasm during interviews—two characteristics employers seek in candidates. Employees, in turn, tend to most enjoy their work when it coincides with their expectations and goals. Be sure to identify what it is you really want to do in

reference to employers' needs. Make sure your goals are **employer-centered** rather than self-centered. For example, a typical self-centered goal might be this:

> *"An increasingly responsible management position that leads to career advancement with a large nonprofit organization."*

While this may represent a personally honest objective, it does not impress an employer as much as this employer-centered objective:

> *"A management position with responsibility for building a strong membership base that will more than double contributions within the next three years."*

This objective clearly speaks to the specific needs of many nonprofit employers. If you fail to develop an objective, you may appear unfocused and thus organize your job search in a very disorganized manner.

3. **Conduct research on appropriate nonprofit organizations, employers, and positions.** Knowledge is power when looking for a job. Without research you will lack power in the nonprofit job world. Unfortunately, few applicants really do their homework to learn about the job market, organizations, employers, and specific positions suitable for their particular interests, skills, and abilities. They send

> **Make sure your goals are employer-centered rather than self-centered.**

resumes and go to interviews knowing little or nothing about the employer's needs. Worst of all, they get to the salary negotiation stage uninformed about current salary ranges for comparable positions. Fortunately, there is a wealth of information available on nonprofit organizations, and it's readily available to anyone with a minimum amount of effort—visiting Web sites, reviewing printed materials in the library, placing phone calls, or sending faxes and e-mail. You should start by spending a few hours on the Internet surveying major Web sites that focus on nonprofit organizations and the nonprofit job market. We identified several such sites on page 24 of Chapter 2. Major gateway sites, such as *www.idealist.org* and *www.clark.net/pub/pwalker*, provide a wealth of links to major organizations that define the nonprofit sector. Most major libraries include directories to nonprofit organizations, such as the *National Directory of Nonprofit Organizations* (The Taft Group), *National Trade and Professional Associations* (Columbia Books), *Encyclopedia of Associations* (Gale Research), *Good Works* (Barricade Books), *100 Best Nonprofits to Work For* (Arco/Simon & Schuster), *In Search of America's Best Nonprofits* (Jossey-Bass), and *The International Jobs Directory* (Impact Publications). These directories provide names, addresses, telephone and fax numbers, and Web sites as well as annotated descriptions on thousands of nonprofit organizations. They are good starting points for identifying nonprofit organizations that most appeal to you given your interests, skills, and motivations. For comparable salary information, consult *Compensation in Nonprofit Organizations* (Abbott, Langer, and Associates). Other useful resources help identify job vacancies: *The Non-Profits and Education Job Finder* (Planning/Communication), *Community Jobs: The National Employment Newspaper For the Non-Profit Sector* (202/785-4233) and *The Chronicle of Philanthropy* (800/347-6969). Many professional groups and associations, such as The Taft Group, U.S. Chamber of Commerce, American Society of Association Executives, and the Society for Nonprofit Organizations, maintain databases on nonprofit organizations as well as provide job assistance to members. But your best resource will be you, yourself, talking with individuals who are knowledgeable about the nonprofit sector. Talk to people who are involved with nonprofit organizations, from board members to full-time staff and volunteers; who know what it's really like working for organizations X, Y, and Z; and who can give you useful information, advice, and contacts. The point here is that you need both knowledge and realistic expectations about your future employer. You can gain invaluable information by conducting library research and by interviewing people who are knowledgeable about your areas of concern. If you neglect to do such research—spend at least two to three weeks gathering useful information before applying for jobs—you will neglect one of the most important phases of getting a job. If done properly, your research will reveal a wealth of useful information that will help you target your job search on specific employers. Best of all, your research will help you identify organizations, employers, and positions you should avoid as well as actively seek out.

4. **Write dynamite resumes and letters that grab the attention of individuals interested in your experience.** Your single most important calling card for nonprofit employers will be your resume. It says who you are and what you can likely do for them. Always write your resume with the needs of employers in mind. They want to know what it is you have done, can do, and will do for them. They look for experience and **patterns of accomplishments** that may be directly relevant to their operations. Since employers are busy people who have limited time to digest a lengthy resume, keep your resume to one or two pages—the shorter and more succinct the better. You may want to write two types of resumes—conventional and electronic. The conventional resume is designed to be read by hiring personnel. Electronic resumes are designed to be electronically scanned. The principles for writing such resumes, including examples of effective resumes and letters, are found in our *Dynamite Resumes, Dynamite Cover Letters,* and *High Impact Resumes and Letters* and in Peter Weddle's *Internet Resumes* as well as on pages 93-104 of Chapter 6 of this book.

5. **Conduct informational interviews and network for information, advice, and referrals.** While current job listings in newspapers, trade journals, specialized newsletters, and Web sites are a convenient way of identifying job vacancies, they by no means represent the true universe of job opportunities with nonprofit organizations. Since the nonprofit sector tends to be a highly networked community, one of the best ways to find quality jobs is through networking. Indeed, many jobs with

nonprofits are never advertised or they are assigned to head-hunters who specialize in recruiting executive-level personnel. Thousands of jobs are found and filled through informal means—word-of-mouth, friends, family, and the ubiquitous "connection." Therefore, you are well advised to plug into the informal word-of-mouth communication channels by initiating a well-organized networking campaign designed for yielding quality information, advice, and referrals. At the heart of this networking process is the informational interview. Conducted over the telephone or in face-to-face settings, the informational interview helps you penetrate the unadvertised job market where many quality jobs will be found. Focused on individuals who are well-positioned to give useful information, advice, and referrals, the informational interview can yield an enormous amount of information that can be critical to the overall direction of

> **Many jobs with nonprofits are never advertised.**

your job search. Details on the informational interview, including sample dialogues, appear in two of our other books, *Dynamite Networking For Dynamite Jobs* and *Interview for Success*. See pages 88-91 for examples.

6. **Target specific organizations and employers.** It is always preferable to target specific organizations and employers rather than cast a very broad and unfocused net. When you target your job search, you focus only on those organizations and employers that have jobs appropriate for your interests and skills. Targeting enables you to focus your attention on a manageable number of employers. For example, rather than broadcast your resume and cover letter to 1000 nonprofit organizations, identify 20 key organizations you would like to work for. Devote at least five hours to learning about each organization. Spend another five hours on each organization networking for information, advice, and referrals; developing presentation packages and delivering them to the appropriate hiring personnel; and following up with letters, phone calls, faxes, and e-mail. You'll quickly discover that job search success comes from understanding the hiring details of each

organization and persisting in working those details to your advantage. Above all, it requires persistence in following-through with information, advice, and referrals acquired through your networking activities.

7. **Write lots of letters, make numerous phone calls, and learn to communicate effectively by fax and e-mail.** Communication, communication, communication lies at the heart of any successful job search, and written communication plays an even more important role today given the widespread use of faxes and e-mail. Effective communication takes many different forms and mediums. Remember, you are a stranger to most hiring personnel in nonprofit organizations. Your job is to persuade them to notice you as well as take your candidacy seriously. Above all, you must communicate your qualifications loud and clear —and error free—to strangers who

> **Employers want to know what it is you have done, can do, and will do for them.**

have the power to hire. You need to convince them that you have the requisite skills and talent to make a positive contribution to their operations. You also need to project a positive personality—you are a thoughtful and likable person who will get along well with others in the organization. But how do you do this? Which communication mediums appear to be most effective with hiring personnel? You initially communicate these qualities in letters as well as over the telephone and in faxes and e-mail. You will need to write a variety of letters—which also can be converted into faxes and e-mail messages—throughout your job search—cover, approach, resume, follow-up, and thank-you. One of the most effective letters you can write is the thank-you letter. Make sure you follow-up with such letters. They say a lot about you as an individual—qualities hiring personnel look for when screening candidates. For a comprehensive treatment of such letters, including writing principles and examples, see our *Dynamite Cover Letters* and *201 Dynamite Job Search Letters*. Also, make sure you use the telephone, fax machine, and e-mail systems. Busy people have difficulty responding to letters and telephone messages. If you send a letter of inquiry or a cover letter and resume, be sure to follow-up with a telephone call, fax, or e-mail within five working days. In fact, many people now prefer receiving faxes or e-mail rather than telephone calls because fax and e-mail messages are easier to sort, respond to, and control. Given the widespread use of voice mail systems, many telephone calls get recorded rather than received by a real person. Since busy people are often confronted with 20 or more voice mail messages each day, it's virtually impossible for them to return all of their calls. If they did, they would have little time for other pressing work. On the other hand, a well-crafted fax or e-mail message may be more effective in getting a response from the person. Faxes and e-mail get the immediate attention of recipients who feel obligated to respond to what appears to be time-sensitive communication. Our advice for today's rapidly changing communication mediums: become a good fax and e-mail communicator! For information on the use of telephones, faxes, and e-mail systems in your job search, see our *Dynamite Tele-Search: 101 Telephone Techniques and Tips For Getting Job Leads and Interviews*.

> **If you send a letter, be sure to follow-up with a telephone call, fax, or e-mail within five working days.**

8. **Develop effective interview and salary negotiation skills and schedule job interviews.** The most critical step in landing a job is the actual job interview. You must take initiative in order to get job interviews. This requires regularly following-up your job search communication and scheduling job interviews. Be prepared for different types of interviews, from the telephone screening interview to panel and stress interviews. The best way to prepare is to anticipate the types of questions you are likely to be asked about your goals, education, experience, and personality. Outline answers to such questions with both positive form and content. For example, can you give very positive answers to these questions? *"Tell me about yourself"* and *"Why should we hire you?"* Can you talk intelligently about your goals in reference to the employer's needs as

well as discuss relevant accomplishments in previous jobs? If you can't, or if you are uncertain, now is the time to prepare for such questions. At the same time, you should be prepared to ask intelligent questions. Indeed, the quality of your questions may be just as important to landing the job as the quality of your answers to the interviewer's questions. In the job interview, you simply won't have a second chance to make a good first impression! And that's what the job interview is all about—making good impressions verbally and nonverbally. For details on how to handle the job interview, see our *101 Dynamite Answers to Interview Questions* and *Interview For Success* as well as Richard Fein's *101 Dynamite Questions You Should Ask At the Job Interview* (Impact Publications).

9. **Follow-up, follow-up, follow-up.** The weakest link in the job search tends to be the follow-up process. Many people write terrific resumes and letters and are good at networking for information, advice, and referrals. But they fall down at the stage where everything must come together—follow-up. You simply must develop an effective follow-up campaign if you expect get attention and positive responses to your job search initiatives. Assume that

> You constantly want to be remembered as someone who should be called for a job interview.

most hiring personnel are busy people who have little time to take your candidacy seriously. The one thing you can do that will separate you from the pack of other applicants is to engage in certain follow-up activities that will get results. At the very minimum, you should follow-up all written, mailed, and e-mailed communication with a telephone call. If you sent a cover letter and resume, call within five working days to inquire if the individual received your materials and ask when you might expect to hear from them. Follow-up that follow-up call with a nice thank-you letter for taking the time to speak with you and reiterate your interest in the position. If you don't hear within another two weeks, make a similar telephone call reiterating your interest in the position and asking again when you might anticipate hearing from them. The key to effective follow-up activities is to keep your name and application active in the mind of the recipient without becoming a pushy, annoying pest. You constantly want to be **remembered** as someone who should be called for a job interview. Therefore, your follow-up calls must project you as someone who is interested, friendly, enthusiastic, and competent. And remember, every time you initiate a telephone follow-up, you're probably engaging yourself in a telephone interview. So be prepared to respond to potential screening interview questions.

10. **Start out on the right foot by "doing the right things" with your new boss.** Being hired is just the first step in what hopefully will be a long and rewarding job with this particular nonprofit organization. Both you and your boss hope you've collectively made the right decisions. It's not over until you are on the payroll and demonstrating that you can really do the job you say you can do. In other words, can you assure your boss that you really are the person you and your reference claimed you were? Keep in mind that most employers immediately look for on-the-job performance indicators to confirm the fact that they indeed made a good hiring decision. Don't disappoint your new boss by raising questions about your capabilities. During the first 90 days you should clearly communicate that you are the perfect hire. Start out on the right foot by making a thoughtful gesture to your boss—send a nice thank-you letter indicating your genuine appreciation for the employer's trust in you, reaffirming your commitment to the organization, and expressing your enthusiasm for the job. Try to forge a close personal relationship that will keep the lines of communication open between you and your boss. How you handle these first 90 days will set the tone for your future with your boss and the organization.

> Try to forge a close personal relationship that will keep the lines of communications open between you and your boss.

20 Habits For Success

The principles for job search success with nonprofit organizations are the same as those for success with most other types of organizations. They constitute a set of habits for success.

Success is determined by more than just a good plan getting implemented. We also know success is not determined primarily by intelligence, time management, or luck. Based upon experience, theory, research, common sense, and acceptance of some self-transformation principles, we believe you will achieve job search success by following many of the following 20 habits:

1. **You should work hard at finding a job with a nonprofit organization:** Make this a daily endeavor and involve your family.

2. **You should not be discouraged with set-backs:** You are playing the odds, so expect disappointments and handle them in stride. You will get many "no's" before finding the one "yes" which is right for you.

3. **You should be patient and persevere:** Expect three to six months of hard work before you connect with the job that's right for you.

4. **You should be honest with yourself and others:** Honesty is always the best policy. But don't be naive and stupid by broadcasting your negatives and shortcomings to others.

5. **You should develop a positive attitude toward yourself:** Nobody wants to employ guilt-ridden people with inferiority complexes. Focus on your positive characteristics—not your negatives.

6. **You should associate with positive and successful people:** Finding a job depends on how well you relate to others. Avoid associating with negative people who complain a lot and have a "you-can't-do-it" attitude. Run with winners who have a positive "can-do" outlook on life.

7. **You should set goals:** You should have a clear idea of what you want and where you are going. Without these, you will present a confusing and indecisive image to others. Clear goals help direct your job search into productive channels. Moreover, setting high goals will help make you work hard in getting what you want.

8. **You should plan:** Convert your goals into action steps that are organized as short, intermediate, and long-range plans.

9. **You should get organized:** Translate your plans into activities, targets, names, addresses, telephone numbers, and materials. Develop an efficient and effective filing system and use a large calendar to set time targets, record appointments, and compile useful information.

10. **You should be a good communicator:** Take stock of your oral, written, and nonverbal communication skills. How well do you communicate? Since your job search involves communicating with others—and communication skills are one of the most sought-after skills—always present yourself well both verbally and nonverbally.

11. **You should be energetic and enthusiastic:** Employers are attracted to positive people. They don't like negative and depressing people who toil at their work. Generate enthusiasm both verbally and nonverbally. Check on your telephone voice—it may be more unenthusiastic than your voice in face-to-face situations.

12. **You should ask questions:** Questions play a powerful role. A candidate who fails to ask questions appears to lack initiative. At the same time, your best information about the job and the employer comes from asking questions. Learn to develop intelligent questions that are non-aggressive, polite, and interesting to others. The quality of your questions indicates your level of interest, enthusiasm, and intelligence—qualities readily sought by employers. But don't ask too many questions and thereby become a bore.

13. **You should be a good listener:** Being a good listener is often more important than being a good questioner or talker. Learn to improve your face-to-face listening behavior (nonverbal cues) as well as remember and use information gained from others. Make others feel they enjoyed talking with you, i.e., you are one of the few people who actually *listens* to what they say.

14. **You should be polite, courteous, and thoughtful:** Treat gatekeepers, especially receptionists and secretaries, like human beings. Avoid being aggressive or too assertive. Try to be polite, courteous, and gracious. Your social graces are being observed. Remember to send thank-you letters—a very thoughtful thing to do in a job search. Even if rejected, thank your employer for the "opportunity" given to you. After all, they may later have additional opportunities, and they will remember you.

> Remember to send thank-you letters—a very thoughtful thing to do in a job search.

15. **You should be tactful:** Watch what you say to others about other people and your background. Don't be a gossip, back-stabber, or confessor.

16. **You should maintain a professional stance:** Be neat in what you do and wear, and speak with the confidence, authority, and maturity of a professional.

17. **You should demonstrate your intelligence and competence:** Present yourself as someone who gets things done and achieves results—a *producer*. Employers generally seek people who are bright, hard working, responsible, communicate well, have positive personalities, maintain good interpersonal relations, are likable, observe dress and social codes, take initiative, are talented, possess expertise in particular areas, use good judgment, are cooperative, trustworthy, and loyal, generate confidence and credibility, and are conventional. In other words, they like people who

score in the "excellent" to "outstanding" categories of the annual performance evaluation.

18. **You should not overdo your job search:** Don't engage in overkill and bore everyone with your "job search" stories. Achieve balance in everything you do. Occasionally take a few days off to do nothing related to your job search. Develop a system of incentives and rewards—such as two non-job search days a week, if you accomplish targets A, B, C, and D.

19. **You should be open-minded and keep an eye open for "luck":** Too much planning can blind you to unexpected and fruitful opportunities. You should welcome serendipity. Learn to re-evaluate your goals and strategies. Seize new opportunities if they appear appropriate.

20. **You should evaluate your progress and adjust:** Take two hours once every two weeks and evaluate what you are doing and accomplishing. If necessary, tinker with your plans and reorganize your activities and priorities. Don't become too routinized and thereby kill creativity and innovation.

These habits or principles for success should provide you with an initial orientation for starting your job search in the nonprofit sector. As you become more experienced, you will develop your own set of operating principles that should work for you in particular employment situations.

What to Do If You Lack Experience

Nonprofit organizations provide numerous entry-level opportunities for individuals without work experience. If you are graduating from college with little or no work experience, or re-entering the job market after a lengthy absence, nonprofit organizations may offer some ideal job opportunities for you. This is not to say that nonprofits disproportionately hire the inexperienced or unskilled. Rather, given the nature of their organizations, they offer numerous opportunities to acquire work experience which may not be available with other types of organizations. If you are inexperienced, we recommend doing the following:

1. **Offer skills nonprofits really need for success in today's new economy.** The watchwords are "business," "technology," "marketing," "public relations," "Internet," and "fund raising." Nonprofits at present tend to employ a disproportionate number of people who lack these skills for success. If you have such skills, regardless of your experience, you should appear especially attractive to many nonprofits that have finally recognized that they really need these skills to function in the 21st century.

2. **Be willing to volunteer your services, acquire an internship, or work part-time.** Many nonprofit organizations consist of four major employment groups: board members, volunteers, part-time staff, and full-time staff. Many also offer internship opportunities. In some organizations, especially charitable, the number of volunteer positions may out-number the full-time staff positions. An excellent way to gain experience is to acquire a volunteer position or an internship. When you contact a nonprofit organization, be sure to ask if they have a volunteer program, volunteer positions, internships, or part-time positions. A good starting point is to examine the latest edition of *Invest Yourself: The Catalogue of Volunteer Opportunities* (Commission on Voluntary Service and Action) which outlines more than 200 organizations offering volunteer opportunities in the U.S. and abroad. You may discover that while the organization is not hiring at present for full-time positions, it does have a very active volunteer program. Such a program may be an opportunity to literally "get your foot in the door." Many volunteers later move on to full-time staff positions with nonprofit organizations. Indeed, volunteering not only gives you invaluable experience, but this experience also will help you decide if nonprofit organizations are the right career track for you. With a minimum investment of your time, you may quickly learn whether or not this employment arena is right for you. Better still, such an experience

may put you into important networks that can lead to the perfect job as well as future career advancement within the nonprofit sector.

3. **Always demonstrate your enthusiasm, energy, and competence.** Employers like individuals who are enthusiastic and energetic self-starters. Better still, they like those who demonstrate their competence in solving problems, taking initiative, and operating well with a limited amount of supervision. You can make up for your lack of experience by communicating these qualities to employers. They are the qualities of individuals who can learn and grow within organizations.

4. **Apply for as many jobs as possible.** There's a big nonprofit world out there with hundreds of job opportunities for which you probably qualify. While it is always preferable to target your job search on a few employers, individuals with little or no relevant work experience first need to land a job in order to acquire experience. Therefore, try to apply for as many jobs as possible in order to learn about nonprofit employers and to get experience interviewing for nonprofit jobs. While you may end up with a job that may not be a perfect "fit," it is a job nonetheless. And a job will give you experience for refining your goals.

Organize and Sequence Your Job Search

While we recommend that you plan your job search, we also caution you to avoid the excesses of too much planning. Planning should not be all-consuming. Planning makes sense because it focuses attention and directs action toward specific goals and targets. It requires you to set goals and develop strategies for achieving the goals. However, too much planning can blind you to unexpected occurrences and opportunities—that wonderful experience called serendipity. Given the nature of the job market, you want to do just enough planning so you will be in a position to take advantage of what will inevitably be unexpected occurrences and opportunities arising from your planned job search activities. Therefore, as you plan your job search, be sure you are flexible enough to take advantage of new opportunities.

Based on our previous discussion of the sequence of job search steps, we outline on page 54 a hypothetical plan for conducting an effective job search. This plan incorporates the individual job search activities over a six-month period. If you phase in the first five job search steps during the initial three to four weeks and continue the final four steps in subsequent weeks and months, you should begin receiving job offers within two to three months after initiating your job search. Interviews and job offers can come anytime—often unexpectedly—as you conduct your job search. An average time is three months, but it can occur within a week or take as long as five months. If you plan, prepare, and persist at the job search, the pay-off will be job interviews and offers.

While three months may seem a long time, you can shorten your job search time by increasing the frequency of your individual job search activities. If you are job hunting on a full-time basis, you may be able to cut your job search time in half. But don't expect to get a job—especially a job that's right for you—within a week or two. Job hunting requires time and hard work—perhaps the hardest work you will ever do—but if done properly, it pays off with a job that is right for you.

Take Risks and Handle Rejections

You can approach a job or career change in various ways. Some actions have higher pay-offs than others. Many people waste time by doing nothing, reconstructing the past, worrying about the future, and thinking about what they should have done. They simply fail to take productive actions. This negative approach impedes rather than advances careers.

A second approach is to do what most people do when looking for a job. They examine classified ads, respond to vacancy announcements, and complete applications in personnel offices. While this approach is better than doing nothing, it is relatively inefficient as well as ineffective. You compete with many others who are using the same approach. Furthermore, the vacancy announcements do not represent the true number of job vacancies nor do they offer the best opportunities. You should use this approach to some degree, but it should not preoccupy your time. Responding to vacancy announcements is a game of chance, and the odds are usually against you. It makes you too dependent upon others to give you a job.

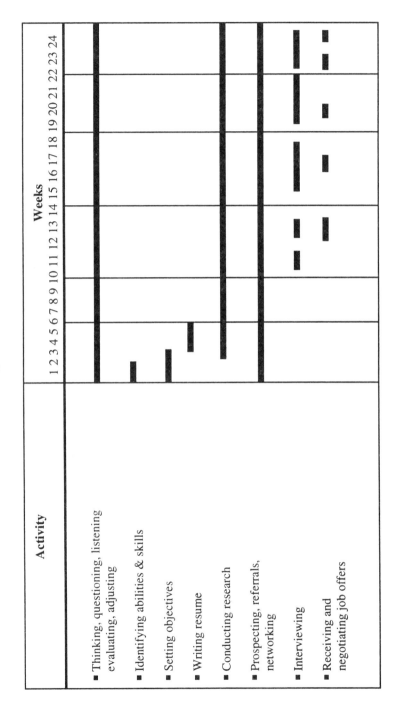

ORGANIZATION OF JOB SEARCH ACTIVITIES

The third approach to finding a nonprofit job requires *taking creative action* on your part. You must become a self-reliant risk-taker. You identify what it is you want to do, what you have acquired skills to do, and organize yourself accordingly by following the methods outlined in this chapter. You don't need to spend much time with classified ads, employment agencies, and personnel offices. And you don't need to worry about your future. You take charge of your future by initiating a job search which pays off with job offers. Your major investment is *time*. Your major risk is being turned down or rejected.

> **Being rejected or having someone say "no" to you will probably be your greatest job hunting difficulty.**

Job hunting is an ego-involving activity. You place your past, abilities, and self-image before strangers who don't know who you are or what you can do. Being rejected or having someone say "no" to you will probably be your greatest job hunting difficulty. We know most people can handle two or three "no's" before they get discouraged. If you approach your job search from a less ego-involved perspective, you can take "no's" in stride; they are a normal aspect of your job search experience. Be prepared to encounter 10, 20, or 50 "no's." Remember, the odds are in your favor. For every 20 "no's" you get, you also should uncover one or two "yeses." The more rejections you get, the more acceptances you also will get. Therefore, you must encounter rejection *before* you get acceptances.

This third approach is the approach we recommend for finding a profitable job with nonprofits. Experience with thousands of clients shows that the most successful job seekers are those who develop a high degree of self-reliance, maintain a positive self-image, and are willing to risk being rejected time after time without becoming discouraged. This approach will work for you if you follow our advice on how to become a self-reliant risk-taker in today's job market. Better yet, if you use networking strategies, you can significantly decrease the number of "no's" you receive on your way to a nonprofit job that's right for you!

5

Key Nonprofit Job Finding Resources

Where exactly should you begin your job search? Should you
look in the classified sections of newspapers or trade publications for job listings? Is there a central clearinghouse for
nonprofit job vacancy information? What about professional
associations? Do they offer placement services, operate job banks, or
advertise vacancies? Can many jobs be found on the Internet? Would you be
better off contacting a nonprofit organization directly for information on job
opportunities?

Organizational and Job Vacancy Information

A wealth of information is readily available on job opportunities with
nonprofit organizations. Indeed, once you discover how to access this
information, you may be overwhelmed with having to sort through so
many alternatives!

You can easily access information on nonprofit organizations and job
vacancies in your local library, over the telephone, or by using a
computer. If you buy only one other book on nonprofit organizations, we
strongly suggest acquiring the latest edition of Daniel Lauber's *Non-
Profits and Education Job Finder* (Planning/Communications). This

book is literally a directory to all the major job listing sources relevant to nonprofit organizations. Organized by occupational areas and states, this comprehensive and affordable resource includes newspapers, trade journals, job banks, and online services available at the local, state, and national levels. If you can't find any appropriate job vacancies relevant to your skills and experience through this directory, chances are none are available. Lauber's book should function as a companion directory to this book. His book is available in most libraries and in many bookstores, or it can be ordered directly from Impact Publications by completing the order form at the end of this book or visiting their Web site.

> **You can easily access information on nonprofits and job vacancies in your local library, over the telephone, or by using your computer.**

Key Books and Directories

Any job search relating to nonprofit organizations should begin with the following books and directories. Most are readily available in major libraries or through Impact Publications (see order form at end of this book or Impact's online bookstore: *www.impactpublications.com*). They constitute an "essential career library" relevant to nonprofits:

➤ *100 Best Nonprofits to Work For* (Macmillan/Simon & Schuster). Authored by Leslie Hamilton and Robert Tragert, this relatively new book (1998) is one of the few attempts to identify the best nonprofits that should be of interest to job seekers. Includes two- to three-page annotations on each nonprofit which cover budget, number of employees, mission, and other useful information. Organized alphabetically. Appendix identifies several useful resources on nonprofits. A great place to start your job search.

➤ *Business Phone Book USA 1999* (Detroit, MI: Omnigraphics). One of our favorite resources, this two-volume work is the ultimate telephone directory for job seekers. Published annually, this massive telephone/fax directory includes more than 137,000 listings, 125,000 fax numbers, 25,000 toll-free numbers, and more than 1,000 Web sites. Organized alphabetically and arranged by subject for different types of businesses and organizations.

Includes hundreds of nonprofit organizations along with listings of businesses and industries nationwide. Major nonprofit categories include:

- Alcoholism and Drug Abuse Treatment Centers
- Associations and Organizations
- Blood Banks
- Colleges and Universities
- Credit Unions
- Foundations
- Hospitals
- Libraries
- Museums and Art Galleries
- Political Action Committees
- Political Parties
- Research Organizations and Services

It's well worth spending some time examining various listings for ideas.

➤ *Compensation in Nonprofit Organizations* (Crete, IL: Abbott, Langer & Associates, Tel. 708/672-4200, Fax 708/672-4674, or visit their Web site: *www.abbott-langer.com*). An annual survey of salaries for over 40,000 positions (87 job categories) in more than 2,000 nonprofit organizations.

➤ *CyberHound's® Guide to Associations and Nonprofit Organizations On the Internet* (Detroit, MI: Gale Research). Includes 2,500 significant associations and nonprofit organizations. Rates sites by stringent and objective rating critera: covering content, technical merit, and design. Useful directory for checking out a site before going online. Published in 1997 but now out of print.

➤ *Directory of Executive Recruiters* (Fitzsimmon, NH: Kennedy Information). This annual directory is the indispensable guide to 6,700 executive recruiters, many of whom recruit for major nonprofit organizations. Includes names, addresses, telephone/fax numbers, e-mail addresses of 4,000 offices of 2,900 firms in the U.S., Canada, and Mexico.

➤ *Encyclopedia of Associations: National Organizations* (Detroit, MI: Gale Research). One of the most useful directories for researching nonprofit organizations. This four-volume annual directory annotates nearly 25,000 associations. Provides a wealth of information on each organization: name, address, phone and fax number, name of primary officials, founding date, staff size, number of members, activities, budget information, official publications, and regional, state, and local groups. Includes useful geographic and executive indexes. Most libraries routinely carry the newest annual edition which is published in July of each year. Many libraries also have the CD-ROM version of this directory (*Associations Unlimited CD-ROM*) which helps in quickly sorting information for targeting specific nonprofit associations. Additional volumes also include regional, state, and local associations and international associations. An annual supplement is published in November of each year. Fabulous and revealing "must review" resource.

➤ *Encyclopedia of Associations: Regional, State, and Local Organizations* (Detroit, MI: Gale Research). Similar in organization and content to the national version of the *Encyclopedia of Association* but focuses on more than 113,000 nonprofit membership organizations that operate at the regional, state, and local levels. Includes trade and professional associations, social welfare and public affairs organizations, and religious sports, and hobby groups with voluntary members. Also available on CD-ROM as part of the *Associations Unlimited CD-ROM* program.

➤ *Finding a Job in the Nonprofit Sector* (Washington, DC: The Taft Group). Somewhat dated (1991) and with no plans for a future updated edition, nonetheless, this directory to nonprofit employers is still useful. Profiles nearly 1,000 nonprofit organizations. Many listings include name, address, phone number, activity, and range of annual income. Coverage of individual organizations is often spotty and income data is mostly useless given the large ranges specified for each organization. Includes a few introductory essays. Entries organized alphabetically. Includes two useful indexes—activity and state. Can still be found in many major libraries.

➤ *The Foundation Directory* (New York: The Foundation Center). This annual directory provides summary information on over 6,300 foundations with assets of at least $2 million or annually disperse $200,000+ in grants. Each entry includes name, address, phone/fax number, assets, support activities, orientation, and key officers. Includes useful geographic and subject indexes. This is the "bible" of the foundation industry. You also may want to visit the Foundation Center's useful Web site: *www.fdncenter.org*

➤ *From Making a Profit to Making a Difference: Careers in Non-Profits For Business Professionals* (River Forest, IL: Planning/ Communications). Authored by Richard M. King, this new book (1999) reveals the inside secrets for switching to nonprofits from the world of business: "strategic volunteerism," building a non-profit contacts network, gaining credibility in the nonprofit community, learning how nonprofit leaders think and hire, writing effective resumes even when you lack any nonprofit experience, compensation standards, classifying your nonprofit interests, transferring business skills to the nonprofit world, and adjusting to the different mindset at nonprofit organizations.

➤ *Good Works: A Guide to Careers in Social Change*, Donna Colvin, ed. (New York: Barricade Books). The latest edition (1994) of this unique directory profiles over 1,000 nonprofit organizations dealing with issues of social change. Each entry includes name, address, phone number, purpose, issues/projects, operations, publications, funding sources, contact person, budget, staff numbers, salaries, and vacancy information. Indexed by state and activity. This publication is associated with Ralph Nader's Common Cause. It's one of the major anchors for one of the better Web sites for nonprofit jobs: *www.essential.org/goodworks*

➤ *In Search of America's Best Nonprofits* (San Francisco: Jossey-Bass). Authored by Richard Steckel and Jennifer Lehman, this book is designed for a diverse audience of managers, fundraisers, and corporate givers. While it does not specifically deal with employment issues, other than a short chapter on nonprofit employers, this is a very useful book for getting an overview of what many "insiders" feel are the best run nonprofits in America.

Includes such large and high profile nonprofits as Alzheimer's Foundation, American Red Cross, Boy Scouts of America, Children's Defense Fund, Girl Scouts of the U.S.A., Habitat For Humanity, International Rescue Committee, Salvation Army, and Planned Parenthood.

➤ *Invest Yourself: The Catalogue of Volunteer Opportunities* (New York: Commission on Voluntary Service and Action, 1998). A comprehensive annotated directory of over 200 organizations that provide volunteer opportunities. Covers everything from agriculture, children, community service, disaster relief, and education to disabled, health care, legal, labor, and public policy groups. Includes several U.S.-based organizations that operate abroad. Summaries operations, skills required, and whom to contact. Useful indexes organized by skill/interest and geographic location.

➤ *Job Hotlines USA* (Harleysville, PA: Career Communications, Inc.). Latest edition (1995) includes over 2,000 job hotlines nationwide—those hard-to-find telephone numbers that lead to recorded job vacancy and application information on a large variety of organizations. Major nonprofit organizations include education, health/medical, and utilities. If you're interested in vacancies with hospitals, this directory is a goldmine of job hotline numbers with such organizations. Listings organized alphabetically and by state and industry. Each entry includes a main address and telephone number along with a highlighted job hotline number.

➤ *National Directory of Nonprofit Organizations 1999* (Washington, DC: The Taft Group). Published biannually, this two-volume directory is the "bible" for locating thousands of nonprofit organizations that are required to file 990 returns with the Internal Revenue Service (IRS). Using the classification system and data available through the IRS, the directory lists each organization alphabetically. The first volume includes all nonprofits with annual incomes exceeding $100,000. The second volume focuses on nonprofits with annual incomes between $25,000 and $99,000. Each listing includes the name, address, annual income, IRS classification, and whether or not contributions to the organization are tax deductible. The directory also classifies the organizations by two useful indexes—activity and geography. For example, it categorizes all nonprofits whose primary mission is dealing with AIDS, child care, employee benefits, grants, health planning, loans to students, peace issues, veterans affairs, and several other activity areas. If you are only interested in working for an emergency service organization in the state of Florida, this directory will help you pinpoint specific nonprofits.

➤ *National Job Hotline Directory* (Planning/Communications). Comprehensive and user-friendly, this new list of job hotlines (telephone numbers that lead to recorded messages on job vacancies) for over 6,500 companies, government agencies, and nonprofit organizations includes instructions on how to effectively use job hotlines as part of a balanced job search. Many of the job hotline numbers are toll-free.

➤ *National Trade and Professional Associations* (Washington, DC: Columbia Books). Published annually, this popular directory looks like a mini-version of the *Encyclopedia of Associations: National Organizations*. Includes addresses, phone/fax numbers, incomes, and employees of nearly 7,500 trade and professional associations. Useful indexes classify organizations by activities, budget size, and geographic location. Available in most libraries.

➤ *Nonprofits and Education Job Finder* (River Forest, IL: Planning/Communications). Key directory to over 2,200 job listing resources dealing with nonprofits. Receives our highest recommendation on pages 56-57.

➤ *Research Centers Directory* (Detroit, MI: Gale Research). Published biannually, this two-volume directory provides annotated descriptions on over 14,300 nonprofit research centers in all fields. Groups entries into 17 chapters that cover five broad subject categories.

Most categories of nonprofit organizations have their own organizational directories. For example, if you're interested in nonprofit environmental organizations, you should examine the *Gale Environmental Sourcebook* and the *Environmental Information Directory*, both published by Gale Research. If you are interested in minority organizations, consult *Minority Organizations* (Ferguson Publishing) and a series of minority directories produced by Gale Research: *Asian Americans Information Directory, Black American's Information Directory, Hispanic Americans Information Directory*, and *Native Americans Information Directory*. For women's organizations, consult two directories also published by Gale Research: *Women's Information Directory* and *Encyclopedia of Women's Associations Worldwide*. A good resource for locating these and other relevant directories is the latest edition of Bernard Klein's *The Directory of Directories* (West Nyack, NY: Todd Publications).

Associations

Several associations provide job information and assistance for individuals interested in nonprofit organizations. Examples of some major such associations related to various categories of nonprofits include:

American Association of Museums
1575 Eye Street NW, Suite 400
Washington, DC 20005
Tel. 202/289-1818 or Fax 202/289-6578
Web site: *www.aam-us.org*

American Association of University Women
1111 16th Street NW
Washington, DC 20036
Tel. 202/785-7700 or Fax 202/872-1425
Web site: *www.aauw.org*

American Federation of Teachers
555 New Jersey Avenue NW
Washington, DC 20001
Tel. 202/879-4400 or Fax 202/879-4556
Web site: *www.aft.org*

American Hospital Association
1 N. Franklin, Suite 27
Chicago, IL 60606
Tel. 312/422-3000 or Fax 312/422-4519
Web site: *www.aha.org*

American Library Association
500 E. Huron Street
Chicago, IL 60611
Tel. 312/944-6780 or Fax 312/280-3255
Web site: *www.ala.org*

American Public Health Association
1015 15th Street NW, Suite 300
Washington, DC 20005
Tel. 202/789-5600 or Fax 202/789-5661
Web site: *www.apha.org*

American Society of Association Executives
1575 Eye Street NW
Washington, DC 20005-1168
Tel. 202/626-2742 or Fax 202/408-9633
Web site: *asaenet.org*

Council on Foundations
1828 L Street NW, Suite 300
Washington, DC 20036
Tel. 202/466-6512 or Fax 202/785-3926
Web site: *www.cof.org*

Independent Sector
1828 L Street NW, Suite 1200
Washington, DC 20036
Tel. 202/223-8100 or Fax 202/416-0580
Web site: *www.indepsec.org*

National Association of Social Workers
750 1st Street NE, Suite 700
Washington, DC 20002-4241
Tel. 202/408-8600 or Fax 202/336-8312
Web site: *naswdc.org*

National Congress For Community Economic Development
11 Dupont Circle, Suite 325
Washington, DC 20036-1207
Tel. 202/234-5009 or Fax 202/234-4510

National Committee on Planned Giving
233 McCrea St., Suite 400
Indianapolis, IN 46225
Tel. 317/269-6274 or Fax 317/269-6276
Web site: *www.ncpg.org*

National Education Association
1201 16th Street NW
Washington, DC 20036
Tel. 202/833-4000 or Fax 202/822-7767
Web site: *www.nea.org*

National Society of Fund Raising Executives
1101 King Street, Suite 700
Alexandria, VA 22314
Tel. 703/684-0410 or Fax 703/684-0540
Web site: *www.nsfre.org*

Nonprofit Management Association
315 W. 9th Street, Suite 1100
Los Angeles, CA 90015
Tel. 213/623-7080 or Fax 213/623-7460

Points of Light Foundation
1400 I Street NW
Washington, DC 20005
Tel. 202/729-8000 or Fax 202/729-8100
Web site: *pointsoflight.org*

Society For Nonprofit Organizations
6314 Odana Road, Suite 1
Madison, WI 53719
Tel. 608/274-9777 or Fax 608/274-9978
Web site: *www.danenet.wicip.org/snpo*

U.S. Chamber of Commerce
1615 H Street NW
Washington, DC 20062
Tel. 202/659-6000 or Fax 202/463-5836
Web site: *www.uschamber.org*

Numerous other professional associations maintain in-house job banks, operate placement services, and list jobs in trade publications and newsletters. The major such associations are identified in Chapter 8.

Vacancy Announcements in Print

Since most nonprofits are very small community-based organizations, many of them will run classified ads or display ads for job openings in the employment section of local newspapers. Therefore, it may be worth monitoring this section of your local newspaper. At the same time, more and more nonprofits have their own Web sites on which they list current job vacancies or they may participate in an online job service for nonprofits, such as *www.nonprofitjobs.org*. Be sure to check both types of Web sites for vacancy announcements.

Nonprofits which are national in scope advertise many of their professional positions in major newspapers, such as the *Washington Post, New York Times, Chicago Tribune,* or *The Los Angeles Times,* especially in the Sunday editions. Many of these nonprofits also recruit online by posting job announcements on major Internet job sites as well as on their own Web sites.

Several newspapers specialize in job listings for nonprofit organizations. The major such newspapers include:

➤ *Association Trends* (Association Trends, 7910 Woodmont Avenue, #1150, Bethesda, MD 20814-3062, Tel. 301/652-8666). This weekly newspaper is one of the major sources of employment information on associations. It includes numerous job listings in each issue. It also maintains a job referral service. Individuals can take out classified ads announcing their availability for positions. Send $95 for 50 issues. Web site: *www.associationtrends.com*

➤ *The Chronicle of Philanthropy* (P.O. Box 1989, Marion, OH 43304, Tel. 800/347-6969 or 202/466-1032). Includes 60 to 90 job listings in each biweekly issue for all types of professional nonprofit positions. Send $36 for a 12-issue subscription or $67.50 for a 24-issue subscription. Web site: *www.philanthropy. com*

➤ *Community Jobs: The Employment Newspaper For the Non-Profit Sector* (Access: Networking in the Public Interest, 1001 Connecticut Avenue NW, Suite 838, Washington, DC 20036, Tel. 202/785-4233). A "must" resource for anyone looking for a job with nonprofits. Each issue of this 40-page monthly newspaper is filled with informative articles, job hunting tips, and nearly 400 job listings for individuals interested in working in the nonprofit sector. Individuals can subscribe by sending $39 for 6 months or $76 for one year. The articles and job listings also are available through Access's Web site: *www.communityjobs.org*.

➤ *Chronicle of Higher Education* (1255 23rd St. NW, Suite 700, Washington, DC 20037, Tel. 202/466-1000). This weekly newspaper includes informative articles on higher education as well as hundreds of classified ads for recruiting university administrators and faculty as well as professional positions with associations and foundations. Send $75.00 for an annual subscription (48 issues) or $3.25 per issue. Web site: *http://chronicle.com*

➤ *National Business Employment Weekly* (P.O. Box 300, Princeton, NJ 08543, Tel. 609/520-4313). This weekly newspaper includes hundreds of classified and display ads for all types of positions. The first and third issues of each month include a special section with 40 or more ads for professionals in the nonprofit sector which are supplied by Access (*Community Jobs*). Send $38 for 2 month, $52 for 3 months, $112 for 6 months, or $199 for an annual subscription. Web site: *www.nbew.com*

➤ *The NonProfit Times* (240 Cedar Knolls Road, Suite 318, Cedar Knolls, NJ 07927, Tel. 201/734-1700). This monthly publication includes 20-30 job listings in its "National NonProfit Employment Marketplace" for numerous types of nonprofit positions. Send $59 for an annual subscription. Check out their Web site for useful links to nonprofits: *www.nptimes.com*

In-House Job Services of Professional Associations

Several professional associations offer a variety of career services for individuals interested in working in the nonprofit sector. These range from job banks and placement programs to electronic online services. Many professional associations—such as the American Society of Association Executives, American Public Health Association, National Organization of Women, National Association of Broadcasters, Catalyst, U.S. Chamber of Commerce, Urban Coalition, and the American Chemical Society—operate their own in-house career and placement services. Be sure to check with various professional associations to see if they maintain a job bank or offer career services. If they do, chances are many nonprofits come directly to these organizations to use their job banks for recruiting personnel. You'll want to make sure you have a current resume in their resume database as well as periodically review new job listings. More and more employers turn to these professional associations to recruit key personnel.

> **Be sure to check with various professional associations to see if they maintain a job bank or offer career services.**

Key Off-Line Resume Databases

In the early 1990s—before the Internet became the key medium for accessing job information—off-line electronic resume databases became very popular with many job seekers and employers who found them to be very efficient employment arenas. Individuals paid monthly or yearly fees to belong to a resume database which was accessed by employers in search of individuals with certain skills and experience. Individuals submitted an electronic version of their resumes to be scanned in a resume database. Employers, in turn, did keyword searches to identify qualified candidates.

However by the mid-1990s, the rapid movement of such databases to the Internet, as well as the rise of new online commercial employment services which included resume databases and special search futures, put many off-line databases out of business. Primarily financed by employers and advertising fees, these online services allowed individuals to post their resumes in an online database and search job listings free of charge. Consequently, fee-based resume databases that charged job seekers for their services became less popular than the free online employment services that charged employers advertising and access fees. However, several off-line resume databases still operate. Many of them also have an online feature. You may want to start with some of the most popular electronic resume database firms. While they include all types of jobs, they also include some nonprofit jobs:

❏ **Career Net Graduate:** INET. 643 W. Crosstown Parkway, Kalamazoo, MI 49008, Tel. 616-344-3017. Designed for college students and recent graduates, this service makes resumes available to thousands of employers. This is now a free service to job seekers. You can enter your career profile online at *www.careernet.com*

❏ **Cors:** One Pierce Place, Suite 300 East, Itasca, IL 60143, Tel. 800-323-1352, 708-250-8677 or Fax 708-250-7362. Claims to have 2.5 million resumes in its database. Contracts with employers to recruit candidates from database. Charges one-time $25 fee for entering resume in database. Allows unlimited updates. Can complete an online form and submit it by e-mail over their Web site: *www.cors.com/corspro.htm*

❏ **Electronic Job Matching:** Human Resource Management Center, 1915 N. Dale Mabry Highway, Suite 307, Tampa, FL 33607, Tel. 813-879-4100 or Fax 813-870-1883. Includes applicant resumes in database that can be accessed by employers who pay search fees. Free of charge for job seekers. Represents many different occupational fields and several experience levels. For more information, visit their Web site: *www.hrmc.com*

❏ **Resume-Link:** 5995 Wilcox Place, Dublin, OH 43016. Tel. 614-923-0600 or Fax 614-923-0610. Specializes in the computer and engineering fields. Includes thousands of resumes in its database. Free to job seekers who belong to a relevant professional society ($50 a year for nonmembers). Employers pay access fees. Web site: *www.resume-link.com*

❏ **SkillSearch:** 3354 Perimeter Hill Drive, Suite 235, Nashville, TN 37211-4129, Tel. 615-834-9448 or Fax 615-834-9453. Sponsored by 100 university alumni associations, alumni associated with each sponsoring university can have their resumes included in the database for $49 a year. The SkillSearch database includes nearly 35,000 resumes. Employers pay a per-search fee to use the database. For more information, visit their Web site: *www.skillsearch.com*

❑ **University ProNet:** 2445 Faber Place, Suite 200, Palo Alto, CA 94303-3394, Tel. 650-845-4000 or Fax 650-845-4019. Participation restricted to alumni of 20 member universities: California Institute of Technology, Carnegie-Mellon University, Columbia University, Cornell University, Duke University, Georgia Tech, Massachusetts Institute of Technology, Ohio State University, Purdue University, Stanford University, University of California at Berkeley, University of California at Los Angeles, University of Chicago, University of Illinois, University of Michigan, University of Pennsylvania, University of Texas at Austin, University of Wisconsin, U.S. Naval Academy, and Yale University. Employers, which consists of 300 corporate subscribers, pay an annual subscription fee to participate in the database. Alumni charged a one-time $35 registration fee. Operated by the alumni associations at each participating university. Can register online by going to the University ProNet Web site which links to each member university: *www.universitypronet.com*

Web Sites and Online Services

During the past three years, nonprofits have begun to embrace the Internet. As they become more and more technologically sophisticated and Internet savvy, they are turning to the Internet to recruit personnel. They are discovering what many employers in the private sector have learned in the past few years: the Internet provides a relatively inexpensive and efficient arena for finding talented personnel. Consequently, you are strongly urged to focus a great deal of your job search attention on the Internet in order to:

1. Research various nonprofits that have their own Web sites to identify which ones best fit your interests and skills.

2. Survey online job listings found on a variety of sites.

3. Enter your resume in various online resume databases.

Except for some specialized executive-level services, most of these sites and online employment services are free to job seekers. Employers pay for both posting job listings online and accessing resumes in an online resume database. You are well advised to also embrace the Internet. Chances are your next job will be initially found via the Internet. While classified ads in newspapers and trade journals still play an important role in locating vacancies, they are quickly becoming a secondary market to online job postings.

If you are new to conducting an online job search, we highly recommend starting with these major Internet employment sites which include a variety of job listings, online job banks (resume databases), and useful information on conducting an online job search. Many of these sites include jobs with nonprofit organizations.

Major Internet Employment Sites

Within the past three years, hundreds of new career-related services have appeared on the Internet's World Wide Web, and several of those which used to be accessed only through the commercial online services, such as AOL, are now available on the World Wide Web. In fact, this is where most online career networking is taking place these days.

The following organizations now operate databases and career services on the Internet's World Wide Web. Most of them offer a combination of free and fee-based services and products. Some primarily operate as job listing bulletin boards (BBS) or newsgroups:

❑ **America's Job Bank:** *www.ajb.dni.us.* Here's the ultimate "public job bank" that could eventually put some private online entrepreneurs out of business. Operated by the U.S. Department of Labor, this is the closest thing to a comprehensive nationwide computerized job bank. Linked to state employment offices, which daily post thousands of new job listings filed by employers with their offices, individuals should soon be able to explore more than a million job vacancies in both the public and private sectors at any time through this service. Since this is your government at work, this service is free. While the jobs listed cover everything from entry-level to professional and managerial positions, expect to find a disproportionate number of jobs requiring less than a college education listed in this job bank. This service is also available at state employment offices as well as at other locations (look for touch screen kiosks in shopping centers and other public places) which are set up for public use. Useful linkages.

❑ **CareerBuilder:** *www.careerbuilder.com.* A real up and coming site which uses a different approach—heavily advertises on radio, especially early in morning when individuals are commuting to work. Gets lots of hits during the noon hours when employees search their site for job listings! Employers list job vacancies in anticipation of getting hits from job seekers. Also, job seekers complete a questionnaire and receive e-mail messages when a position fits their keywords. Does not operate a resume database since they contact you.

❑ **CareerCity:** *www.careercity.com.* Operated by one of the major publishers of career books, this online service includes job listings, discussion forums (conferences, workshops, Q&A sessions), specialized career services, and publications.

❑ **Career Magazine:** *www.careermag.com.* A very user-friendly and useful site with lots of advice, newsgroups, and links. Includes a directory of executive recruiters as well as a resume database.

❑ **CareerMosiac:** *www.careermosiac.com.* This job service is appropriate for college students and professionals. Includes hundreds of job listings in a large variety of fields, from high-tech to retail, with useful information on each employer and job. Includes a useful feature whereby college students can communicate directly with employers (e-mail) for information and advice—a good opportunity to do "inside" networking.

❑ **CareerPath:** *www.careerpath.com.* Over 30 major newspapers across the country participate in this site which primarily consists of newspaper classified ads being put online. Many job announcements are for nonprofits. Includes lots of advice as well as Richard Nelson Bolles' *What Color Is Your Parachute?* site which serves as a gateway site to many other Internet employment sites.

❑ **CareerWeb:** *www.careerweb.com.* Operated by Landmark Communications (Norfolk, Virginia) which also publishes several newspapers and operates The Weather Channel and InfiNet, this service is a major recruitment source for hundreds of companies nationwide. Free service for job seekers who can explore hundreds of job listings, many of which are in high-tech fields. Covers some nonprofits. Includes company profile pages to learn about a specific company. A quality operation.

❑ **E.span:** *www.espan.com.* This full-service online employment resource includes hundreds of job listings in a variety of fields as well as operates a huge database of resumes. Job seekers can send their resumes (e-mail or snail mail) to be included in their database of job listings and search for appropriate job openings through the Interactive Employment Network. Also includes useful career information and resources.

❑ **JobTrak:** *www.jobtrak.com.* This organization posts over 500 new job openings each day from companies seeking college students and graduates. Includes company profiles, job hunting tips, and employment information. Good source for entry-level positions, including both full-time and part-time positions, and for researching companies. Very popular with college students.

❑ **JobWeb:** *www.jobweb.org.* A comprehensive online service targeted for the college scene. Operated by the National Association of Colleges and Universities (formerly the College Placement Council), this service is designed to do everything: compiles information on employers, including salary surveys; lists job openings; provides job search assistance; and maintains a resume database.

❑ **Monster Board:** *www.monster.com.* One of the Internet's largest and most popular sites. Lots of job listings and company profiles. Owned by TMP, an advertising recruitment firm, which also owns the Online Career Center.

❑ **Online Career Center:** *www.occ.com/occ.* This is the grandaddy of career centers on the Internet. It's basically a resume database and job search service. Individuals send their resume (free if transmitted electronically) which is then included in the database. Individuals also can search for appropriate job openings. Employers pay for using the service. Also available through online commercial services.

Many other Web sites also have resume databases. At the very minimum, you also should visit these sites:

4Work.com	*www.4work.com*
America's Employers	*www.americasemployers.com*
Best Jobs U.S.A.	*www.bestjobsusa.com*
Black Collegian	*www.black-collegian.com*
CareerCast	*www.careercast.com*
Career.com	*www.career.com*
CareerMart	*www.careermart.com*
CareerSite	*www.careersite.com*
Careers.wsj.com	*www.careers.wsj.com*
College Central	*www.collegecentral.com*

College Grad Job Hunter	*www.collegegrad.com*
Headhunter.net	*www.headhunter.net*
Internet Job Locator	*www.joblocator.com/jobs*
JobBank USA	*www.jobbankusa.com*
JobDirect	*www.jobdirect.com*
NationJob Network	*www.nationjob.com*
TOPjobs USA	*www.topjobsusa.com*
Town Online Working	*www.townonline.com/working*
Westech Virtual Job Fair	*www.vjf.com*
World.Hire Online	*www.world.hire.com*
Yahoo! Classifieds	*classifieds.yahoo.com/employment.html*

If you are with the military, or you are a veteran, you may want to get your resume in the resume databases of these excellent sites:

Green to Gray Online	*www.greentogray.com*
Blue to Gray Online	*www.bluetogray.com*
Transition Assistance Online	*www.taonline.com*

If you want to send your resume to executive recruiters or headhunters, try these two sites:

| DICE | *www.dice.com* |
| Recruiters Online Network | *www.ipa.com* |

If you want to electronically broadcast your resume to hundreds of companies, try these sites. All are free except for CareerSearch which charges a fee:

CareerSearch	*www.careersearch.net*
CompaniesOnline	*www.companiesonline.com*
E.span	*www.espan.com*
Resumail	*www.resumail.com*
ResumePath	*www.resumepath*

Hundreds of other Web sites, many of which are occupationally specialized, also operate resume databases. And don't forget to contact your professional association. More and more professional associations are developing their own online services and résumé databases to better serve the career needs of their members. You may find these Web sites more useful since they are targeted toward your profession and primarily involve employers who are looking for your occupational specialty.

Sites Specializing in Employment With Nonprofits

During the past three years, several nonprofits have organized their own Web sites. In addition to including information about the organization, members, services, and funding, many of these sites have a job or employment section which lists job vacancies with the organization. Some operate their own resume databases. You are well advised to visit several of these Web sites since they constitute a key network for finding jobs with nonprofits. They will probably prove more useful than the more general commercial online employment services outlined above. Start with these sites:

❑ **Nonprofit Career Network:** *www.nonprofitcareer.com.* One of the largest networks for job seekers and nonprofits. Includes national and international job listings with nonprofit organizations as well as a resume database with a useful search engine—can specify either full-time or part-time positions by preferred location. A nonprofit directory section allows you to search for nonprofits by name; provides essential contact information (address, telephone and fax numbers, Web addresses).

❑ **Community Career Center:** *www.nonprofitjobs.org.* Includes hundreds of job listings with nonprofits. Site also allows candidates to advertise their interests and qualifications ($25 for six months). Search engine enables user to specify preferred salary range, location, skills, and field or mission of interest. Lists numerous members with Web linkages.

❑ **Access/Community Jobs:** *www.communityjobs.org.* Access is a noted clearinghouse for employment and careers with nonprofits. It publishes the popular monthly newspaper, *Community Jobs* ($25 for 3 months; $39 for 6 months; $76 for 12 months). This site includes numerous employment articles that appear in recent issues of the newspaper as well as job listings, career information, and a book-store. The site also advertises job counseling through Access ($55 for resume and cover letter review and $75 for each 1.5 hours of career counseling). Its job listings also are linked to the Wall Street Journal's online employment partner (*www.careers.wsj.com*). Since this is primarily an off-line print operation (newspaper with classified ads and articles), Access does not maintain a resume database nor have a search engine. Can review print job listings that have been simultaneously posted to their Web site. One of the best employment resources relevant to the nonprofit job market.

❏ **Philanthropy Journal Online:** *www.pj.org.* Includes a wealth of information on nonprofit organizations, from current trends to job listings.

❏ **Chronicle of Philanthropy:** *www.philanthropy.com.* Includes numerous job listings that appear in the *Chronicle* as well as many linkages to nonprofit organizations.

❏ **Good Works:** *www.essential.org/goodworks.* This is the Web site for the book *Good Works*, a national directory of nearly 1,000 social change organizations. Includes many job listings with nonprofits which are organized by state.

Important Gateway Sites to Nonprofits

The following Web sites function as important gateway sites to the world of nonprofits. While many of them also include job listings, their primary focus tends to be on information in general:

❏ **Action Without Borders:** *www.idealist.org.* A terrific gateway site to the world of nonprofits. Includes a powerful search engine to locate over 15,000 nonprofit organizations, many of which have their own homepages with job listings. You'll want to visit and revisit this site frequently.

❏ **Nonprofit Resources Catalog/Philip H. Walker:** *www.clark.net/ pub/pwalker.* One of the most important gateway sites to the nonprofit world. Expansive classification system which includes hundreds of links to key nonprofit sites. A great place to start any investigation of the nonprofit sector. Can easily get lost in the myriad of information linked to this exhaustive site!

❏ **GuideStar:** *www.guidestar.org.* Includes a wealth of resources on nonprofit organizations, especially volunteer groups, along with job listings and links to other nonprofit sites.

❑ **Internet Nonprofit Center:** *www.nonprofits.org*. Functions as an information center for nonprofits, donors, and volunteers interested in the nonprofit world. Includes lots of linkages to nonprofits in its "Gallery of Organizations" and has a "Nonprofit Locator" to search for any charity in the U.S. Its "Nonprofit Directory" links to the useful Action Without Borders site: *www.idealist.org*

❑ **Opportunity NOCs:** *www.opnocs.org*. This site has a decided regional focus—nonprofits in New England. Includes biweekly job listings for nonprofit organizations operating in New England as well as lots of linkages to nonprofits throughout the region. If you're interested in working for a nonprofit in Boston, this site should be very useful in your job search.

❑ **Council on Foundations:** *www.cof.oprg*. Major gateway site to the world of foundations. This is the nonprofit membership organization of 1,500 grantmaking foundations and corporations that contribute more than $6 billion to various grant programs that fund a large portion of the nonprofit sector.

❑ **Foundation Center:** *www.fdncenter.org*. This is the site for the premier foundation training and education organization. Includes lots of useful information on foundations.

❑ **Independent Sector:** *www.indepsec.org*. This is an important gateway site to some of the major nonprofit organizations. Made up of a national coalition of nearly 800 voluntary organizations, foundations, and corporate giving programs. Includes links to member organizations.

❑ **National Center For Nonprofit Boards:** *www.ncnb.org*. Includes lots of useful information on the governing boards of nonprofit organizations as well as many useful linkages.

❑ **National Council of Nonprofit Associations:** *www.ncna.org*. Major gateway site to state associations of nonprofits which also serve as gateways to community-based nonprofits.

❑ **Information For Nonprofits:** *www.nonprofit-info.org*. Gateway site to many local nonprofits, especially in the state of Washington.

❑ **Impact Online:** *www.impactonline.org*. Provides online matching services for voluntary and nonprofit organizations. Includes advice, services, volunteer opportunities, and linkages to many state non-profit organizations.

❏ **Charity Village:** *www.charityvillage.com*. Major gateway site to Canadian charities.

Connecting to Community-Based Nonprofits

While the most popular nonprofits tend to be national in scope, in reality the bulk of nonprofits operate at the state and local levels. Each state has one or two organizations or associations that maintain contacts with hundreds and thousands of community-based nonprofits. More and more of the state coalitions have developed their own Web sites that include directories of local nonprofits, linkages to member Web sites, and job listings. By visiting these sites, you should be able to gather a great deal of information on nonprofits in your own community. At present the following state nonprofit organizations and associations have Web sites worth visiting for information and linkages:

Alabama
Nonprofit Resource Center of Alabama
Web site: *www.nonprofit-al.org*

Arkansas
Nonprofit Resources, Inc.
Web site: *www.aristotle.net/~nonprofit*

California
California Association of Nonprofits
Web site: *www.canonprofits.org*

Colorado
Colorado Association of Nonprofit Organizations
Web site: *www.canpo.org*

Delaware
Delaware Association of Nonprofit Agencies
Web site: *www.delawarenonprofit.org*

Florida
Florida Association of Nonprofit Organizations
Web site: *www.special-event.com/FANO*

Illinois
Donors Forum of Chicago
Web site: *www.donorsforum.org*

Maryland
Maryland Association of Nonprofit Organizations
Web site: *www.mdnonprofit.org*

Massachusetts
Massachusetts Council of Human Service Providers
Web site: *www.providers.org*

Michigan
Michigan League For Human Services
Web site: *www.msu.edu/user.mlhs*

Minnesota
Minnesota Council of Nonprofits
Web site: *www.mncn.org*

New Hampshire
Granite State Association of Nonprofits
Web site: *www.nbnonprofits.org*

New Jersey
Center For Non-Profit Corporations
Web site: *www.njnonprofits.org*

New York
Nonprofit Coordinating Committee of New York
Web site: *www.npccny.org*

North Carolina
North Carolina Center For Nonprofits
Web site: *www.ncnonprofits.org*

North Dakota
North Dakota Association of Nonprofit Organizations
Web site: *www.ncna.org/ND*

Pennsylvania
Pennsylvania Association of Nonprofit Organizations
Web site: *www.pano.org*

Rhode Island
Nonprofit Resources of Southern New England
Web site: *www.ncna.org/RI*

South Carolina
South Carolina Association of Nonprofit Organizations
Web site: *www.ncna.org/SC*

Tennessee
Tennessee Nonprofit Association
Web site:
   www.nastn.citysearch.com/E/V/NASTN/0003/59/71/12.html

Texas
Texas Association of Nonprofit Organizations
Web site: *www.tano.org*

Utah
Utah Nonprofit Association
Web site: *www.nonprofit.utah.org*

Washington
The Evergreen State Society
Web site: *www.tess.org*

Washington
West Nonprofit Resources
Web site: *www.tran.org/nnr*

For further information on nonprofits operating at the regional, state, and local levels, consult the latest edition of the *Encyclopedia of*

Associations: Regional, State, and Local Organizations (Gale Research). This directory annotates more than 113,000 nonprofits. If you live in a large urban area, chances are many of the major nonprofits have formed a local association, council, or consortium of nonprofits. Your local government (Department of Social Services) or local chapter of the United Way should have information on such an organization. The National Council of Nonprofit Associations (1001 Connecticut Avenue, Suite 900, Washington, DC 20036-5504, Tel. 202/833-5740) maintains current information on community-based nonprofits. Look for useful linkages on their Web site: *www.ncna.org*

Reviewing Web Sites of Major Nonprofits

While we've attempted to include as many Web site addresses as possible in our annotated listings of nonprofits in Chapters 7-9, you may want to quickly examine several of the following Web sites. They are operated by some of today's largest and best known nonprofit organizations. Most of them include an employment section as well as information on their organization and links to other relevant organizations and services in the nonprofit sector. This set of Web addresses will give you a quick overview of the types of information you can easily access over the Internet:

ACCION International	*www.accion.org*
American Association of Retired Persons (AARP)	*www.aarp.org*
American Bar Association	*www.aba.org*
American Chemical Society	*www.acs.org*
American Heart Association	*www.americanheart.org*
American Hospital Association	*www.aha.org*
American Lung Association	*www.lungusa.org*
American Medical Association	*www.ama.org*
American Petroleum Institute	*www.api.org*
American Red Cross	*www.redcross.org*
American Society of Association Executives	*www.asaenet.org*
Americares Foundation	*www.americares.org*
Amnesty International, USA	*www.amnesty.org*
Alzheimer's Association	*www.alz.org*

Arthritis Foundation	*www.arthritis.org*
Big Brothers Big Sisters of America	*www.bbbsa.org*
Boy Scouts of America	*www.basa.counting.org*
CARE	*www.care.org*
Catholic Relief Services	*www.devcap.org/crs*
Chamber of Commerce of the U.S.A.	*www.uschamber.org*
Children's Defense Fund	*www.childrensdefense.org*
Close Up Foundation	*www.closeup.org*
Environmental Defense Fund	*www.edf.org*
Food For the Hungry	*www.fh.org*
Girl Scouts of the U.S.A.	*www.girlscouts.org*
Goodwill Industries International	*www.goodwill.org*
Greenpeace	*www.greenpeaceusa.org*
Habitat For Humanity International	*www.habitat.org*
Institute of International Education	*www.iie.org*
Insurance Institute of America	*www.aicpu.org*
International Rescue Committee	*www.intrescom.org*
Make-a-Wish Foundation	*www.wish.org*
Mercy Corps International	*www.mercycorps.org*
Metropolitan Museum of Art	*www.matmuseum.org*
Mothers Against Drunk Driving	*www.madd.org*
NAACP	*www.naacp.org*
National Association of Manufacturers	*www.nam.org*
National Broadcasting Service	*www.pbs.org*
National Education Association	*www.nea.org*
National Organization of Women	*www.now.org*
National Public Radio	*www.pbs.org*
National Rifle Association	*www.nra.org*
National Urban League	*www.nul.org*
National Wildlife Federation	*www.nwf.org*
Nature Conservancy	*www.tnc.org*
Outward Bound	*www.outwardbound.org*
Oxfam America	*www.oxfamamerica.org*
People For the American Way	*www.pfaw.org*
Plan International	*www.plan-international.org*
Planned Parenthood Federation	*www.ppfa.org*
Population Council	*www.popcouncil.org*
Salvation Army	*www.salvationarmy.org*

Save the Children Federation   *www.savethechildren.org*
Share Our Strength   *www.strength.org*
Sierra Club   *www.sierraclub.org*
Special Olympics   *www.specialolympics.org*
Technoserve   *www.technoserve.org*
United Way of America   *www.unitedway.org*
Veterans of Foreign Wars   *www.vfw.org*
Volunteers of America   *www.voa.org*
Wilderness Society   *www.wwf.org*
World Visions   *www.worldvision.org*
World Wildlife Fund   *www.wilderness.org*

Useful Electronic Job Search Resources

If you are new to conducting an online job search, you're in good luck. You'll find several excellent resources that focus on everything from identifying key employment sites on the Internet to creating electronic and e-mail versions of your resume and managing an online job search. However, given the rapid changes taking place on the Internet, many of these resources quickly become outdated. Among some of the most useful such resources are:

Criscito, Pat, *Resumes in Cyberspace* (Hauppauge, NY: Barrons, 1997)

Crispin, Gerry and Mark Mehler, *CareerXroads 1999* (Kendall Park, NJ: MMC Group, 1999)

Dixon, Pam, *Job Searching Online For Dummies* (Foster City, CA: IDG Books, 1998)

Jandt, Fred E. and Mary Nemnick, *Cyberspace Resume Kit: How to Make a Snazzy Online Resume!* (Indianapolis, IN: JIST Works, 1999)

Jandt, Fred E. and Mary Nemnick, *Using the Internet and the World Wide Web in Your Job Search* (Indianapolis, IN: JIST Works, 1997)

Karl, Shannon and Arthur Karl, *How to Get Your Dream Job Using the Web* (Scottsdale, AZ: Coriolis Group Books, 1997)

Kennedy, Joyce Lain, *Hook Up, Get Hired* (New York: Wiley & Sons, Inc., 1995)

Kennedy, Joyce Lain, *Resumes For Dummies* (Foster City, CA: IDG Books, 1998)

Kennedy, Joyce Lain and Thomas J. Morrow, *Electronic Job Search Revolution* (New York: Wiley & Sons, Inc., 1996)

Kennedy, Joyce Lain and Thomas J. Morrow, *Electronic Resume Revolution* (New York: Wiley & Sons, Inc. 1996)

Oakes, Elizabeth H., *Career Exploration On the Internet* (Chicago, IL: Ferguson Publishing, 1998)

Riley, Margaret, Frances Roehm, and Steve Oserman, *The Guide to Internet Job Searching* (Lincolnwood, IL: NTC Publishing, 1998)

Weddle, Peter D., *Internet Resumes* (Manassas Park, VA: Impact Publications, 1998)

These and other relevant resources are available directly from Impact Publications by completing the order form at the end of this book or by visiting Impact's online career bookstore: *www.impactpublications.com*

Executive Search Firms and Resources

Many nonprofit organizations recruit their top talent through professional associations and executive search firms. If you seek an executive-level position, you should join as well as contact the American Society of Association Executives (1575 Eye Street NW, Washington, DC 20005, Tel. 202/626-2723. This organization provides in-house career services. It also maintains one of the best libraries on nonprofit organizations—a terrific resource for job hunters. For more information, visit their Web site: *www.asaenet.org*

We also recommend getting a copy of the latest edition of *The Directory of Executive Recruiters* (Kennedy Information). This is a "bible" for anyone interested in contacting executive recruiters. Many of the firms listed in this directory recruit executive-level professionals for key positions in trade and professional associations as well as in other nonprofit organizations.

CEO Update (1575 Eye Street NW, Suite 1190, Washington, DC 20005, Tel. 202/408-7900) specializes in job vacancy announcements for executives working with nonprofits. Focuses on jobs that pay above $50,000 a year. This biweekly publications includes nearly 200 vacancies per issue. Subscriptions rates: 7 issues for $90.00; 13 issues for $160.00; 26 issues for $300.00. For more information, review their Web site: *www.associationjobs.com* or *www.careeropps.com*

The Search Bulletin (The Beacon Group, P.O. Box 641, Great Falls, VA 22066, Tel. 1-800-486-9220) is a 30-40 page biweekly newsletter listing 350-400 executive-level positions in the $70,000-$300,000+ range. It includes some listings for nonprofit organizations. Subscriptions are available at the following rates: 6 issues for $115.00; 12 issues for $187.00. Web site: *www.searchbulletin.com*

Most of the online resources for nonprofit jobs we discussed earlier on pages 75-76 will include executive level positions.

Individuals interested in working with international nonprofit organizations should review the specialized resources identified in Chapter 9.

6

The World of Nonprofit Employers and Your Job Search

ith over 1 million nonprofit organizations spending nearly $500 billion each year and generating over 10 million jobs, it's virtually impossible to provide complete or representative coverage of nonprofit employers. Nor is it necessarily desirable for you and others interested in finding a nonprofit job to have such a definitive guide to nonprofit employers. Indeed, such a book would be unwieldy and confined to the reference section of only a few libraries. It would probably consist of several volumes running thousands and thousands of pages—and would still be incomplete!

And if we only examined the largest nonprofits, we would disproportionately cover hospitals, credit unions, educational institutions, and utility companies—organizations that satisfy IRS regulations but are not considered "real nonprofits" by many fellow nonprofit organizations. Such groups are of little interest to those who want to pursue a nonprofit career with smaller organizations that function as advocacy, charitable, or philanthropic groups.

Our Choices

Our coverage of nonprofit organizations follows a very simple principle —we chose to profile those organizations which we thought would be of greatest interest to our readers. In this sense, our choices are somewhat arbitrary and follow the stereotypes of many types of nonprofits—organizations that have social agendas, that deal with interesting and important public issues, and whose operations are primarily national or international in scope. These are the types of purposeful organizations many individuals get passionate about. We also include several professional associations and international nonprofits—some which do not have special IRS nonprofit status—because they offer excellent opportunities for individuals pursuing other types of nonprofit interests and causes. Although there are exceptions, most nonprofits we've listed employ 10 or more people and have budgets of at least $500,000.

Our omissions are obvious and quite intentional: we cover few local nonprofits. Furthermore, we skip most hospitals, credit unions, educational institutions, and utility companies. While ostensibly nonprofits, for all intents and purposes, these organizations are large businesses that adhere to special provisions of the Federal Tax Code (Sections 501 c and d) that allow them to financially operate as nonprofits. While they deal with many interesting public issues, these nonprofits have less discernible social and political agendas.

> **Our nonprofits are primarily located in Washington, DC, New York City, Chicago, and San Francisco—the major centers for national and international nonprofit organizations.**

By excluding most small local nonprofits and including professional associations and international nonprofits, the nonprofit organizations which are profiled in the remainder of this book are primarily located in Washington, DC, New York City, Chicago, and San Francisco. While these cities are the major centers for national and international nonprofit organizations, they by no means represent the overall geographic dispersion of nonprofits. Again, nonprofit organizations are found in every community. Larger communities will have a larger number of nonprofits, reflecting the overall diversity and complexity of such communities.

A Nonprofit Starter Kit

Most of the nonprofit organizations identified in this book should give you a glimpse into the employment world of nonprofit organizations.

You may find four or five organizations of particular interest to you and thus you follow-through by contacting the organizations for more information on employment opportunities. You may even go so far as to find a job with one of the organizations. If you do, that's great; you will have exceeded our expectations. In most cases, however, we expect users to examine our listings for ideas and as a starting place to network for finding a job with particular types of organizations. For example, if you are especially interested in working for an environmental group, you'll find we include information on only 40 nonprofit employers focused on environmental issues. Use these 40 listings as your starting point for exploring these and many other related environmental organizations. Treat our organizations as only the tip of the iceberg—you'll want to also look at the *Gale Environmental Sourcebook, Environmental Information Directory, Encyclopedia of Associations,* and the *National Directory of Nonprofit Organizations* (see pages 57-62) for information on hundreds of additional nonprofit organizations dealing with environmental issues.

The same principle applies to all of our other listings—these should be starting points for heading you in the right direction in finding your own suitable nonprofit employer. In this sense, the remainder of the book should become your starter kit for further learning, exploration, and discovery. If you approach the listings in this manner, you will find the right path to a nonprofit organization that is right for you. The result should be a good "fit".

Initiate Contacts and Follow-Up

As we noted in Chapter 4, your job search should follow a certain sequence and be based on key principles for success. Assuming you know what you want to do, you have conducted preliminary research, have written a dynamite resume, and understand where to find various job listings, your next step is to make direct contact with potential employers. Once you identify an employer you wish to contact, the first thing you should do is to verify the address and contact person. The best way to do this is to literally pick up the telephone and call for information and advice. In the process, you should try to get other important employment information. Projecting an upbeat, cheery, and enthusiastic voice (you're an assertive but very likable person), your conversation should go something like this:

OPENER: *Hi, this is Marcia Taylor. I need some information on your organization.* (The response is likely to be, what type of information can I help you with?)

CONTACT: *Whom should I contact about employment opportunities with your organization?* (Assuming you get a name of a person, go to the next question.)

                Could you please transfer me to him? Thanks.

REQUEST: *Hi, this is Marcia Taylor. I'm in the process of gathering information on career opportunities with environmental organizations. How do you go about hiring for positions in your organization? Do you normally advertise in the local newspaper or a particular trade journal or do you maintain a resume bank?* (Assuming the answer is both, go on to the next question.)

                Are you doing any hiring at present?

                For what types of positions? Full-time, part-time, volunteer?

                How often do vacancies normally occur?

                Could I send you a copy of my resume? I'm really interested in your organization and would love to have an opportunity to interview for a position.

ADDRESS: *Should I send my resume directly to you? Are you still located at: _____?*

REFERRAL: *Since you're not hiring at present, do you know any other environmental groups that might be hiring now or perhaps in the near future?*

CLOSE: *Thanks so much. I really appreciate the information. I'll send you my resume tomorrow and hopefully speak with you soon.*

By just picking up the telephone and using this type of direct approach, you should be able to get four critical things for improving your employability with this type of nonprofit organization:

1. Accurate information about the organization's hiring structure and practices, including whether or not they are currently hiring, and if they compile an in-house resume bank for future reference.

2. Permission to submit your resume and application to a specific person in a position of screening and/or hiring responsibility.

3. Advice and referrals relevant to other organizations in the same occupational field—you tap into the current grapevine of information on who's hiring where for what positions.

4. A relationship established over the telephone with someone who may help you in the future and who hopefully will remember you as that "nice person" they spoke with recently.

Be sure to follow-up this phone call with a nice cover letter and a copy of your resume. These materials should be sent within 24 hours. Wait until two days after the person should have received your letter and then make this follow-up call:

OPENER: *Hi, this is Marcia Taylor. I spoke with you a few days ago about jobs with environmental organizations. I really appreciated your advice. Did you receive the materials you requested I sent you last Tuesday?* (Assuming the answer is yes, go on to the next line of questioning.)

CONNECT: *Do you have any questions about my background and interests in environmental issues?* (If the recipient has not read your cover letter and resume carefully, he may look at it now while you are speaking with him over the phone. This question directly connects him to your resume and letter. He's now about to remember you in greater depth

by learning more about you as a person and professional.)

REQUEST: *Would you recommend that I contact some other
environmental groups?* (It's worth a try to get a
referral again. This person may have heard about
a vacancy with another group during the past
week, since you last asked the question.)

CLOSE: *Again, I want to thank you for looking at my
resume and keeping me in your database for
future reference. Do let me know if any positions
become available for someone with my qualifications. I'm really interested in promoting the
wonderful work of your organization.* (Depending
on your situation, you might also inquire about
part-time or volunteer positions to literally get
your foot in the door.)

This type of follow-up call may accomplish four things related to a
possible candidacy:

1. You verify the fact that your materials have indeed been
   received and entered into the recipient's system.

2. You are again remembered as that "nice person" he spoke
   with before.

3. The recipient may conduct a preliminary screening interview
   at this time by asking you a few questions about your background and interests based upon your cover letter and resume.
   Your answers may result in getting your resume moved into a
   "should interview sometime" file.

4. You may get a referral to another environmental organization
   which has a vacancy or pending vacancy appropriate for your
   qualifications. This is a great way to develop your networks
   and plug into the word-of-mouth system that is important to
   the nonprofit job market.

Write Dynamite Resumes and Letters

Your communication skills tell potential employers a lot about how well you will do in their organizations. Nonprofit organizations are particularly sensitive to communication skills because their livelihoods depend on how well they communicate with their constituencies. They must hire people who have excellent communication skills. Therefore, your resume and letters as well as your telephone conversations and face-to-face interviews are important indicators of your communication skills. Make sure you shine in all of these communication areas.

Some of the most important written communication you will engage in during your job search relates to resumes and letters. Whether sent in the mail, transmitted by fax, or e-mailed, your resume and letters should be well focused on your overall goal—get job interviews through direct application or referrals. As you use our organizational listings, or those of others, keep in mind that you will need to write to the contact person you verified in your telephone call. Be sure you always send a resume and/or letter to a specific name. And since individuals move a lot from position to position, and from organization to organization, you must verify the name by telephone **before** you send or transmit information.

On pages 93-104 we include sample resumes and letters based upon principles of effective communication. You should write similar resumes and letters during various stages of your nonprofit job search.

Whenever you send a letter or resume, make sure you follow-up with a phone call. If you have an active application for a specific position, this follow-up call should be aimed at getting a decision in your favor. You want to be remembered, and you want action:

REQUEST: *When would you expect to make a decision?*

Would it be okay if I called you next Friday if I've not heard from you in the meantime?

This line of questioning not only may give you useful information on the decision-making process, it potentially makes you more visible in the eyes of the employer. The individual will remember you as someone he needs to respond to in a timely and specific manner. He'll probably look over your application again—just to be sure he hasn't missed anything.

CHRONOLOGICAL RESUME

SARAH TAYLOR
2720 Euclid Drive
Philadelphia, PA 19110   215/721-1982

OBJECTIVE: A research and public relations position with an association, where strong communication, research, and analytical skills will be used for furthering the goals of the association.

EXPERIENCE: Planning Analyst, City of Philadelphia, Pennsylvania. Developed community-wide plans for public housing and conducted research in response to requests for zoning variances. Regularly met with community groups to identify housing needs, communicate city's policies, and advise on policies and procedures. Wrote policy papers and reports on city planning issues. Worked closely with citizen groups, landlords, contractors, and lawyers representing interests of various local groups. Developed a new information system for responding quickly to requests for planning information. 1995-present

Research Associate, Coalition for Community Service Agencies, Philadelphia, Pennsylvania. Conducted research, analyzed data, wrote reports, and lobbied government agencies at both the local and state levels on various aspects of community service organizations. Research involved interviewing government officials and representatives of community service groups. Several reports were responsible for providing greater public assistance to strengthen community service organizations at the local level. Reports cited by supervisor as "outstanding contributions to making community service organizations a central issue on the local government agenda." 1991-1994

EDUCATION: M.A., Public Administration, Temple University, Philadelphia, PA, 1991.

B.A., Political Science, State University of New York, Plattsburg, NY 1988.

REFERENCES: Available upon request.

COMBINATION RESUME

SARAH TAYLOR
2720 Euclid Drive
Philadelphia, PA 19110   215/721-1982

OBJECTIVE   A research and public relations position with an association, where strong communication, research, and analytical skills will be used for furthering the goals of the association.

AREAS OF EFFECTIVENESS

RESEARCH   Conducted 22 research projects on various aspects of planning and community service groups. Developed research design, conducted field interviews, and analyzed data. Research resulted in several reports which were responsible for changing local government policies. Consistently cited by supervisors as making "outstanding" contributions to both understanding and action.

PUBLIC RELATIONS   Developed press releases, issued reports, and met regularly with community groups, government officials, contractors, and the press. Devised an innovative information system to respond quickly to requests for information.

COMMUN-ICATION   Authored numerous position papers and major reports on public policy issues for government agencies and community groups. Frequent speaker before community organizations. Conducted several briefings for supervisors, city council members, and the press.

WORK HISTORY   Planning Analyst, City of Philadelphia, PA, 1995-present.

Research Associate, Coalition for Community Service Agencies, Philadelphia, PA, 1991-1994.

EDUCATION   M.A., Public Administration, Temple University, Philadelphia, PA, 1991.

B.A., Political Science, State University of New York, Plattsburg, NY 1988.

PERSONAL   Enjoy developing innovative approaches to public issues which involve research, writing, and frequent contact with government officials and community groups.

COMBINATION RESUME—continued

SUPPLEMENTAL INFORMATION　　　　　　SARAH TAYLOR

CONTINUING EDUCATION AND TRAINING

- Completed 15 graduate level hours of research and communication courses directly related to the public service.

- Recently attended several workshops on strengthening research, communication, and community relations skills:

  "Survey Research Methods in Local Government," International City Manager Association, June 4-6, 1998

  "Briefing Techniques," American Management Associations, May 8, 1996

  "Public Speaking," Greater Philadelphia Chamber of Commerce, February 20-21, 1995

  "Effective Report Writing for Public Employees," November 12-13, 1994

  "Planning as a Community Process," American Planning Association, March 21-25, 1994

MAJOR RESEARCH CONDUCTED AND REPORTS AUTHORED

"Making Community Service Organizations Work More Effectively," Coalition for Community Service Agencies, 1998.

"Serving the Community: A Practical Manual for Working With Government and Other Community Organizations," Coalition for Community Service Agencies, 1996.

"Planning Our Housing Future: A Comprehensive Approach to Balanced Growth," City of Philadelphia, 1994.

"City Planning Research: A Manual for Conducting Survey Research in the City of Philadelphia," City of Philadelphia, 1993.

PROFESSIONAL AFFILIATIONS

American Society for Public Administration
American Society of Association Executives
Toastmasters International

EDUCATIONAL HIGHLIGHTS

Working toward Ph.D. in Public Policy with concentration on policy formation and community management.

Earned 4.0/4.0 grade point average in graduate studies.

FUNCTIONAL RESUME

SARAH TAYLOR
2720 Euclid Drive
Philadelphia, PA 19110   215/721-1982

OBJECTIVE: A research and public relations position with an association,
where strong communication, research, and analytical skills will
be used for furthering the goals of the association.

EDUCATION: M.A., Public Administration, Temple University, Philadelphia,
Pennsylvania, 1991.

B.A., Political Science, State University of New York,
Plattsburg, New York, 1988.

MAJOR   Research
STRENGTHS:
Conducted 22 research projects on various aspects of planning
and community service groups. Developed research design,
conducted field interviews, and analyzed data. Research resulted in several reports which were responsible for changing local
government policies. Consistently cited by supervisors as
making "outstanding" contributions to both understanding and
action.

Public Relations

Developed press releases, issued reports, and met regularly
with community groups, government officials, contractors, and
the press. Devised an innovative information system to respond
quickly to requests for information.

Communication

Authored numerous position papers and major reports on
public policy issues for government agencies and community
groups. Frequent speaker before community organizations.
Conducted several briefings for supervisors, city council members, and the press.

PERSONAL: Enjoy developing innovative approaches to public issues which
involve research, writing, and frequent contact with government
officials and community groups.

RESUME LETTER

2720 Euclid Drive
Philadelphia, PA 19110
April 17, _____

James Weston, Assistant Director
American Association of
  Community Service Organizations
7210 Connecticut Avenue, Suite 223
Washington, DC 20036

Dear Mr. Weston:

AACSO is one of the most important groups providing assistance to community organizations. I know, because I have worked with these groups for several years at both the local and state levels.

My work has been very exciting, but I would now like to contribute to the work of the national association. My experience includes:

Research: Conducted 22 research projects on local planning and community service groups. Research resulted in several reports which significantly altered local government policies.

Public relations: Developed press releases, issued reports, and met regularly with community groups, government officials, contractors, and the press. Devised an innovative information system to respond quickly to requests for information.

Communication: Authored numerous position papers and major reports on public policy issues for agencies and community groups. Frequent speaker before community organizations. Conducted several briefings for supervisors, city council members, and the press.

In addition, I am completing my Ph.D. in Public Policy with emphasis on policy formation and community management.

I would like to meet with you to discuss how my experience and skills relate to the work of AACSO. Since I will be in Washington, DC next month, I would appreciate an opportunity to meet with you at that time. I will call your office on Thursday morning, April 24, to see if we might be able to arrange a mutually convenient time to meet. I especially want to share with you some of the innovative research and public relations work I have done with community service organizations.

I look forward to meeting with you.

Sincerely,

Sarah Taylor

Sarah Taylor

COVER LETTER

2720 Euclid Drive
Philadelphia, PA 19110
April 15, _____

James Weston, Assistant Director
American Association of
    Community Service Organizations
7210 Connecticut Avenue, Suite 223
Washington, DC 20036

Dear Mr. Weston:

I enclose my resume in response to your announcement in The Washington Post for a Community Research Analyst.

I am especially interested in this position for several reasons. First, I have six years of thoroughly enjoyable experience in working closely with community service organizations at the local and state levels. Second, I have conducted several practical studies of community service organizations which have resulted in strengthening their roles at the local level. Finally, my research work has placed me at the center of the policy process where I have worked effectively with government officials and other community groups.

I would appreciate an opportunity to meet with you to discuss how my experience might best relate to your needs. My combined research and community relations approach may be of special interest to you since it has resulted in some innovative approaches to community action. I will call your office on Tuesday morning April 22, to see if your schedule would permit such a meeting.

I look forward to learning more about your research needs and sharing some of my experiences with you.

Sincerely,

Sarah Taylor

Sarah Taylor

APPROACH LETTER: REFERRAL

2720 Euclid Drive
Philadelphia, PA 19110
April 8, _____

James Weston, Assistant Director
American Association of
   Community Service Organizations
7210 Connecticut Avenue, Suite 223
Washington, DC 20036

Dear Mr. Weston:

Alice White suggested that I contact you about my interest in community service organizations. She enthusiastically mentioned you as one of the best people to talk to about careers in this public service field.

I am leaving local government after three years of progressively responsible experience in community planning where I worked extensively with community service organizations. But before I decide to seek a career in this field as well as relocate, I believe I would benefit greatly from your professional experience and insights. Your advice would be very helpful at this stage in my career.

I will be in Washington during the seek of April 21-25. Would it be possible for us to meet briefly to discuss my career plans? I have several concerns you might be most helpful in clarifying. I will call your office on Thursday morning, April 15, to see if your schedule would permit such a meeting.

Sincerely,

Sarah Taylor

Sarah Taylor

APPROACH LETTER: Cold Turkey

2720 Euclid Drive
Philadelphia, PA 19110
March 23, _____

James Weston, Assistant Director
American Association of
  Community Service Organizations
7210 Connecticut Avenue, Suite 223
Washington, DC 20036

Dear Mr. Weston:

I have been most impressed by your work with community service organizations in Philadelphia. Indeed, the recent article appearing in Association Trends on your promotion to assistant director of AACSO stressed what I learned a long time ago here in Philadelphia—you have an exceptional talent to get the local organization to work together in pursuing the national agenda of AACSO. Congratulations on a well deserved promotion!

Your public service career with community service organizations is one I hope to emulate. After six enjoyable years of working with these organizations at the local and state levels, I am convinced I want to pursue a long-term career in this field and especially from a much broader national perspective. My research and public relations work with these groups may also be of interest to you.

Would it be possible for us to meet briefly to discuss my career interests in this field? I believe your advice would be most valuable in helping me better define my future with community service organizations.

I will be in Washington, DC during the week of April 21-25. Perhaps your schedule would permit a meeting during that week. I will call your office on Tuesday morning, April 8, to see if such a meeting would be possible.

I look forward to meeting you and learning from your experience.

Sincerely,

Sarah Taylor

Sarah Taylor

THANK-YOU LETTER:
Post-Informational Interview

2720 Euclid Drive
Philadelphia, PA 19110
March 23, _____

James Weston, Assistant Director
American Association of
  Community Service Organizations
7210 Connecticut Avenue, Suite 223
Washington, DC 20036

Dear Mr. Weston:

Our meeting yesterday was truly informative and extremely useful in helping me clarify various concerns regarding careers with community service organizations. Your experience and knowledge of this field is most impressive.

I want to thank you again for taking the time from your busy schedule to meet with me. Your suggestions for strengthening my resume were very helpful. I am now revising the resume in light of your thoughtful advice. I will send you a copy of the revised resume next week.

Following your advice, I will contact Marilyn Plante tomorrow to see if she might have or know of any opportunities for someone with my interests and qualifications. I will give her your regards.

I hope to have a chance to meet with you again sometime.

Sincerely,

Sarah Taylor

Sarah Taylor

THANK-YOU LETTER:
Post-Job Interview

2720 Euclid Drive
Philadelphia, PA 19110
March 23, _____

James Weston, Assistant Director
American Association of
    Community Service Organizations
7210 Connecticut Avenue, Suite 223
Washington, DC 20036

Dear Mr. Weston:

I want to thank you again for the opportunity to interview for the Community Research Analyst position. You and your staff were most helpful in clarifying many questions about this position and AACSO.

Our meeting further convinced me that this position is ideally suited for my interests, skills, and experience. My prior research and public relations work with community service agencies at the local and state levels has prepared me well for this position. I am committed to giving AACSO my very best effort.

I look forward to meeting with you again to further discuss my candidacy.

Sincerely,

Sarah Taylor

Sarah Taylor

THANK-YOU LETTER:
Job Rejection

2720 Euclid Drive
Philadelphia, PA 19110
March 23, _____

James Weston, Assistant Director
American Association of
   Community Service Organizations
7210 Connecticut Avenue, Suite 223
Washington, DC 20036

Dear Mr. Weston:

I want to thank you again for considering me for the Community Research Analyst position. Although I am disappointed with the outcome, I appreciated the opportunity and learned a great deal about AACSO. I am especially pleased with the highly professional manner in which you and your staff conducted the interview.

Please keep me in mind for future vacancies. I have a strong interest in AACSO which will certainly continue in the future. I believe I could contribute a great deal to AACSO. I am sure I would work well with you and your staff.

Best wishes.

Sincerely,

Sarah Taylor

Sarah Taylor

THANK-YOU LETTER:
Job Offer Acceptance

2720 Euclid Drive
Philadelphia, PA 19110
March 23, _____

James Weston, Assistant Director
American Association of
   Community Service Organizations
7210 Connecticut Avenue, Suite 223
Washington, DC 20036

Dear Mr. Weston:

I am pleased to accept your offer and look forward to joining AACSO later this month.

The Community Research Analyst position is ideally suited to my interests, skills, and experience. I will give you and AACSO my very best effort.

I understand I will begin work on May 14. Please contact me if I need to complete any paperwork prior to this starting date.

Thank you again for your consideration and confidence.

Sincerely,

Sarah Taylor

Sarah Taylor

7

Start-Up Directory to Thousands of Great Nonprofit Organizations

The 200 organizations profiled in this chapter represent some of the most popular types of nonprofits. Each listing includes the organization's purpose, activities, budget, and number of employees. Many of the employment figures may vary considerably from one year to another, depending on the number of part-time, volunteer, and intern positions an organization decides to include with its full-time personnel. We include the organization's name, address, and phone number as well as its Web site, if available.

If you decide to contact an organization after you have had a chance to research it, do what we advised in Chapter 6—call the organization to verify its current address and to get the name of the individual who handles personnel matters. In the case of very small nonprofits, this individual may be the director of the organization. With larger organizations, this person may be a personnel manager or the director of the human resources department. In any case, be sure you get a specific name to whom you will direct your communication.

We've classified the following organizations into ten general categories that correspond to the major interests and missions of most job seekers. For additional interest and mission areas, please refer to the *Encyclopedia of Associations*.

Arts and Entertainment

The nonprofit organizations profiled in this section represent a wide variety of interests related to the arts and entertainment—children, women, minorities, producers, artists, free speech, communication, and legal issues. While most of these organizations are small—operating on budgets in the $150,000 to $500,000 range and using many volunteers and interns—some are large, such as the Lincoln Center for the Performing Arts with an annual budget of $56,000,000 and 492 employees. Typical positions associated with these groups include director, program assistants, program coordinators, grantwriters, publicists, writers, editors, grassroots and foundation fundraisers, issue experts, lobbyists, administrative assistants, attorneys, office managers, bookkeepers, accountants, stage managers, and receptionists. Entry-level positions tend to pay $15,000 to $22,000 a year. Other positions may pay in the $25,000 to $35,000 range. These nonprofits are especially in need of two types of fundraisers—grassroots and foundation. Being small organizations, much of the work will be multi-faceted and entail a great deal of responsibility.

CALIFORNIA LAWYERS FOR THE ARTS
Fort Mason Center, Building C, Room 255
San Francisco, CA 94123
Tel. 415/775-7200 or Fax 415/775-1143

PURPOSE: To provide legal services, education, and self-help information to artists, performers, and arts organizations of all disciplines. Programs respond to the needs of the California arts community and help artists understand and apply legal concepts. Also provides alternative dispute resolution services.
ACTIVITY: Legal services, education, research, training.
BUDGET: $545,000
EMPLOYEES: Full-time: 9; Part-time: 3; Volunteers: 15; Interns: 5

CHILDREN'S ART FOUNDATION
P.O. Box 83
Santa Cruz, CA 95063
Tel. 408/426-5557 or Fax 408/426-1161
Web site: *www.stonesoup.com*

PURPOSE: To encourage childrens' creativity through educational and publication programs. Publishes *Stone Soup*, an international bi-monthly magazine of stories, poems, and art by young people ages 6 through 13. The Web site includes exemplary writing and art samples as well as supplementary materials for teachers, parents, and children.

ACTIVITY: Art school and publications.
BUDGET: $400,000
EMPLOYEES: Full-time: 3; Part-time: 6; Volunteers: 4; Interns: none

EMPOWERMENT PROJECT
3403 Highway 54 West
Chapel Hill, NC 27516
Tel. 919/967-1963 or Fax 919/967-1863
Web site: *www.webcom.com/~empower*

PURPOSE: To provide facilities, training and other support for independent producers, artists, activists and organizations to work toward democratizing access to the media and to provide the resources necessary to put the power of media in the hands of those working to further important human purposes.
ACTIVITY: Community organizing, training and technical assistance, direct action, research.
BUDGET: $130,000
EMPLOYEES: Full-time: 2; Part-time: 1; Volunteers: 30

FILM NEWS NOW FOUNDATION
100 Bleecker Street, Suite 12D
New York, NY 10012
Tel. 212/998-3768

PURPOSE: To advance the presence and involvement of people of color and women in the media field by assisting, encouraging, and providing services and consultations to minority as well as women producers.
ACTIVITY: Research, publications, public education, training and technical assistance, lobbying, and community organizing.
BUDGET: $900,000
EMPLOYEES: Full-time: 3; Part-time: 2; Volunteers: 2; Interns: 2

LINCOLN CENTER FOR THE PERFORMING ARTS, INC.
70 Lincoln Center Plaza
New York, NY 10023
Tel. 212/875-5000 or Fax 212/875-5414
Web site: *www.lincolncenter.org*

PURPOSE: Promote the performing arts in New York City by producing over 300 performances each year and sponsoring education programs for children.
ACTIVITY: Productions, educational programs, publications.
BUDGET: $56,000,000
EMPLOYEES: 492

LIVING STAGE THEATRE COMPANY
6th and Main Avenue, SW
Washington, DC 20024
Tel. 202/554-9066
Web site: *www.arenastage.org*

PURPOSE: To use improvisational theater techniques in a performance/workshop format working with groups of youth and adults in the inner city, helping them to rediscover their creativity, thereby promoting more positive life choices.
ACTIVITY: Human services, training, technical assistance.
BUDGET: $650,000
EMPLOYEES: Full-time: 17; Part-time: 1; Volunteers: 3; Interns: 3

MINNEAPOLIS TELECOMMUNICATIONS NETWORK
125 SE Main Street
Minneapolis, MN 55414
Tel. 612/331-8575
Web site: *www.mtn.org*

PURPOSE: To train people to use and create programs which promote free speech, communication within cultures, educate the general public about neighborhoods and other cultures.
ACTIVITY: Provide training and technical assistance, promote community organizing and public education.
BUDGET: $650,000
EMPLOYEES: Full-time: 15; Part-time: 7; Volunteers: 500; Interns: 5

NATIONAL CAMPAIGN FOR FREEDOM OF EXPRESSION
918 F Street NW, Suite 609
Washington, DC 20004
Tel. 202/393-2787 or Fax 202/347-7376
Web site: *www.artswire.org~ncfe*

PURPOSE: To fight censorship and to protect and extend the First Amendment right to freedom of artistic expression.
ACTIVITY: Research, lobbying, litigation, publications, community organizing, public education, media education/advocacy.
BUDGET: $278,000
EMPLOYEES: Full-time: 3; Part-time: 3; Volunteers: varies; Interns: 1

VERY SPECIAL ARTS
1300 Connecticut Avenue NW
Suite 700
Washington, DC 20036
Tel. 202/628-2800 or Fax 202/737-0725
Web site: *www.vsarts.org*

PURPOSE: To ensure that people with disabilities have access to educational programs in the arts. Coordinating committee for arts programs in 86 countries.
ACTIVITY: Research, information exchange, referrals, workshops, training, technical assistance, and sponsors competitions.
BUDGET: $6,670,000
EMPLOYEES: 55

VOLUNTEER LAWYERS FOR THE ARTS
1 East 53rd Street
6th Floor
New York, NY 10022
Tel. 212/319-2787 or Fax 212/752-6575

PURPOSE: To provide arts-related legal assistance to artists and arts organizations in all creative fields who cannot afford private counsel. VLA also works to prevent legal entanglements through education programs, including seminars, publications, and the maintenance of an Art Law Library.
ACTIVITY: Legal services to indigent artists and emerging or small arts organizations. Research, publications, public education and lobbying.
BUDGET: $500,000
EMPLOYEES: Full-time: 7; Part-time: 3; Volunteers: 5, 800 lawyers; Interns: 35

WOLF TRAP FOUNDATION FOR THE PERFORMING ARTS
1624 Trap Road
Vienna, VA 22182
Tel. 703/255-1920 or Fax 703/255-1905
Web site: *www.wolf-trap.org*

PURPOSE: To fund and contract programs at Wolf Trap Farm Park for the Performing Arts which presents opera, musical comedy, ballet, theater, modern dance, and classical and pop concerts.
ACTIVITY: Fundraising, workshops, performances.
BUDGET: $15,000,000
EMPLOYEES: 55

WOMEN MAKE MOVIES
462 Broadway, Room 500
New York, NY 10013
Tel. 212/925-0606 or Fax 212/925-2052

PURPOSE: To facilitate production, promotion and distribution of women's films and videotapes. Also provide support services to emerging and established women film and video artists. Functions as the nation's leading distributor of media by and about women.
ACTIVITY: Training and technical assistance, publications, community organizing, and lobbying.
BUDGET: $750,000
EMPLOYEES: Full-time: 9; Part-time: 2; Volunteers: 4; Interns: 4

YOUNG AUDIENCES
115 E. 92nd Street
New York, NY 100128
Tel. 212/831-8110 or Fax 212/289-1202
Web site: *www.youngaudiences.com*

PURPOSE: Promote live educational programs in music, dance, and theater to children in grades K-12 during regular school hours.
ACTIVITY: Research, program development, training, and technical assistance.
BUDGET: $12,000,000
EMPLOYEES: 8

Civil Rights, Liberties, and Disabilities

Who defends civil liberties, fights for civil rights, and assists the disabled? Some might say lawyers or the down-trodden themselves. The truth is that many nonprofit groups are organized to deal with these issues. The nonprofit organizations appearing in this section represent a wide variety of interests and groups related to civil rights, liberties, and disabilities—freedom, immigration, AIDS, law, handicapped, human rights, minorities, and women. Many of these groups, such as the AIDS Project of Los Angeles and Americans for Democratic Action, also should appear in the sections on medical/health care and political/government reform.

Most of the organizations in this section also are relatively small, with budgets under $2 million and with fewer than 25 employees. However, a few of these organizations are medium in size, with budgets over $20 million and staffs in excess of 200.

Many of our civil liberties and civil rights organizations have been at the forefront in fighting for change. Some have made significant contributions to the nation's civil rights movement. Individuals working for these organizations tend to be passionately committed to change. Most of these nonprofits are relatively liberal groups seeking to make major changes.in government policies.

AFRICA FUND
50 Broad Street, Suite 711
New York, NY 10004
Tel. 212/785-1024 or Fax 212/785-1078
Web site: *www.prarient.org/acas/afund.html*

PURPOSE: To support the struggle for democracy, economic justice, and human rights in Africa.
ACTIVITY: Research, public education, and publications.
BUDGET: $450,000
EMPLOYEES: Full-time: 6; Part-time: 3; Volunteers: varies; Interns: varies

AIDS PROJECT—LOS ANGELES
1313 N. Vine Street
Los Angeles, CA 90028
Tel. 323/993-1600 or Fax 323-993-1592
Web site: *www.apla.org*

PURPOSE: To be a direct provider of, and resource for, HIV/AIDS services and information, and an advocate to government for people with HIV/AIDS.
ACTIVITY: Lobbying, publications, human services community organizing, public education, training and technical assistance.
BUDGET: $19,000,000
EMPLOYEES: Full-time: 220; Part-time: 20; Volunteers: 2,500; Interns: varies

AMERICAN BAR ASSOCIATION
(Public Services Division)
740 15th Street NW
Washington, DC 20036-5802
Tel. 202/331-2276 or Fax 202/662-1032
Web site: *www.abanet.org*

PURPOSE: To provide leadership in identification, development and reform of law and law-related policies that promote the ideals of a just society and ensure equal rights and protections for all, particularly vulnerable populations.
ACTIVITY: Research, publications and videos, public education, training and technical assistance nationwide, symposia, workshops and conferences, model legislation, policy development for ABA, speeches and professional papers.

BUDGET: $2,000,000
EMPLOYEES: Full-time: 30; Part-time: 5; Volunteers: 5; Interns: varies

AMERICAN CIVIL LIBERTIES UNION (ACLU)
125 Broad Street
18th Floor
New York, NY 10004-2400
Tel. 212/549-2500 or Fax 212/549-2646
Web site: *www.aclu.org*

PURPOSE: To safeguard rights provided in the Bill of Rights of the U.S. Constitution: freedom of speech, press, assembly, and religion; due process of law; fair trials; and application of laws regardless of race, color, sexual orientation, national origin, political opinion, or religious belief.
ACTIVITY: Litigation, advocacy, and public education.
BUDGET: $20,000,000
EMPLOYEES: 125

AMERICAN CIVIL LIBERTIES UNION OF SOUTHERN CALIFORNIA
1616 Beverly Blvd.
Los Angeles, CA 90026
Tel. 213/977-9500
Web site: *www.aclu-sc.org*

PURPOSE: To assure that the Bill of Rights and amendments to the Constitution that guard against unwarranted governmental control, are preserved.
ACTIVITY: Litigation, lobbying, community organizing, public education, research, and publications.
BUDGET: $2,500,000
EMPLOYEES: Full-time: 31; Part-time: None; Volunteers: 5; Interns: 20 law students (summer)

AMERICAN COUNCIL OF THE BLIND
1155 15th Street NW, Suite 720
Washington, DC 20005
Tel. 202/467-5081 or Fax 202/467-5085
Web site: *www.acb.org*

PURPOSE: To promote the independence, dignity and well-being of blind, and visually impaired people.
ACTIVITY: Lobbying, litigation, publications, direct action, public education, community organizing, and human services.
BUDGET: $2,009,000
EMPLOYEES: Full-time: 10; Part-time: None; Volunteers: None; Interns: varies

AMERICAN FOUNDATION FOR THE BLIND
11 Penn Plaza, Suite 300
New York, NY 10001
Tel. 212/502-7600 or Fax 212/502-7777
Web site: *www.afb.org*
(Regional centers in Chicago, Dallas, San Francisco
and Washington, DC)

PURPOSE: To enable persons who are blind or visually impaired to achieve equality of access and opportunity that will ensure freedom of choice in their lives.
ACTIVITY: Research, lobbying, publications, public education, training and technical assistance.
BUDGET: $33,264,000
EMPLOYEES: Full-time: 125; Part-time: varies; Volunteers: varies; Interns: varies

AMERICANS FOR DEMOCRATIC ACTION
1625 K Street, NW, Suite 210
Washington, DC 20006
Tel. 202/785-5980 or Fax 202/785-5969
Web site: *www.adaction.org*
(Other offices in Winston-Salem, NC; Tempe, AZ; and Chicago)

PURPOSE: To educate the American public as to the significant issues; to lobby on behalf of these issues; to work through their public action committee (PAC) in supporting candidates whose views are similar to ADA's; to produce publications and analysis for mass distribution.
ACTIVITY: Lobbying, publications, community organizing, public education, and direct action.
BUDGET: $1,000,000
EMPLOYEES: Full-time 9; Part-time: 3; Volunteers: varies; Interns: 5

ANTI-DEFAMATION LEAGUE
823 United Nations Plaza
New York, NY 10017
Tel. 212/490-2525 or Fax 212/867-0779
Web site: *www.adl.org*

PURPOSE: Halt the defamation of Jewish people as well as ensure justice and fair treatment to all citizens.
ACTIVITY: Education, training, assistance, publications, lobbying, and award recognition
BUDGET: $28,000,000
EMPLOYEES: 400

CENTER FOR IMMIGRANTS RIGHTS
48 Saint Marks Place
4th Floor
New York, NY 10003
Tel. 212/505-6890 or Fax 212/995-5876

PURPOSE: To provide legal assistance, community outreach and education, policy advocacy and technical support in defending the rights of immigrant newcomers, documented and undocumented, in the areas of immigration, employment rights, access to public entitlements/health and civil rights.
ACTIVITY: Public education, training and technical assistance, community organizing, publications, litigation, lobbying and research.
BUDGET: $330,000
EMPLOYEES: Full-time: 6; Part-time: 2; Volunteers: 5, Interns: 5

CENTER ON BUDGET AND POLICY PRIORITIES
777 N. Capitol Street, NE
Suite 705
Washington, DC 20002
Tel. 202/408-1080 or Fax 202/408-1056
Web site: *www.cbpp.org*

PURPOSE: To provide research and analysis which focuses on the impact of changes in Federal and state policies on low-income Americans.
ACTIVITY: Publications, training and technical assistance, research, public education, and lobbying.
BUDGET: $3,400,000
EMPLOYEES: Full-time: 40; Part-time: 7; Volunteers: none; Interns 5

CITIZENS ACTION COALITION OF INDIANA
3951 N. Meridian Street
Suite 300
Indianapolis, IN 46208
Tel. 317/921-1120 or Fax 317/921-1210
Web site: *www.citact.org*
(Other offices in Fort Wayne, South Bend, and New Albany)

PURPOSE: To advocate public interest in energy, utility, health care, and environmental policies and issues concerning small farmers.
ACTIVITY: Research, lobbying, community organizing, public education, litigation, and publications.
BUDGET: $2,500,000
EMPLOYEES: Full-time: 85; Part-time: 30; Volunteers: 30; Interns: none, but will accept applications

COMMITTEE TO PROTECT JOURNALISTS
330 7th Avenue, 12th Floor
New York, NY 10001
Tel. 212/465-1004 or Fax 212/465-9568
Web site: *www.cpj.org*

PURPOSE: To promote press freedoms around the world.
ACTIVITY: Publications, research and direct action, consisting of monitoring events around the world, confirming facts, protesting where appropriate, sharing information with other professional groups, publicizing cases and publishing reports and periodicals.
BUDGET: $1,800,000
EMPLOYEES: Full-time: 20; Part-time: 1; Volunteers: varies; Interns: varies

DISABILITY RIGHTS EDUCATION AND DEFENSE FUND
2212 6th Street
Berkeley, CA 94710
Tel. 510/644-2555 or Fax 510/841-8645
(Other office in Washington, DC)
Web site: *www.dredf.org*

PURPOSE: To provide legal advice and representation for people with disabilities and parents of children with disabilities, especially civil rights in regards to school, employment, housing, and educating local, state and national representatives regarding disabilities.
ACTIVITY: Training and technical assistance, national policy monitoring, litigation, and community organizing.
BUDGET: $1,545,000
EMPLOYEES: Full-time: 19; Part-time: None; Volunteers: varies; Interns: 5-10

DRUG POLICY FOUNDATION
4455 Connecticut Avenue NW
Suite B-500
Washington, DC 20008-2328
Tel. 202/537-5005 or Fax 202/537-3007
Web site: *www.dpf.org*

PURPOSE: To promote alternative drug policy approaches, such as legalization, decriminalization, and medicalization of illegal drugs.
ACTIVITY: Lobbying, education, training, research, publications, and legal aid.
BUDGET: $2,000,000
EMPLOYEES: 10

EQUAL RIGHTS ADVOCATES
1663 Mission Street
Suite 550
San Francisco, CA 94103
Tel. 415/621-0672 or Fax 415/621-6744
Web site: *www.equalrights.org*

PURPOSE: To address sex and race-based discrimination including legal representation, public education, advice and counseling, coalition building, media relations and public policy advocacy.
ACTIVITY: Litigation, public education, advice and counseling, publications, community organizing, training and technical assistance, public policy advocacy, and grassroots lobbying.
BUDGET: $1,100,000
EMPLOYEES: Full-time: 15; Part-time: 3; Volunteers: varies; Interns: varies

FRIENDS COMMITTEE ON NATIONAL LEGISLATION
245 Second Street NE
Washington, DC 20002
Tel. 202/547-6000 or Fax 202/547-6019
Web site: *www.scnl.org/pub/fcnl*

PURPOSE: To bring Quaker values to bear on public policy. FCNL's goals are world peace, equity and justice for all, civil rights, environmental quality, and economic justice.
ACTIVITY: Lobbying, research and education, and publications.
BUDGET: $1,000,000
EMPLOYEES: Full-time: 18; Part-time: varies, Volunteers: many; Interns: 4

HUMAN RIGHTS CAMPAIGN (HRC)
1101 14th Street NW
Suite 200
Washington, DC 20005
Tel. 202/628-4160 or Fax 202/347-5323
Web site: *www.hrc.org*
(Other offices in Atlanta and Chicago)

PURPOSE: To secure full civil rights for lesbians and gay men and responsible policies on AIDS.
ACTIVITY: Research, lobbying, publications, community organizing and public education.
BUDGET: $11,000,000
EMPLOYEES: Full-time: 60; Part-time: none; Volunteers: 10; Interns: 5

INDIAN LAW RESOURCE CENTER
602 N. Ewing Street
Helena, MT 59601
Tel. 406/449-2006 or Fax 406/449-2031
Web site: *www.indianlaw.org*

PURPOSE: To provide legal help without charge to Indian nations and tribes in major cases of important Indian rights.
ACTIVITY: Research, litigation, training and technical assistance, publications, and public education.
BUDGET: $1,000,000
EMPLOYEES: Full-time: 10; Part-time: 0; Volunteers: 0; Interns: 1

LAWYERS' COMMITTEE FOR CIVIL RIGHTS UNDER THE LAW
1450 G Street NW
Suite 400
Washington, DC 20005
Tel. 202/662-8600 or Fax 202/783-0857

PURPOSE: To provide quality legal services for poor and minorities on major civil and Constitutional rights cases. Represents clients in suits alleging unlawful racial discrimination and influence the development and application of civil rights law.
ACTIVITY: Research, litigation in cases involving voting rights, discrimination, education, housing, and minority business enterprise.
BUDGET: $3,500,000
EMPLOYEES: Full-time: 27 Part-time: 2; Volunteers: none; Interns: 8

MEXICAN AMERICAN LEGAL DEFENSE AND EDUCATIONAL FUND
634 South Spring Street, 11th Floor
Los Angeles, CA 90014
Tel. 213/629-2512
Web site: *www.maldef.org*
(Other offices in San Francisco; Washington, DC; San Antonio; Chicago; Sacramento; Fresno; Santa Ana; and Detroit)

PURPOSE: To promote and protect the civil rights of U.S. Latinos through class action litigation, advocacy and community education.
ACTIVITY: Lobbying, litigation, publications, direct action, public education, leadership and development.
BUDGET: $4,300,000
EMPLOYEES: Full-time: 60; Part-time: none; Volunteers: varies; Interns: varies

NATIONAL ASSOCIATION FOR THE ADVANCEMENT OF COLORED PEOPLE (NAACP)
4805 Mt. Hope Drive
Baltimore, MD 21215
Tel. 410/358-8900 or Fax 410/358-3818
Web site: *www.naacp.org*

PURPOSE: To achieve equal rights and eliminate racial prejudice in housing, employment, voting, school, court system, transportation, recreation, prisons, and business.
ACTIVITY: Lobbying, education, training, assistance, publications, and referral services.
BUDGET: $11,909,000
EMPLOYEES: 132

NAACP LEGAL DEFENSE AND EDUCATIONAL FUND—LOS ANGELES
315 W. 9th Street, Suite 208
Los Angeles, CA 90015
Tel. 213/624-2405
Web site: *www.idfla.org*

PURPOSE: To undertake civil rights litigation and advocacy in a variety of discrimination areas including: education, housing, voting rights, employment, health, environmental justice, poverty, and criminal justice.
ACTIVITY: Litigation, training and technical assistance.
BUDGET: $9,500,000
EMPLOYEES: Full-time: 9; Part-time: none; Volunteers: 1; Interns: 5

NAACP LEGAL DEFENSE AND EDUCATIONAL FUND, INC.
99 Hudson Street, 16th Floor
New York, NY 10013
Tel. 212/219-1900 or Fax 212/226-7592

PURPOSE: To bring civil rights litigation on behalf of African Americans in areas of employment, housing, voting, education, health care, poverty and justice and capital punishment.
ACTIVITY: Litigation, research, lobbying, community organizing, and scholarships.
BUDGET: $8,900,000
EMPLOYEES: Full-time: 68; Part-time: 3; Volunteers: none; Interns: 3

NATIONAL CAUCUS AND CENTER ON BLACK AGED
1424 K Street NW, Suite 500
Washington, DC 20005
Tel. 202/637-8400 or Fax 202/347-0895
Web site: *www.ncba-blackaged.org*
(Other offices in Atlanta, Chicago, Baltimore,
Cleveland, Philadelphia, Raleigh, NC, and Stuttgart, AZ)

PURPOSE: To improve the quality of life for African American elderly—especially those who are low income.
ACTIVITY: Lobbying, publications, human services, direct action, public education, training and technical assistance.
BUDGET: $14,000,000
EMPLOYEES: Full-time: 26; Part-time: 2; Volunteers: none; Interns: 7

NATIONAL PARTNERSHIP FOR WOMEN AND FAMILIES
1875 Connecticut Avenue NW, Suite 710
Washington, DC 20009
Tel. 202/986-2600 or Fax 202/986-2539
Web site: *www.nationalpartnership.org*

PURPOSE: To help women become full and equal participants in their public and private lives; advocates public policies that focus on work and family concerns. Formerly known as the Women's Legal Defense Fund.
ACTIVITY: Lobbying, litigation, publications, community organizing, public education, training and technical assistance.
BUDGET: $2,330,000
EMPLOYEES: Full-time: 28; Part-time: varies; Volunteers: varies; Interns: varies

NATIONAL URBAN LEAGUE, INC.
120 Wall Street
New York, NY 10005
Tel. 212/310-9000 or Fax 212/344-5332
Web site: *www.nul.org*

PURPOSE: To assist African Americans in the achievement of social and economic equality in such crucial areas as educational attainment, employment and economic self-sufficiency.
ACTIVITY: Advocacy, research, human services, community organizing, publications, public education, training and technical assistance.
BUDGET: $18,900,000
EMPLOYEES: Full-time: 200; Part-time: varies; Volunteers: 30,000+; Interns: varies

PEOPLE FOR THE AMERICAN WAY
2000 M Street NW
Suite 400
Washington, DC 20036
Tel. 202/467-4999 or Fax 202/293-2672
Web site: *www.pfaw.org*

PURPOSE: To promote and protect individual liberties including First Amendment rights and the right to privacy.
ACTIVITY: Research, lobbying, litigation, publications, community organizing, and public education.
BUDGET: $4,200,000
EMPLOYEES: Full-time: 49; Part-time: 3; Volunteers: 25; Interns: 10

PUERTO RICAN LEGAL DEFENSE AND EDUCATION FUND
99 Hudson Street
14th Floor
New York, NY 10013
Tel. 212/219-3360 or Fax 212/431-4276

PURPOSE: To protect the civil rights of Puerto Ricans and other Latinos and to ensure their equal protection under the law.
ACTIVITY: Litigation, legal education training, community education, and advocacy.
BUDGET: $1,624,000
EMPLOYEES: Full-time: 20; Part-time: none; Volunteers: varies; Interns: varies

SOUTHERN CHRISTIAN LEADERSHIP CONFERENCE
334 Auburn Avenue NE
Atlanta, GA 30303
Tel. 404/522-1420 or Fax 404/659-7390

PURPOSE: To improve civic, religious, economic, and cultural conditions of African-Americans. Works primarily in 16 southern and border states. Uses nonviolent methods such as voter registration, social protest, boycotts, and picketing. Also functions as a coordinating and service agency for local organizations.
ACTIVITY: Educator, training, nonviolent protest, technical assistance, lobbying, and publishing.
BUDGET: $3,200,000
EMPLOYEES: 12

SOUTHERN POVERTY LAW CENTER
P.O. Box 2087
Montgomery AL 36102
Tel. 334/264-0286 or Fax 334/264-0629
Web site: *www.splcenter.org*

PURPOSE: To protect and advance the legal and civil rights of poor people, regardless of race.
ACTIVITY: Education and litigation.
BUDGET: $9,500,000
EMPLOYEES: 60

THE URBAN INSTITUTE
2100 M Street NW
5th Floor
Washington, DC 20037
Tel. 202/833-7200 or Fax 202/429-0687
Web site: *www.urban.org*

PURPOSE: To conduct research, evaluations, and policy analysis related to social and economic issues facing the U.S. (or related to the same issues in developing nations); to improve government decisions and their implementation; and to facilitate informed debate and decision-making by policy makers.
ACTIVITY: Research, publications, training and technical assistance.
BUDGET: $21,000,000
EMPLOYEES: Full-time: 200; Part-time: 10; Volunteers: varies; Interns: 10

WORLD INSTITUTE ON DISABILITY
510 16th Street
Oakland, CA 94612
Tel. 510/763-4100 or Fax 510/763-4109
Web site: *www.wid.org*

PURPOSE: To use research, public education, training and model program development as a means to create a more accessible and supportive society for all people—disabled and nondisabled alike.
ACTIVITY: Public education, research, training and technical assistance, publications, direct action, and community organizing.
BUDGET: $2,090,000
EMPLOYEES: Full-time: 30; Part-time: 3; Volunteers: 5; Interns: 4

Consumer Advocacy

The organizations presented in this section fit the stereotypical nonprofit organization profile—advocate a particular consumer issue and employ individuals who are passionately committed to consumer issues. Here you will find everything from the Center for Auto Safety to the Older Persons Action Group. These groups do a great deal of research and lobbying. They sponsor some of the most important legislation affecting consumers. Many of these groups have been at the forefront in getting laws changed concerning housing, health care, insurance reform, public education, food labeling, utility rates, business practices, and environmental control. Most of these nonprofits are relatively small organizations with budgets under $2 million and staffs under 20. However, you'll find exceptions to this rule, such as the Consumers Union which operates with a $478 million budget and with a staff of 420 full-time employees.

CALIFORNIA PUBLIC INTEREST RESEARCH GROUP
926 J Street, Suite 523
Sacramento, CA 95814-2707
Tel. 916/448-4516 or Fax 916/448-4560
Web site: *www.pirg.org/calpirg*

PURPOSE: To conduct research and advocacy on environmental and consumer issues in California.
ACTIVITY: Research, lobbying, litigation, publications, community organizing, and public education.
BUDGET: $750,000
EMPLOYEES: Full-time: 62; Part-time: 15; Volunteers: varies; Interns: varies

CENTER FOR AUTO SAFETY
2001 S Street NW, Suite 410
Washington, DC 20009
Tel. 202/328-7700 or Fax 202/387-0140
Web site: *www.autosafety.org*

PURPOSE: To conduct research and advocacy regarding fuel efficiency and emissions, vehicle safety, economy and reliability.
ACTIVITY: Research, public education, training and technical assistance, publications, and litigation.
BUDGET: $800,000
EMPLOYEES: Full-time: 15; Interns: 6

CENTER FOR SCIENCE AND THE PUBLIC INTEREST
1875 Connecticut Ave., NW, Suite 300
Washington, DC 20009-5728
Tel. 202/332-9110 or Fax 202/265-4954
Web site: *www.cspinet.org*

PURPOSE: To ensure food safety by initiating legal actions to ban unsafe and poorly tested food additives; improve food labeling; ban deceptive food advertising; and influence public policy affecting health and diet.
ACTIVITY: Research, lobbying, litigation, public education, publishing, and projects.
BUDGET: $17,000,000
EMPLOYEES: 65

CITIZENS ADVICE BUREAU, INC.
2054 Morris Avenue
Bronx, NY 10453
Tel. 212/365-0910
(Other office in New York City)

PURPOSE: To assist low-income families and senior citizens to meet survival needs and to support policy efforts aimed at eradication of poverty.
ACTIVITY: Human services, training and technical assistance, and community organizing.
BUDGET: $1,300,000
EMPLOYEES: Full-time: 200; Volunteers: 6; Interns: 8

CITIZENS UTILITY BOARD
208 South LaSalle
Suite 1760
Chicago, IL 60604
Tel. 312/263-4282
Web site: *www.cuboard.org*
(Other office in Springfield, IL)

PURPOSE: To represent the interests of residential and small business utility ratepayers in matters before regulatory agencies, the Illinois General Assembly and other jurisdictions.
ACTIVITY: Litigation, community organizing, public education, lobbying, publications, research, and human services.
BUDGET: $1,800,000
EMPLOYEES: Full-time: 11; Part-time: 5; Volunteers: 1; Interns: 3

CO-OP AMERICA
1612 K Street NW, Suite 600
Washington, DC 20006
Tel. 202/872-5307 or Fax 212/331-8166
Web site: *www.coopamerica.org*

PURPOSE: To create a just and sustainable society by working in four program areas: to encourage corporate responsibility; to help socially responsible businesses emerge and thrive; to educate consumers about creating social change; and to create sustainable communities.
ACTIVITY: Research, public education, publications, networking and creating an "alternative marketplace."
BUDGET: $2,500,000
EMPLOYEES: Full-time: 24; Part-time: 4; Interns: 25

CONSUMER FEDERATION OF AMERICA, CONSUMER RESEARCH COUNCIL
1424 16th Street NW, Suite 604
Washington, DC 20036
Tel. 202/387-6121 or Fax 202/265-7989
Web site: *www.stateandlocal.org*

PURPOSE: To advocate and educate for the advancement of pro-consumer policy on a variety of issues before Congress, regulatory agencies and the courts. Consists of a federation of 259 pro-consumer groups with combined membership of 50 million.
ACTIVITY: Advocacy, education, and member services.
BUDGET: $2,200,000
EMPLOYEES: Full-time: 20; Part-time: 4; Interns: 3

CONSUMERS UNION
101 Truman Avenue
Yonkers, NY 10703
Tel. 914/378-2000 or Fax 914/378-2900
Web site: *www.consumerreports.org*
(Other offices in Washington, DC; San Francisco; and Austin, TX)

PURPOSE: To provide consumers with information and advice on goods, services, health and personal finance and to initiate/cooperate with individual and group efforts to maintain and enhance the quality of life for consumers.
ACTIVITY: Research, lobbying, litigation, publications, community organizing, direct action, public education, training and technical assistance.
BUDGET: $478,000,000
EMPLOYEES: Full-time: 420; Part-time, Volunteers, and Interns: varies

COUNCIL OF BETTER BUSINESS BUREAUS
4200 Wilson Blvd., Suite 800
Arlington, VA 22203-1804
Tel. 703/276-0100 or Fax 703/525-8277
Web site: *www.bbb.org*

PURPOSE: Promotes ethical business practices amongst the 260,000 businesses that are members of 135 local Better Business Bureaus. Provides support to the local Better Business Bureaus as well as information to the public on how to avoid scams and frauds. Helps settle, through arbitration and other means, many of the 1.8 million consumer complaints received by local Better Business Bureaus each year.
ACTIVITY: Public education, arbitration and mediation, research, publishing.
BUDGET: $14,000,000
EMPLOYEES: 140

HEALTH CARE FOR ALL
30 Winter Street, Suite 1010
Boston, MA 02108
Tel. 617/350-7279
Web site: *www.hcfa.org*

PURPOSE: To promote reform of the health care system on both state and national levels.
ACTIVITY: Community organizing, public education, human services, research, publications, lobbying, direct action, and litigation.
BUDGET: $400,000
EMPLOYEES: Full-time: 8; Part-time: 2; Volunteers: 10; Interns: 6

HOUSING AND CREDIT COUNSELING, INC.
1195 SW Buchanan, Suite 203
Topeka, KS 66604-1183
Tel. 913/234-0217
Web site: *www.law.ukans.edu/~hcci/HCCI.htm*
(Other offices in Emporia, Lawrence, Manhattan, and Topeka)

PURPOSE: To facilitate safe, adequate, affordable and equitable housing situations for all—particularly those of low and moderate income; assist with budgeting and debt repayment alternatives so people can handle their finances on their own and avoid bankruptcy.
ACTIVITY: Human services, public education, training and technical assistance, and community organizing.
BUDGET: $500,000
EMPLOYEES: Full-time: 21; Part-time: 1; Volunteers: varies; Interns: varies

MASSACHUSETTS PUBLIC INTEREST RESEARCH GROUP
29 Temple Place
Boston, MA 02111
Tel. 617/292-4800
Web site: *www.pirg.org/masspirg*

PURPOSE: To develop policy, coordinate grassroots campaigns, and win legislation to promote environmental preservation, consumer protection, safe energy and corporate and governmental responsibility.
ACTIVITY: Lobbying, research, community organizing, fundraising, public education, litigation, and publications.
BUDGET: $4,500,000
EMPLOYEES: Full-time: 118; Volunteers: 50; Interns: varies

MINNESOTA PUBLIC INTEREST RESEARCH GROUP
2414 University Avenue Street
Minneapolis, MN 55414
Tel. 612/627-4035
Web site: *www.tc.umn.edu/nlhome/g046/mpirg*
(Other offices in Duluth, Morris, Northfield, and St. Paul)

PURPOSE: To promote the public interest through research and policy development, legislative advocacy, impact litigation, and grassroots organizing.
ACTIVITY: Research, lobbying, litigation, community organizing, and public education.
BUDGET: $400,000
EMPLOYEES: Full-time: 15; Part-time: 5-15; Volunteers: 300-500; Interns: 5-25

NATIONAL CONSUMER LAW CENTER
18 Fremont Street, Suite 400
Boston, MA 02108
Tel. 617/523-8010 or Fax 617/523-7398
Web site: *www.consumerlaw.org*
(Other office in Washington, DC)

PURPOSE: To provide legal and technical assistance to lawyers representing low-income clients on consumer and energy issues and provide direct representation to low-income clients on these issues in cases of national scope.
ACTIVITY: Research, lobbying, litigation, publications, training and technical assistance.
BUDGET: $2,500,000
EMPLOYEES: Full-time: 25; Part-time: varies; Volunteers: varies; Interns: varies

NATIONAL CONSUMERS LEAGUE
1701 K Street NW, Suite 1200
Washington, DC 20006
Tel. 202/835-3323 or Fax 202/835-0747
Web site: *www.fraud.org*

PURPOSE: To provide information to consumers and workers through research, education, and advocacy as well as encourage citizen participation in governmental and business decision-making.
ACTIVITY: Public education, direct action, research, publications, community organizing, lobbying and human services.
BUDGET: $1,600,000
EMPLOYEES: Full-time: 21; Part-time: 4; Volunteers: 2: Interns: 3

NEW JERSEY CITIZEN ACTION
400 Main Street
Hackensack, NJ 07601
201/488-2804
(Other offices in New Brunswick, Trenton, Woodbury, Collingswood)

PURPOSE: To increase citizen participation in the democratic process on issues such as toxic chemicals, fair banking, affordable housing and health care, insurance reform, and family leave.
ACTIVITY: Lobbying, community organizing, direct action, education.
BUDGET: $600,000
EMPLOYEES: Full-time: 63; Part-time: 2; Volunteers: 4; Interns: 6

NEW YORK PUBLIC INTEREST RESEARCH GROUP, INC.
9 Murray Street
New York, NY 10007-2272
Tel. 212/349-6460
Web site: *www.nypirg.org*
(Other offices in Buffalo, Syracuse, Cortland, Binghamton, Albany, New Paltz, Purchase, Oswego, Huntington, Stony Brook, Garden City, Old Westbury, and Washington, DC)

PURPOSE: To advocate for a cleaner environment, consumer protection, fair and open government, mass transit, quality health care, better funding for higher education and issues of social justice.
ACTIVITY: Research, lobbying, student organizing, litigation, publications, community organizing, education, training and technical assistance, legal action.
BUDGET: $4,000,000
EMPLOYEES: Full-time: 98; Part-time: varies; Volunteers: varies; Interns 6-12

OFFICE OF THE CONSUMERS' COUNSEL
77 South High Street, 15th Floor
Columbus, OH 43266-0550
Tel. 614/466-8574

PURPOSE: To represent Ohio's residential public utility consumers before state and federal courts, legislative and regulatory bodies. To provide professional, innovative and accountable advocacy.
ACTIVITY: Litigation and negotiation, research, lobbying, publications, public education, training and technical assistance.
BUDGET: $4,800,000
EMPLOYEES: Full-time: 64; Interns: varies

OHIO CITIZEN ACTION
402 Terminal Tower
50 Public Square
Cleveland, OH 44113
Tel. 216/861-5200
Web site: *www.ohiocitizen.org*
(Other offices in Akron, Cincinnati, Toledo, Columbus, and Dayton)

PURPOSE: To promote and assist citizen action as the basis for democratic change.
ACTIVITY: Research, lobbying, publications, community organizing, direct action, public education, training and technical assistance, elections, and litigation.
BUDGET: $4,000,000
EMPLOYEES: Full-time: 172; Part-time: varies; Volunteers: varies; Interns: varies

OLDER PERSONS ACTION GROUP, INC.
325 E. Third Avenue, Suite 300
Anchorage, AK 99501
Tel. 907/276-1059
(Other office in Wasilla, AK)

PURPOSE: To improve services, develop programs, educate, promote and implement changes to foster self-determination of older Alaskan citizens.
ACTIVITY: Training and technical assistance, publications, research, direct action, and public education.
BUDGET: $800,000
EMPLOYEES: Full-time: 24; Part-time: 21; Volunteers: 15; Interns: will accept applications

OREGON STATE PUBLIC INTEREST RESEARCH GROUP
1536 SE 11th Street
Portland, OR 97214
Tel. 503/231-4181
Web site: *www/pirg.org/ospirg*
(Other office in Eugene, OR)

PURPOSE: To conduct independent research, monitor government and corporate actions, and advocate reforms to benefit the public—primarily in the areas of environmental protection, consumer rights, and government reform.
ACTIVITY: Community organizing, research, public education, lobbying, publications, and direct action.
BUDGET: $500,000
EMPLOYEES: Full-time: 18; Volunteers: varies; Interns: varies

UNITED STATES PUBLIC INTEREST RESEARCH GROUP
218 D Street SE
Washington, DC 20003-1900
Tel. 202/546-9707 or Fax 202/546-2461
Web site: *www.pirg.org*

PURPOSE: To advocate for environmental protection, consumer protection, energy and government reform. A coalition of state PIRGs.
ACTIVITY: Lobbying, community organizing, public education, research and publications.
BUDGET: $1,000,000
EMPLOYEES: 20; Part-time: 16; Interns: 10

Economic Development

Most of the organizations in this section focus on issues relating to poverty, hunger, community development, cooperatives, credit unions, investment, and income generation. These organizations represent a combination of approaches—organizing self-help initiatives to empower individuals and communities to create self-sustaining development and lobbying government for changes in legislation.

While you will find numerous nonprofit organizations involved with economic development issues, most are very small with annual budgets under $1,000,000 and with fewer than 20 full-time employees. These organizations do offer numerous volunteer opportunities.

ACCION INTERNATIONAL
120 Beacon Street
Somerville, MA 02143
Tel. 617/492-4930 or Fax 617/876-9509
Web site: *www.accion.org*
(Other offices in New York, NY: Albuquerque, NM;
San Antonio, TX; and Washington, DC)

PURPOSE: To fight poverty and hunger by encouraging the economic self-reliance of impoverished working men and women in the Americas.
ACTIVITY: Publications and training and technical assistance.
BUDGET: $6,130,000
EMPLOYEES: Full-time: 36; Part-time: 1; Volunteers: varies; Interns: varies

CHICANOS POR LA CAUSA, INC.
1112 East Buckeye Road
Phoenix, AZ 85034-4043
Tel. 602/257-0700 or Fax 602/256-2740
Web site: *www.cplc.org*
(Other offices in Somerton, Nogales, and Tucson)

PURPOSE: To provide greater opportunities for constituents to obtain quality and affordable housing, a good education, and meaningful employment; thereby promoting self-sufficiency and dignity for the residents of South Phoenix.
ACTIVITY: Publications, human services, community organizing, direct action, public education and training and technical assistance.
BUDGET: $7,000,000
EMPLOYEES: Full-time: 250; Part-time: 30; Volunteers: 50; Interns: varies

FEDERATION OF SOUTHERN COOPERATIVES
P.O. Box 95
Epes, AL 35460
Tel. 205/652-9676
Web site: *www.farmworkers.org/fscpage.html*

PURPOSE: To provide services, resources, and advocacy to over 100 cooperatives and credit unions in the rural South to assist the economic development needs of low-income people.
ACTIVITY: Research, lobbying, publications, human services, organizing and training and technical assistance.
BUDGET: $1,800,000
EMPLOYEES: Full-time: 36; Part-time: varies; Interns: varies

INSTITUTE FOR FOOD AND DEVELOPMENT POLICY
398 60th Street
Oakland, CA 94618
Tel. 510/654-4400 or Fax 510/654-4551
Web site: *www.foodfirst.org*

PURPOSE: To empower citizens to solve the problems of hunger, poverty, and environmental decline. Also known as Food First.
ACTIVITY: Research, public education, publications.
BUDGET: $600,000.
EMPLOYEES: Full-time: 67; Part-time: 1; Volunteers: varies; Interns: varies

NATIONAL COMMUNITY REINVESTMENT COALITION
733 15th Street NW
Suite 504
Washington, DC 20005-2112
Tel. 202/986-7898 or Fax 202/986-7475
Web site: *www.youthlink.net/ncrc*

PURPOSE: To increase access to credit and asset accumulation in low-income, minority, and disadvantaged communities through the Community Reinvestment Act (CRA).
ACTIVITY: Research, lobbying, publications, education, training, and technical assistance.
BUDGET: $600,000
EMPLOYEES: Full-time: 7; Part-time: 2; Volunteers: 2; Interns: 2

NORTHEAST-MIDWEST INSTITUTE
218 D Street SE
Washington, DC 20003
Tel. 202/544-5200 or Fax 202/544-0043
Web site: *www.nemw.org*

PURPOSE: To enhance the economic vitality and environmental quality in the Northeast and Midwest.
ACTIVITY: Research and lobbying.
BUDGET: $1,000,000
EMPLOYEES: Full-time: 15; Interns: varies

OREGON FAIR SHARE
702 NE Schuyler Street
Portland, OR 97214
Tel. 503/280-1762
(Other offices in Medford, Independence, Eugene, and Salem)

PURPOSE: To secure greater economic and social justice through nonviolent, grassroots-based citizen action programs.
ACTIVITY: Community organizing, public education, direct action, lobbying, research and publications.
BUDGET: $1,000,000
EMPLOYEES: Full-time: 23; Part-time: 2; Volunteers: hundreds; Interns: 2

OXFAM AMERICA
26 West Street
Boston, MA 02111
617/482-1211 or Fax 617/728-2594
Web site: *www.oxfamamerica.org*
(Other offices in Canada, the United Kingdom, Belgium, Hong Kong, and several countries in the developing world)

PURPOSE: To fund locally-generated grassroots development work and provide disaster relief through a worldwide network of Oxfam organizations that operate in poor countries of Asia, Africa, and the Americas. Emphasis on promoting economic and food self-reliance.
ACTIVITY: Direct action, public education, lobbying, and publications.
BUDGET: $13,500,000
EMPLOYEES: Full-time: 80; Part-time: 5; Volunteers: varies; Interns: 5

PARTNERS FOR LIVABLE COMMUNITIES
1429 21st Street NW
Washington, DC 20036
Tel. 202/887-5990 or Fax 202/466-4845
Web site: *www.livable.com*

PURPOSE: To improve communities—their economic health and quality of life—through collaborative resource management.
ACTIVITY: Research, education, training, technical assistance, publications.
BUDGET: $930,000
EMPLOYEES: Full-time: 10; Part-time: 4; Volunteers: varies; Interns: varies

PARTNERSHIP FOR THE SOUNDS
P.O. Box 55
Columbia, NC 27925
Tel. 919/796-1000 or Fax 919/796-0218
Web site: *www.albermarle-nc.com/pfs*
(Other office in Washington, DC)

PURPOSE: To promote environmental education and sustainable economic development through cultural, historical and nature-based tourism in North Carolina's Albemarle-Pamlico Sounds region.
ACTIVITY: Public education, training and technical assistance, community organizing and lobbying.
BUDGET: $3,000,000
EMPLOYEES: Full-time: 2; Part-time: 2; Interns: 1

PEOPLE FOR PROGRESS, INC.
301 W. Arkansas Street
Sweetwater, TX 79556
Tel. 915/235-8455

PURPOSE: To research, develop and operate community service programs that resolve poverty conditions and enable low-income people to become self-sufficient.
ACTIVITY: Human services, research, community organizing, direct action, public education and training and technical assistance.
BUDGET: $5,000,000
EMPLOYEES: Full-time: 85; Part-time: varies; Volunteers: 5; Interns: 2

WISCONSIN CITIZEN ACTION
152 West Wisconsin Avenue
Suite 308
Milwaukee, WI 53203
Tel. 414/272-2562
(Other offices in Madison, Racine/Kenosha, Eau Claire, and Green Bay)

PURPOSE: To fight for social and economic justice at local, state and federal levels through issue organizing, grassroots lobbying, and electoral action.
ACTIVITY: Lobbying, public education, community organizing, research and direct action.
BUDGET: $1,500,000
EMPLOYEES: Full-time: 47; Part-time: 3; Volunteers: 5; Interns: varies

WOMEN VENTURE
2324 University Avenue
St. Paul, MN 55114
Tel. 612/646-3808 or Fax 612/641-7223
Web site: *www.womenventure.qpg.org*

PURPOSE: To secure a stronger economic future for women through career development, business development and employment programs.
ACTIVITY: Training and technical assistance.
BUDGET: $1,100,000
EMPLOYEES: Full-time: 18; Part-time: varies; Volunteers: 20; Interns: varies

WOODSTOCK INSTITUTE
407 South Dearborn
Chicago, IL 60605
Tel. 312/427-8070
Web site: *www.nonprofit.net/woodstock*

PURPOSE: To promote forms of investment in disadvantaged communities that contribute to economic opportunity, community capacity, equity formation and the creation of economically and racially diverse communities.
ACTIVITY: Technical assistance, research, program design and publications.
BUDGET: $617,000
EMPLOYEES: Full-time: 7; Interns: varies

Education

Nonprofit organizations focused on education issues are involved in everything from citizenship education to providing educational alternatives to young people and minorities. Compared to many other types of nonprofits, these groups tend to be larger and better financed. The largest in this category, the Close Up Foundation, operates with an annual budget of nearly $36 million and a full-time staff of 190.

ACADEMY FOR EDUCATIONAL DEVELOPMENT
1875 Connecticut Avenue, NW
Washington, DC 20009
Tel. 202/884-8000 or Fax 202/884-8400
Web site: *www.AED.org*

PURPOSE: To increase access to learning transfer skills and technology, and support the development of educational institutions.
ACTIVITY: Education, training, research, technical assistance, and publications.

BUDGET: $124,000,000
EMPLOYEES: 600

ADVOCATES FOR CHILDREN OF NEW YORK, INC.
24-16 Bridge Plaza South
Long Island City, NY 11101
Tel. 718/729-8866

PURPOSE: To protect educational entitlements and due process rights of disadvantaged public school children in New York City.
ACTIVITY: Case advocacy, public education, training and technical assistance, litigation, research, publications, community organizing.
BUDGET: $1,000,000
EMPLOYEES: Full-time: 19; Part-time 4; Volunteers: 3; Interns: 2

AMERICAN COUNCIL ON EDUCATION
1 Dupont Circle NW, Suite 800
Washington, DC 20036
Tel. 202/939-9300 or Fax 202/833-4760
Web site: *www.acenet.edu*

PURPOSE: To represent the interests of colleges and universities, educational organizations, and affiliates.
ACTIVITY: Lobbying, education, training, and publications.
BUDGET: $30,000,000
EMPLOYEES: 1,750

ASPIRA ASSOCIATION, INC.
1444 I Street NW, Suite 800
Washington, DC 20005
Tel. 202/835-3600 or Fax 202/223-1253
Web site: *www.aspira.org*
(Other offices operate in Connecticut, Florida, Illinois, New Jersey,
New York, and Puerto Rico)

PURPOSE: To empower the Puerto Rican and Latino youth through education and leadership development. Serves 25,000 students in 400 schools each year.
ACTIVITY: Training and technical assistance, public education, research and publications.
BUDGET: $1,525,000
EMPLOYEES: Full-time: 15; Part-time: 2; Volunteers: varies; Interns: 2

CENTER FOR MARINE CONSERVATION
725 DeSales Street NW
Suite 600
Washington, DC 20036
Tel. 202/429-5609 or Fax 202/872-0619
Web site: *www.cmc-ocean.org*

PURPOSE: To conserve and protect marine wildlife and their habitat through public awareness and education. Formerly the Center For Environmental Education.
ACTIVITY: Resource center, research, publications, organized beach cleanups.
BUDGET: $7,000,000
EMPLOYEES: Full-time: 60; Part-time: 1; Volunteers: 10; Interns: 1

CHILDREN'S EXPRESS FOUNDATION
1331 H Street NW
Suite 900
Washington, DC 20005-4706
Tel. 212/505-7377 or Fax 202/737-0193
Web site: *www.ce.org*
(Other offices in Boston, Indianapolis, New York City,
Oakland, Washington, DC, Australia, and New Zealand)

PURPOSE: To involve young people in journalism in an attempt to change the way children and teens see and value themselves and are seen and valued by others; to encourage reading, writing and understanding; and to stimulate the child's interest in the world.
ACTIVITY: Publications and reporting on children's issues.
BUDGET: $900,000
EMPLOYEES: Full-Time: 11; Part-time: 2; Volunteers: 5; Interns: 2

CLOSE UP FOUNDATION
44 Canal Center Plaza
Alexandria, VA 22314
Tel. 703/706-3300 or Fax 703/706-0000
Web site: *www.closeup.org*

PURPOSE: To promote citizenship education programs primarily for high school students.
ACTIVITY: Educational—primarily through study visits and publications.
BUDGET: $35,676,000
EMPLOYEES: Full-time: 190; Part-time: 4; Interns: none, but will accept applications

COMMUNITY ALLIANCE WITH FAMILY FARMERS
P.O. Box 363
Davis, CA 95616
Tel. 916/756-8518
Web site: *www.caff.org*
(Other office in San Francisco)

PURPOSE: To provide information and technical support to farmers making the transition to ecological farming.
ACTIVITY: Publications, community organizing, public education, training and technical assistance.
BUDGET: $630,000
EMPLOYEES: Full-time: 21; Part-time: 8; Volunteers: 1; Interns: varies

CONSTITUTIONAL RIGHTS FOUNDATION
601 South Kingsley Drive
Los Angeles, CA 90005
Tel. 213/487-5590 or Fax 213/386-0459
Web site: *www.crf-usa.org*

PURPOSE: To instill in America's youth a deeper understanding of citizenship through values expressed in the Constitution and its Bill of Rights, and educate them to become active and responsible participants in society.
ACTIVITY: Training and technical assistance, publications, education.
BUDGET: $2,200,000
EMPLOYEES: Full-time: 47; Part-time: 2; Interns: none, but will accept applications

COUNCIL FOR ADVANCEMENT AND SUPPORT OF EDUCATION (CASE)
11 Dupont Circle NW, Suite 400
Washington, DC 20036
Tel. 202/328-5900 or Fax 202/387-4973
Web site: *www.case.org*

PURPOSE: To serve as a national clearinghouse for corporate matching gift information. Represents its 2,800 members who are in alumni, fundraising, public relations, admissions, publications, and government relations positions with colleges, universities, and independent elementary and secondary schools.
ACTIVITY: Research, training, education, publications, legislative monitoring.
BUDGET: $10,000,000
EMPLOYEES: 86

DOME PROJECT
486 Amsterdam Avenue
New York, NY 10024
Tel. 212/724-1780

PURPOSE: To provide educational alternatives and enrichment to youngsters in greatest need—truants, low achievers and court-involved youth.
ACTIVITY: Human services, education, training and technical assistance.
BUDGET: $750,000
EMPLOYEES: Full-time: 19; Part-time: 10; Volunteers: 12

EAST BAY CONSERVATION CORPS
1021 Third Street
Oakland, CA 94607
Tel. 510/891-3900 or Fax 510/832-5634

PURPOSE: To promote youth development through community service and service-learning while addressing environmental and social issues.
ACTIVITY: Community and human services, education, community organization, training and technical assistance.
BUDGET: $5,748,588
EMPLOYEES: Full-time: 64; Part-time: 6; Volunteers: 1500; Interns: 30

EDUCATION DEVELOPMENT CENTER
55 Chapel Street
Newton, MA 02158
Tel. 617/969-7100 or Fax 617/244-3436
Web site: *www.edu.org*

PURPOSE: Promote the comprehensive improvement of education through work with teachers, administrators, curriculum specialists, researchers, media specialists, academicians, scientists, technicians, and concerned citizens.
ACTIVITY: Education, training, and technical assistance.
BUDGET: $39,000,000
EMPLOYEES: 350

EDUCATION LAW CENTER
801 Arch Street, Suite 601
Philadelphia, PA 19107
Tel. 215/238-6970
Web site: *www.afj.org/mem/edlc.html*
(Other office in Pittsburgh)

PURPOSE: To provide free legal representation to parents and students relating to preschool, primary, and secondary public education issues in Pennsylvania. quality public education for Pennsylvania students.

ACTIVITY: Litigation, case advocacy, public education, training and technical assistance, community organizing.
BUDGET: $700,000
EMPLOYEES: Full-time: 9

EDUCATORS FOR SOCIAL RESPONSIBILITY
23 Garden Street
Cambridge, MA 02138
Tel. 617/370-2515 or Fax 617/864-5164
Web site: *www.esrnational.org*
(Other offices in New York, NY; Madison, WI;
Concord, NH; and Carroboro, NC)

PURPOSE: To help young people develop a commitment to the well-being of others and to make a positive difference in the world.
ACTIVITY: Training and technical assistance, publications, and public education.
BUDGET: $1,200,000
EMPLOYEES: Full-time: 7: Part-time: 7; Volunteers: varies; Interns: varies

---

LOS NINOS
287 G Street
Chula Vista, CA 91910
Tel. 619/426-9110 or Fax 619/426-6664
(Other office in Calexico, CA)

PURPOSE: To improve the quality of life for Mexican children and their families, and to simultaneously provide education on the benefits of self-help community development through cultural interaction.
ACTIVITY: Education, training and technical assistance, human services, community organizing, research and publications.
BUDGET: $500,000
EMPLOYEES: Full-time: 7; Interns: 2

LULAC NATIONAL EDUCATIONAL SERVICE CENTERS
777 North Capitol Street NE, Suite 305
Washington, DC 20002
Web site: *www.lulac.org*
Tel. 202/408-0060
(Other offices in Los Angeles, San Francisco, Denver, Corpus Christi,
Chicago, Kansas City, Miami, Albuquerque, Philadelphia, Houston)

PURPOSE: To improve the educational condition of the Hispanic community in the United States by working with business and government to initiate educational programs at the local and national level.

ACTIVITY: Human services.
BUDGET: $2,700,000
EMPLOYEES: Full-time: 69; Part-time: 11; Volunteers: 20; Interns: 2

NATIONAL ASSOCIATION OF PARTNERS IN EDUCATION
901 N. Pitt Street, Suite 310
Alexandria, VA 22314
Tel. 703/836-4880 or Fax 703/836-6941
Web site: *www.napehq.org*

PURPOSE: To provide leadership in the formation and growth of effective partnerships in education that ensure success for all students.
ACTIVITY: Training and technical assistance, publications, community organizing, direct action, and public education.
BUDGET: $1,500,000
EMPLOYEES: Full-time: 13; Volunteers: 2; Interns: 1

NATIONAL COMMUNITY EDUCATION ASSOCIATION
3929 Old Lee Highway, Suite 91-A
Fairfax, VA 22030
Tel. 703/359-8973 or Fax 703/359-0972
Web site: *www.ncea.com*

PURPOSE: To provide the tools and knowledge for lifelong learning; parent and community involvement in education; community use of schools; leadership training for community members and improve the quality of community life through education and training.
ACTIVITY: Public education, publications, training and technical assistance.
BUDGET: $570,000
EMPLOYEES: Full-time: 4; Part-time: 1; Volunteers: varies; Interns 1

NATIONAL HEAD START ASSOCIATION
1651 Prince Street
Alexandria, VA 22314
Tel. 703/739-0875 or Fax 703/739-0878
Web site: *www.nhsa.org*

PURPOSE: To nurture and to advocate for children and families; to provide the Head Start community the opportunity of expressing concerns; to define strategies on pertinent issues affecting Head Start; to serve as an advocate for Head Start programs; to provide training and professional development opportunities for the Head Start community; and to develop a networking system with other organizations whose efforts are consistent with the National Head Start Association.
ACTIVITY: Research, lobbying, publications, training and technical assistance.

BUDGET: $3,500,000
EMPLOYEES: Full-time: 21; Volunteers: varies

NATIONAL INSTITUTE FOR CITIZEN EDUCATION IN THE LAW
711 G Street SE
Washington, DC 20003
Tel. 202/546-6644 or Fax 202/546-6649

PURPOSE: To increase citizen understanding of law and the American legal system.
ACTIVITY: Training and technical assistance, publications, education.
BUDGET: $1,200,000
EMPLOYEES: Full-time: 15; Part-time: 1; Interns: varies

THE NETWORK, INC.
136 Fenno Drive
Rowley, MA 01969-1004
Tel. 978/948-7764
(Other offices in Washington, DC; Burlington, VT; San Juan, PR)

PURPOSE: To provide support for school improvement efforts; empower clients to achieve their improvement goals; use existing knowledge, research, solutions, and resources toward quality and equity in education.
ACTIVITY: Training and technical assistance, human services, research, publications, lobbying for public education.
BUDGET: $5,000,000
EMPLOYEES: Full-time: 85; Part-time: 10; Interns: 2

NEW LEGAL DEFENSE AND EDUCATION FUND
99 Hudson Street
12th Floor
New York, NY 10013
Tel. 212/925-6635

PURPOSE: To advocate legal issues for women and girls.
ACTIVITY: Litigation, public education, research, technical assistance.
BUDGET: $2,500,000
EMPLOYEES: Full-time: 27; Part-time: 1; Volunteers: 1; Interns: varies

NEW YORK CITY SCHOOL VOLUNTEER PROGRAM
443 Park Avenue South, 9th Floor
New York, NY 10016
Tel. 212/213-3370

PURPOSE: To recruit, train and place volunteers as tutors in pre-kindergarten through 12th grade in New York City public schools.
ACTIVITY: Public education.
BUDGET: $1,603,210
EMPLOYEES: Full-time: 44; Part-time: 17; Volunteers: 12

STUDENT COALITION FOR ACTION IN LITERACY EDUCATION
University of North Carolina, CB #3500
Chapel Hill, NC 27599
Tel. 919/962-1542
Web site: *unc.edu/depts/scale*

PURPOSE: To mobilize college student involvement with literacy education by assisting students to start and strengthen their campus-based literacy program.
ACTIVITY: Community organizing, public education, training and technical assistance, and publications.
BUDGET: $350,000
EMPLOYEES: Full-time: 18; Part-time: 8; Volunteers: varies; Interns: 2

STUDENT PUGWASH USA
815 15th Street NW, Suite 814
Washington, DC 20005
Tel. 202/393-6550 or Fax 202/393-6550
Web site: *www.spusa.org/pugwash*

PURPOSE: To promote concern for the ethical implications of science and technology for students in high school, undergraduate and graduate university level, and professionals.
ACTIVITY: Student and public education and publications.
BUDGET: $300,000
EMPLOYEES: Full-time: 4; Interns: varies

UNITED STATES STUDENT ASSOCIATION
1413 K Street NW, 9th Floor
Washington, DC 20005
Tel. 202/347-8772 or Fax 202/393-5886
Web site: *www.essential.org/ussa*

PURPOSE: To lobby for student interests on Capitol Hill and train students on nationwide campuses in techniques of direct action organizing. USSA's overriding goal is student empowerment and increased access to higher education. ACTIVITY: Training and technical assistance, lobbying, membership services, community organizing, publications, direct action, and public education. BUDGET: $278,000 EMPLOYEES: Full-time: 10; Volunteers: 4; Interns: 5

UP WITH PEOPLE
1 International Court
Broomfield, CO 80021
Tel. 303/460-7100 or Fax 303/438-7301
Web site: *www.upwithpeople.org*

PURPOSE: To give young people, ages 17-25 from the U.S. and abroad (90 countries), a leaning experience relating to global awareness, sensitivity to others, and self-reliance. Uses a two-hour musical production to achieve these purposes. ACTIVITY: Musical productions (5 casts of 145 students each that give 600 performances each year) and community service activities. BUDGET: $13,700,000 EMPLOYEES: N/A (100+)

WORK, ACHIEVEMENT, VALUES, AND EDUCATION
501 School Street SW
Suite 600
Washington, DC 20024-0183
Tel. 202/484-0103 or Fax 202/488-7595

PURPOSE: To provide education, job skills training and motivation to economically and educationally disadvantaged youth—usually between the ages of 16 and 24. ACTIVITY: Human services, training and technical assistance, research, lobbying, publications, and direct action. BUDGET: $3,200,000 EMPLOYEES: Full-time: 28; Volunteers: 500; Interns: 2

WORLDTEACH
Harvard Institute for International Development
14 Story Street
Cambridge, MA 02138
Tel. 617/495-5527
Web site: *www.worldteach.org*

PURPOSE: To assist in education and promote cultural exchange, both in the U.S. and abroad by placing university graduates as teachers in developing countries.

ACTIVITY: Public education, publications, research, training and technical assistance.
BUDGET: $800,000
EMPLOYEES: Full-time: 14; Part-time: 30; Volunteers: 300; Interns: varies

Environment

Environment remains one of the hottest activity areas for nonprofit organizations. Given recent congressional attempts to gut much of the federal environmental legislation as well as downsize the Environmental Protection Agency and the U.S. Department of Interior, environment nonprofits should be very active in the coming months and years. They attract thousands of job seekers who are fervently committed to solving a host of environmental problems. Indeed, within the past 20 years, hundreds of nonprofits have been formed to deal with a large range of environmental issues.

Nonprofits are some of the most important organizations for keeping environmental issues at the forefront of public policy debates. Many of these organizations are mass membership groups committed to public education and lobbying at the federal, state, and local levels. Most environmental nonprofits focus on a particular environmental area, such as rivers, oceans, ground water, forests, pollution, nuclear disarmament, wildlife, public lands, or population growth. Many of these nonprofits are small to medium size, but many others are very big with large dues-paying mass memberships. For example, the 4.4 million member National Wildlife Federation operates with an annual budget of $96 million and a staff of 400. The Nature Conservancy operates with an annual budget of over $130 million and a staff of over 2,000.

For more information on jobs with environmental nonprofits, see *Careers in the Environment* (NTC Publishing), *Environmental Career Guide* (Wiley), *The New Complete Guide to Environmental Careers* (Island Press) and two comprehensive directories published by Gale Research: *Gale Environmental Sourcebook* and *World Guide to Environmental Issues*.

1000 FRIENDS OF OREGON
503 SW Third Avenue, Suite 300
Portland, OR 97204
Tel. 503/223-4396
Web site: *www.friends.org*

PURPOSE: To ensure the proper implementation of Oregon's land use laws.
ACTIVITY: Litigation, community organizing, training and technical assistance, publications, research, lobbying and public education.
BUDGET: $900,000
EMPLOYEES: Full-time: 10; Part-time: 2; Volunteers: varies; Interns: 1

ADIRONDACK COUNCIL, INC.
P.O. Box D-2, Church Street
Elizabethtown, NY 12932
Tel. 518/873-2240 or Fax 518/873-6675
Web site: *www.crisny.org/not-for-profit/adkcncl*

PURPOSE: To protect and preserve the Adirondack Park in northern New York.
ACTIVITY: Public education, publications, research, lobbying and litigation.
BUDGET: $1,250,000
EMPLOYEES: Full-time: 15; Part-time: 3; Interns: varies

ALASKA CONSERVATION FOUNDATION
750 W. 2nd Avenue #104
Anchorage, AK 99501-2167
Tel. 907/276-1917 or Fax 907/274-4145

PURPOSE: To provide financial support and technical assistance to the greater environmental movement in Alaska.
ACTIVITY: Grantmaking, training and technical assistance.
BUDGET: $1,500,000
EMPLOYEES: Full-time: 3; Part-time: 1; Volunteers: 3

AMERICAN COUNCIL FOR AN ENERGY-EFFICIENT ECONOMY
1001 Connecticut Avenue, Suite 801
Washington, DC 20036
Tel. 202/429-8873
Web site: *www.crest.org/aceee*
(Other office in Berkeley, CA)

PURPOSE: To advance energy efficiency as a means of promoting prosperity and environmental protection focusing on national energy policy, efficiency and economic development, utility issues, transportation, buildings, appliances and equipment, industry and international.

ACTIVITY: Research, publications, conference organizing, public education, training and technical assistance.
BUDGET: $1,750,000
EMPLOYEES: Full-time: 15

AMERICAN FORESTS
910 17th Street NW, Suite 600
Washington, DC 20006
Tel. 202/955-4500 or Fax 202/955-4588
Web site: *www.amfor.org*

PURPOSE: To promote and preserve values and benefits of trees and forests in rural and urban areas.
ACTIVITY: Direct action, public education, research, publications, training and technical assistance, lobbying, and community organizing.
BUDGET: $3,600,000
EMPLOYEES: Full-time: 30; Part-time: 2; Volunteers: 2; Interns: varies

AMERICAN RIVERS
1025 Vermont Avenue NW, Suite 720
Washington, DC 20005
Tel. 202/347-9224 or Fax 202/347-9240
Web site: *www.amrivers.org*
(Other offices in Phoenix and Seattle)

PURPOSE: To preserve and restore America's river systems and foster a river stewardship ethic.
ACTIVITY: Litigation, lobbying, direct action, public education, research, community organizing, training and technical assistance.
BUDGET: $3,000,000
EMPLOYEES: Full-time: 24; Volunteers: varies; Interns: varies

CALIFORNIA CONSERVATION CORPS
1530 Capitol Avenue
Sacramento, CA 95814
Tel. 916/445-0307
Web site: *www.ccc.ca.gov*

PURPOSE: To pair two of the state's most precious resources, youth and the environment, to benefit both.
ACTIVITY: Natural resource work; emergency assistance following disasters.
BUDGET: $50,000,000
EMPLOYEES: 400 (75 administrative staff; 325 field staff); Part-time: varies; Volunteers: varies

CALIFORNIA PUBLIC INTEREST RESEARCH GROUP
11965 Venice Blvd., Suite 408
Los Angeles, CA 90066
Tel. 310/397-3404
(Other offices in Berkeley, San Diego, Sacramento,
San Francisco, Santa Cruz, and Santa Barbara)

PURPOSE: To conduct research and advocate on environmental and consumer issues in California.
ACTIVITY: Research, lobbying, litigation, publications, community organizing, and public education.
BUDGET: $750,000
EMPLOYEES: Full-time: 62; Part-time: 15; Volunteers: varies; Interns: varies

CENTER FOR MARINE CONSERVATION
725 DeSales Street NW
Suite 600
Washington, DC 20036
Tel. 202/429-5609 or Fax 202/872-0619
(Other offices in Hampton, VA; St Petersburg, FL;
& San Francisco, CA)

PURPOSE: To protect the marine environment and its wildlife.
ACTIVITY: Research, public education, training and technical assistance, publications, direct action, lobbying and litigation.
BUDGET: $7,000,000
EMPLOYEES: Full-time: 60; Part-time: varies; Volunteers: 10; Interns: 4

CHESAPEAKE BAY FOUNDATION
162 Prince George Street
Annapolis, MD 21401
Tel. 301/268-8816
Web site: *www.cbf.org*
(Other offices in Richmond, VA;
Harrisburg, PA; and Norfolk, VA)

PURPOSE: To restore and preserve the Chesapeake Bay and its natural resources.
ACTIVITY: Direct action, public education, lobbying, litigation, publications and community organizing.
BUDGET: $6,730,000
EMPLOYEES: Full-time: 118; Part-time: 9; Volunteers: 250; Interns: varies

CITIZENS ACTION COALITION OF INDIANA
3951 N. Meridian St. #300
Indianapolis, IN 46208
Tel. 317/921-1120 or Fax 317/921-1143
Web site: *www.citact.org*
(Other offices in South Bend, Ft. Wayne, and Evansville)

PURPOSE: To advocate for public interest policies in energy, utility, health care, environment and issues concerning small farmers.
ACTIVITY: Research, lobbying, community organizing, public education, litigation, and publications.
BUDGET: $2,500,000
EMPLOYEES: Full-time: 85; Part-time: 30; Volunteers: 30; Interns: will accept applications

CITIZENS FOR A BETTER ENVIRONMENT
3255 Hennepin Avenue South, Suite 150
Minneapolis, MN 55408
Tel. 612/824-8537 or Fax 612/824-0506
Web site: *www.cbemw.org*
(Other offices in Milwaukee, WI and Chicago, IL)

PURPOSE: To protect human and environmental health.
ACTIVITY: Public education, community organizing, research, lobbying, litigation, publications, training and technical assistance.
BUDGET: $1,800,000
EMPLOYEES: Full-time: 91; Part-time, Volunteers, Interns: varies

CLEAN WATER ACTION
4455 Connecticut Ave. NW, Suite A300
Washington, DC 20008-2328
Tel. 202/457-1286
(Other offices in Annapolis, MD; Baltimore; Allentown, PA;
Philadelphia; New Brunswick, NJ; Belmar, NJ; Montclair, NJ;
Trenton, NJ; Boston; Amherst, MA; Portsmouth, NH; Providence, RI;
Austin, TX; Denver; Minneapolis; Rochester, MN; Duluth, MN;
Fargo, ND; Lansing, MI; San Francisco; and Miami)

PURPOSE: To work for clean and safe water, control of toxic chemicals, the protection of natural resources and environmental job creation strategies.
ACTIVITY: Public education, community organizing, training and technical assistance, research, lobbying, election, publications and direct action.
BUDGET: $11,000,000
EMPLOYEES: Full-time: 445; Part-time: 100; Volunteers: varies; Interns: varies

COMMUNITY ENVIRONMENTAL COUNCIL
930 Miramonte Drive
Santa Barbara, CA 93109
Tel. 805/963-0583 or Fax 805/962-9080
Web site: *www.grc.org*

Purpose: To conduct environmental research and education.
Activity: Recycling and other operations, public education, research and publications.
BUDGET: $5,000,000
EMPLOYEES: Full-time: 45; Part-time: varies; Volunteers: 10; Interns varies

CONSERVATION LAW FOUNDATION, INC.
62 Summer Street
Boston, MA 02110-1008
Tel. 617/350-0990 or Fax 617/350-4030
Web site: *www.clf.org*
(Other offices in Rockland, ME and Montpelier, VT)

PURPOSE: To confront environmental issues facing the region from court rooms to town halls. Issues include: conserving natural habitats, open space and agricultural lands, improving urban environments, protecting marine resources, reducing environmental threats to human health, preventing water and air pollution, and developing environmentally sound and economically efficient energy, water use and transportation policies.
ACTIVITY: Public education, litigation and publications.
BUDGET: $2,700,000
EMPLOYEES: Full-time: 29; Part-time: 8; Volunteers: 9; Interns: varies

COUNCIL ON THE ENVIRONMENT OF NEW YORK CITY
51 Chambers Street
Room 228
New York, NY 10007
Tel. 212/788-7900

PURPOSE: To promote environmental awareness among New Yorkers and develop solutions to environmental problems.
ACTIVITY: Direct action, training and technical assistance and community organizing.
BUDGET: $2,269,499
EMPLOYEES: varies

DEFENDERS OF WILDLIFE
1101 14th Street NW, Suite 1400
Washington, DC 20005
Tel. 202/682-9400 or Fax 202/682-1331
Web site: *www.defenders.org*
(Other offices in Sacramento, CA; Missoula, MT; and Portland, OR)

PURPOSE: To preserve, enhance and protect the natural abundance and diversity of wildlife, including the integrity of natural wildlife ecosystems.
ACTIVITY: Research, lobbying, litigation, publications, community organizing, direct action, public education, training and technical assistance.
BUDGET: $7,000,000
EMPLOYEES: Full-time: 60; Volunteers: varies; Interns: varies

ENVIRONMENTAL DEFENSE FUND
257 Park Avenue
New York, NY 10010
Tel. 212/505-2100
(Other offices in Boulder, CO; Oakland, CA;
Washington, DC; Raleigh, NC; and Austin, TX)

PURPOSE: To link science, economics and law to create innovative, economically viable solutions to environmental problems.
ACTIVITY: Research, public education, and judicial, administrative and legislative action.
BUDGET: $24,000,000
EMPLOYEES: Full-time: 160; Part-time 10; Interns: varies

ENVIRONMENTAL LAW INSTITUTE
1616 P Street NW
Suite 200
Washington, DC 20036
Tel. 202/939-3800 or Fax 202/939-3868
Web site: *www.eli.org*

PURPOSE: To transform laws into action protecting water, air quality, wildlife, and wetlands and reducing public health threats through training, research and education for communities, governments and businesses.
ACTIVITY: Public education, training and technical assistance, publications, community organizing and research.
BUDGET: $3,000,000
EMPLOYEES: Full-time: 60; Part-time: 5; Volunteers: 2; Interns: varies

ENVIRONMENTAL SOCIETY OF AMERICA
2010 Massachusetts Avenue NW, Suite 400
Washington, DC 20036
Tel. 202/833-8773 or Fax 202/833-8775
Web site: *www.sdsc.edu/~ESA/*

PURPOSE: To promote the better understanding of plants, animals, and people's relationship to their environment. 7,400 members.
ACTIVITY: Research, education, publications, and awards.
BUDGET: $2,700,000
EMPLOYEES: 24

FRIENDS OF THE EARTH
1025 Vermont Avenue NW, Suite 300
Washington, DC 20005
Tel. 202/783-7400 or Fax 202/783-0444
Web site: *www.foe.org*
(Other offices in Seattle, WA and Manila, Philippines)

PURPOSE: To advocate on behalf of global environment issues.
ACTIVITY: Lobbying, publications, research, human services, public education, litigation, direct action and community organizing.
BUDGET: $3,500,000
EMPLOYEES: Full-time: 35; Part-time: 2; Volunteers: 3

GREENPEACE
1436 U Street NW
Washington, DC 20009
Tel. 202/462-1177 or Fax 202/462-4507
Web site: *www.greenpeaceusa.org*
(Other offices in New York, NY; San Francisco, CA;
Seattle, WA; and Chicago, IL)

PURPOSE: To campaign for toxic waste elimination, nuclear disarmament, protection of marine mammals and the oceans, alternatives to environmentally destructive energy consumption, and prevention of further destruction of the ozone layer.
ACTIVITY: Public education, direct action, community organizing, research, lobbying, publications, litigation, training and technical assistance.
BUDGET: $37,000,000
EMPLOYEES: Full-time: 300; Part-time: 10; Volunteers: 50; Interns: 25

INFORM, INC.
120 Wall Street, 16th Floor
New York, NY 10005-4001
Tel. 212/361-2400 or Fax 212/361-2412
Web site: *www.informinc.org*

PURPOSE: To identify and report on practical actions for the preservation and conservation of natural resources and public health.
ACTIVITY: Research, public education, publications, training and technical assistance.
BUDGET: $1,797,0800
EMPLOYEES: Full-time: 22; Volunteers: 1; Interns: varies

IZAAK WALTON LEAGUE OF AMERICA
IWLA Conservation Center
707 Conservation Lane
Gaithersburg, MD 20878
Tel. 301/548-0150 or Fax 301/548-0146
Web site: *www.iwla.org*
(Other office in Minneapolis, MN)

PURPOSE: To pursue conservation goals in areas of clean water, acid rain reduction, improve wildlife habitat, protection of natural areas, improvement of outdoor ethics, public land management and farm conservation.
ACTIVITY: Research, lobbying, litigation, publications, community organizing and public conservation.
BUDGET: $2,000,000
EMPLOYEES: Full-time: 25; Part-time: 1; Interns: varies

LEAGUE OF CONSERVATION VOTERS
1707 L Street NW, Suite 750
Washington, DC 20036
Tel. 202/785-8683 or Fax 202/835-0491
Web site: *www.lcv.org*
(Other office in Portsmouth, NH)

PURPOSE: To help elect pro-environment candidates to the U.S. House of Representatives and Senate.
ACTIVITY: Public education, research, publications, development and membership activities.
BUDGET: $1,000,000
EMPLOYEES: Full-time: 55; Interns: 5

MOUNTAIN INSTITUTE
Main & Dogwood Streets
Franklin, WV 26807
Tel. 304/358-2401 or Fax 304/358-2400
Web site: *www.mountain.org*
(Other offices in Kathmandu, Nepal and Shigalee, Tibet)

PURPOSE: To advance mountain cultures and preserve mountain environments worldwide. Formerly the Woodlands Mountain Institute.
ACTIVITY: Direct action, human services, research, training and technical assistance and membership development.
BUDGET: $2,000,000
EMPLOYEES: Full-time: 25; Part-time: 3

NATIONAL RECYCLING COALITION, INC.
1727 King Street
Suite 105
Alexandria, VA 22314-2720
Tel. 703/683-9025
Web site: *www.nrc-recycle.org*

PURPOSE: To promote recycling.
ACTIVITY: Research, community organizing, publications, direct action, training, and technical assistance.
BUDGET: $321,000
EMPLOYEES: 11

NATIONAL WILDLIFE FEDERATION
8925 Leesburg Pike
Vienna, VA 22184
Tel. 703/790-4000
Web site: *www.nwf.org*
(Other Offices in Anchorage, AK; Ann Arbor, MI;
Missoula, MT; Bismarck, ND; Boulder, CO;
Atlanta, GA; Montpelier, VT; Austin, TX; and Portland, OR)

PURPOSE: To be the nation's most responsible and effective conservation education organization promoting the wise use of natural resources and the protection of the global environment.
ACTIVITY: Lobbying, litigation, publications, public education, direct action and research.
BUDGET: $96,000,000
EMPLOYEES: Full-time: 400; Part-time: 10; Volunteers: 20; Interns: 40

NATURE CONSERVANCY
1815 North Lynn Street
Arlington, VA 22209
Tel. 703/841-5300 or Fax 703/841-1283
Web site: *www.tnc.org*

PURPOSE: To preserve global biological diversity—rare plants, animals and natural communities.
ACTIVITY: Protection, fundraising, stewardship, research and publications.
BUDGET: $131,000,000
EMPLOYEES: Full-time: 2,000; Part-time: 94; Volunteers: low 100,000's; Interns: varies

NORTHEAST-MIDWEST INSTITUTE
218 D Street SE
Washington, DC 20003
Tel. 202/544-5200 or Fax 202/544-0043
Web site: *www.nemw.org*

PURPOSE: To enhance the economic vitality and environmental quality of the 18-state region that makes up the nation's industrial heartland.
ACTIVITY: Research and lobbying.
BUDGET: $1,000,000
EMPLOYEES: Full-time: 15; Interns: varies

PENNSYLVANIA ENVIRONMENTAL COUNCIL
1211 Chestnut Street
Suite 900
Philadelphia, PA 19130
Tel. 215/563-0275
Web site: *www.libertynet.org/pecphila*

PURPOSE: To advocate for environmental legislation and regulation and educate citizens of Pennsylvania about the importance of these measures.
ACTIVITY: Research, lobbying, publications, community organizing, direct action, public education, training and technical assistance.
BUDGET: $900,000
EMPLOYEES: Full-time: 12; Part-time: 5; Volunteers: varies; Interns: varies

RAINFOREST ALLIANCE
650 Bleecker Street
New York, NY 10012
Tel. 212/677-1900 or Fax 212/677-2187
Web site: *www.rainforest-alliance.org*

PURPOSE: To conserve the world's endangered tropical forests and promote economically viable and socially desirable alternatives to the destruction of tropical forests.
ACTIVITY: Research projects, education, publications, partnerships with governments with business, government, and citizens.
BUDGET: $2,700,000
EMPLOYEES: Full-time: 40; Part-time: 9; Volunteers: 20; Interns: varies

ROCKY MOUNTAIN INSTITUTE
1739 Snowmass Creek Road
Old Snowmass, CO 81654
Tel. 970/927-3851 or Fax 970/927-3420
Web site: *www.rmi.org*

PURPOSE: To foster the efficient and sustainable use of resources as a path to global security. Program areas include energy, water, forests, corporate sustainability, climate changes, economic renewal and energy security, transportation and Green Development services.
ACTIVITY: Research, technical assistance, public education, publication of research findings, direct action and community organizing.
BUDGET: $2,500,000
EMPLOYEES: Full-time: 45; Part-time: 10; Volunteers: varies; Interns: varies

SIERRA CLUB
85 2nd Street
2nd Floor
San Francisco, CA 94105-3459
Tel. 415/977-5500 or Fax 415/977-5799
Web site: *sierraclub.org*
(Other offices in Washington, DC; Saratoga Springs, NY;
Annapolis, MD; Birmingham, AL; Madison, WI; Sheridan. WY;
Dallas, TX; Boulder, CO; Phoenix, AZ; Salt Lake City, UT;
Los Angeles, CA; Oakland, CA; Seattle, WA; Anchorage, AK;
and North Palm Beach, FL)

PURPOSE: To explore, enjoy and protect the wild places of the earth; to practice and promote the responsible use of the earth's ecosystems and resources; to educate and enlist humanity to protect and restore the quality of the natural and human environment; and to use all lawful means to carry out these objectives.
ACTIVITY: Research, lobbying, publications, community organizing, education.

BUDGET: $43,000,000
EMPLOYEES: Full-time: 294; Part-time, Volunteers, and Interns: varies

TRUST FOR PUBLIC LAND
116 New Montgomery, 4th Floor
San Francisco, CA 94105
Tel. 415/495-4014 or Fax 415/495-4103
Web site: *www.tpl.org/topl*
(Other offices in Washington, DC; Norwich, CT; Sacramento, CA;
Austin, TX: Costa Mesa, CA; Los Angeles; New York;
Morristown, NJ; Minneapolis; Boston; Tallahassee, FL;
Atlanta; South Miami, FL; Santa Fe, NM; Seattle; Portland, OR)

PURPOSE: To conserve land for people to enjoy.
ACTIVITY: Research, lobbying, litigation, publications, public education, training and technical assistance, land acquisition and Open space financing.
BUDGET: $18,000,000
EMPLOYEES: Full-time: 180; Part-time: varies; Interns: varies

WORLD RESOURCES INSTITUTE
1709 New York Avenue NW, 7th Floor
Washington, DC 20006
Tel. 202/638-6300 or Fax 202/638-0036
Web site: *www.wri.org*

PURPOSE: To provide accurate information about global resources and environmental conditions, analyze emerging issues, and develop creative yet workable policy responses.
ACTIVITY: Research, publications, outreach on research and publications, training and technical assistance and public education.
BUDGET: $14,228,000
EMPLOYEES: Full-time: 85; Interns: varies

WORLD WILDLIFE FUND/
THE CONSERVATION FOUNDATION
1250 24th Street NW
Washington, DC 20037
Tel. 202/293-4800 or Fax 202/293-9211
Web site: *www.wwf.org*
(Other office in Gland, Switzerland)

PURPOSE: To protect endangered wildlife and wildlands especially in the tropical forests of Latin America, Asia and Africa. A mass membership organization with 1.2 million members.
ACTIVITY: Training and technical assistance, direct action, research, community organizing, publications, human services and public education.

BUDGET: $156,000,000
EMPLOYEES: N/A (600+)

WORLDWATCH INSTITUTE
1776 Massachusetts Avenue NW
Washington, DC 20036
Tel. 202/452-1999 or Fax 202/296-7365
Web site: *www.workwatch.org*

PURPOSE: To alert policymakers and the general public to emerging global trends in the availability and management of resources, both human and natural.
ACTIVITY: Research and publications.
BUDGET: $3,827,000
EMPLOYEES: Full-time: 32; Part-time: 1

ZERO POPULATION GROWTH
SEATTLE
4426 Burke Avenue N.
Seattle, WA 98103
Tel. 206/548-0152
Web site: *www.cn.org/zpg*
(Other office in Los Angeles, CA)

PURPOSE: To achieve a sustainable balance of population, resources and the environment—both in the United States and worldwide.
ACTIVITY: Research, lobbying, publications, community organizing, public education, training and technical assistance.
BUDGET: $2,500,000
EMPLOYEES: Full-time: 25; Part-time: 3; Volunteers: 3; Interns: varies

Food and Nutrition

Food and nutrition are important activities for numerous nonprofit organizations. Some of the largest nonprofit organizations primarily deal with these issues in Third and Fourth World countries (see Chapter 9 for additional listings). However, some nonprofits focus on food and nutrition issues in the United States. Most of these organizations are relatively small with annual budgets under $2 million and with staffs of fewer than 15 employees.

BREAD FOR THE CITY
1525 7th Street NW
Washington, DC 20001
Tel. 202/332-0440
Web site: *www.breadz.org*

PURPOSE: To provide emergency food, clothing and social services to low-income residents of the District of Columbia.
ACTIVITY: Human services, training and technical assistance, and lobbying.
BUDGET: $850,000
EMPLOYEES: Full-time: 14; Part-time: 3; Volunteers: 70; Interns: varies

BREAD FOR THE WORLD
1100 Wayne Avenue
Suite 1000
Silver Spring, MD 20910
Tel. 301/608-2400 or Fax 301/608-2401
Web site: *www.bread.org*
(Other offices in Minneapolis, Chicago and Los Angeles)

PURPOSE: To help the world's hungry by lobbying U.S. decision-makers.
ACTIVITY: Research, publications, community organizing, public education, and lobbying by members.
BUDGET: $2,500,000
EMPLOYEES: Full-time: 50; Part-time: 5; Volunteers: 22; Interns: 8

CENTER FOR SCIENCE IN THE PUBLIC INTEREST
1875 Connecticut Avenue NW
Suite 300
Washington, DC 20009-5728
Tel. 202/332-9110 or Fax 202/265-4954
Web site: *www.cspinet.org*

PURPOSE: To conduct research, educate and advocate about nutrition, diet, food safety, alcohol and related food issues.
ACTIVITY: Public education, supporting services, publications, research, litigation, and lobbying.
BUDGET: $17,000,000
EMPLOYEES: Full-time: 65; Part-time: 1; Volunteers: 1; Interns: varies

FOOD RESEARCH AND ACTION CENTER
1875 Connecticut Avenue NW
Suite 540
Washington, DC 20009
Tel. 202/986-2200 or Fax 202/986-2525
Web site: *www.frac.org*

PURPOSE: To end hunger and malnutrition in the United States.
ACTIVITY: Research, lobbying, litigation, publications, organizing, public education, training and technical assistance.
BUDGET: $1,800,000
EMPLOYEES: Full-time: 16; Part-time: varies; Interns: varies

SHARE OUR STRENGTH
1511 K Street NW
Suite 623
Washington, DC 20005
Tel. 202/393-2925 or Fax 202/347-5868
Web site: *www.strength.org*

PURPOSE: To raise funds (working primarily through the restaurant industry) and awareness for the relief of hunger, homelessness and illiteracy in the U.S. and overseas.
ACTIVITY: Grants program through which funds are distributed to public education, community organizing, publications, and research.
BUDGET: $14,000,000
EMPLOYEES: Full-Time: 40; Volunteers: 6; Interns: will accept applications

Housing and the Homeless

Housing and the homeless represent important social issues for hundreds of nonprofit organizations. Nonprofits focusing on these issues deal with tenants rights, housing discrimination, community development, employment, minorities, construction, neighborhood preservation, legal services, ex-offenders, and shelter. While most of these organizations are community-based and relatively small in size, some, such as Habitat for Humanity, are relatively large and have a national and international presence. Nonprofits working in these areas tend to be heavily involved in providing direct services to the poor and homeless.

ASIAN COUNSELING AND REFERRAL SERVICE
720 8th Avenue S.
Suite 200
Seattle, WA 98104
Tel. 206/461-3606 or Fax 206/695-7606
Web site: *www.acrs.org*
(Other office in Bellevue, WA)

PURPOSE: To provide and advocate for human services to empower Asian and Pacific Islander individuals and communities to obtain social and economic well being.
ACTIVITY: Human services, public education, community organizing, direct action, training and technical assistance.
BUDGET: $3,100,000
EMPLOYEES: Full-time: 45; Volunteers: varies; Interns: varies

ASSISTED LIVING FEDERATION OF AMERICA
10300 Eaton Place
Suite 400
Fairfax, VA 22030
Tel. 703/691-8100 or Fax 703/691-8106
Web site: *www.alfa.org*

PURPOSE: To promote the interests of the 15,000 member assisted living industry as well as improve the quality of life for the population it services.
ACTIVITY: Education, speakers, research, trade shows, conferences, and publications.
BUDGET: $3,000,000
EMPLOYEES: 15

BALTIMORE NEIGHBORHOODS, INC.
77 East Main Street
Suite 113 (Long well Building)
Baltimore, MD 21157
Tel. 410/857-8417

PURPOSE: To promote justice in housing, advocate tenants rights, and eliminate illegal discrimination.
ACTIVITY: Litigation, direct action, human services, and community organizing.
BUDGET: $300,000
EMPLOYEES: Full-time: 10; Volunteers: 100

CENTER FOR COMMUNITY CHANGE
1000 Wisconsin Avenue NW
Washington, DC 20007
Tel. 202/342-0519 or Fax 202/342-1132
(Other office in San Francisco)

PURPOSE: To help poor Americans help themselves by building strong community organizations, help them create jobs, build affordable housing, raise money and develop effective community programs.
ACTIVITY: Training and technical assistance, research and development, public policy, research, publications, and lobbying.
BUDGET: $4,500,000
EMPLOYEES: Full-time: 46; Part-time: 3; Interns: varies

CHICANOS POR LA CAUSA, INC.
1112 East Buckeye Road
Phoenix, AZ 85034-4043
Tel. 602/257-0700 or Fax 602/256-2740
Web site: *www.cplc.org*
(Other offices in Somerton, AZ; Nogales, AZ; and Tucson, AZ)

PURPOSE: To provide greater opportunities for constituents to obtain quality and affordable housing, education, and meaningful employment.
ACTIVITY: Publications, human services, community organizing, direct action, public education, training and technical assistance.
BUDGET: $7,000,000
EMPLOYEES: Full-time: 250; Part-time: 30; Volunteers: 50; Interns: varies

COOPERATIVE HOUSING FOUNDATION
8300 Colesville Road
Suite 420
Silver Spring, MD 20910
Tel. 301/587-4700 or Fax 301/587-2626
Web site: *www.chfhq.org*

PURPOSE: To assist in the development of cooperative and self-help housing. Helps families invest own resources for improving their housing situation and living conditions as well as strengthens assistance capabilities of governments, communities, donor agencies, and businesses.
ACTIVITY: Training, technical assistance, project involvement, and lobbying.
BUDGET: $8,000,000
EMPLOYEES: 44

ENTERPRISE FOUNDATION
10227 Wincopin Circle
Suite 500
Columbia, MD 21044-3400
Tel. 410/964-1230 or Fax 410/964-1918
Web site: *www.enterprisefoundation.org*

PURPOSE: To assist nonprofit neighborhood housing organizations in providing decent and affordable housing for low-income families.
ACTIVITY: Education, training, and technical assistance.
BUDGET: $18,000,000
EMPLOYEES: 280

HABITAT FOR HUMANITY INTERNATIONAL
121 Habitat Street
Americas, GA 31709-3498
Tel. 912/924-6935 or Fax 912/924-6541
Web site: *www.habitat.org*

PURPOSE: To eliminate poverty from the world and make decent housing a matter of conscience and action. Christian housing organization that works in partnership with people throughout the world in building shelters that are sold through no-interest loans.
ACTIVITY: Direct action, human services, public education and publications.
BUDGET: $65,000,000
EMPLOYEES: Full-time: 433; Part-time: varies: Volunteers: 100; Interns: varies

HOUSING AND CREDIT COUNSELING, INC.
1500 Walnut Street
Suite 601
Philadelphia, PA 19102
Tel. 913/234-0217 or Fax 215/790-9132
(Other offices in Lawrence, KS and Manhattan, KS)

PURPOSE: To facilitate safe, adequate, affordable and equitable housing situations for all people—particularly those of low and moderate income and to assist with budgeting and debt repayment alternatives.
ACTIVITY: Human services, public education, training and technical assistance, and community organizing.
BUDGET: $500,000
EMPLOYEES: Full-time: 21; Part-time: 1; Volunteers: varies; Interns: 2

HOUSING ASSISTANCE COUNCIL
1025 Vermont Avenue NW, Suite 606
Washington, DC 20005
Tel. 202/842-8600 or Fax 202/347-3441
Web site: *www.ruralhome.org*
(Other offices in Atlanta, GA; Mill Valley, CA; Albuquerque, NM)

PURPOSE: To assist in the provision of decent, sanitary, affordable housing for the rural poor.
ACTIVITY: Training, technical assistance, direct action, research, publications.
BUDGET: $2,000,000
EMPLOYEES: Full-time: 25; Interns: 2

HOUSING ASSOCIATION OF DELAWARE VALLEY
1314 Chestnut Street, Suite 900
Philadelphia, PA 19107
Tel. 215/545-6010

PURPOSE: To end racism and exploitation in housing and ensure decent housing for all residents of the Delaware Valley regardless of race or income.
ACTIVITY: Research, publications, public education, training and technical assistance, housing counseling and housing development.
BUDGET: $2,790,000
EMPLOYEES: Full-time: 12; Interns: varies

LAWYERS ALLIANCE FOR NEW YORK
99 Hudson Street
New York, NY 10013
Tel. 212/219-1800 or Fax 212/941-7458
Web site: *www.lany.org*

PURPOSE: To promote low-income housing development and neighborhood preservation and provide legal services to nonprofit organizations.
ACTIVITY: Training and technical assistance, publications, direct action, fundraising and volunteer placement.
BUDGET: $1,000,000
EMPLOYEES: Full-time: 16; Part-time: 2; Volunteers: 1; Interns: 3

MASSACHUSETTS HALF-WAY HOUSES, INC.
Back Bay Annex, P.O. Box 348
Boston, MA 02117
Tel. 617/437-1864

PURPOSE: To provide residential and non-residential support services to ex-offenders with the goal of achieving successful reintegration into the community after incarceration.

ACTIVITY: Human services, training and technical assistance.
BUDGET: $4,500,000
EMPLOYEES: Full-time: 118; Volunteers: 50; Interns: varies

NATIONAL COALITION FOR THE HOMELESS
1621 K Street NW, Suite 1004
Washington, DC 20006-2802
Tel. 202/775-1322 or Fax 202/775-1316
Web site: *www.nch.ari.net*

PURPOSE: To address and end homelessness through a multi-level strategy of securing rights, services and housing for homeless people.
ACTIVITY: Lobbying, research, litigation, publications, human services, community organizing, direct action, education, training, and technical assistance.
BUDGET: $550,000
EMPLOYEES: Full-time: 8; Part-time: 2; Volunteers: 5; Interns: varies

PROJECT NOW COMMUNITY ACTION AGENCY
418 19th Street
Rock Island, IL 61201
Tel. 309/793-6391 or Fax 309/793-6352

PURPOSE: To develop, mobilize, and utilize to the maximum extent possible all available human and material resources on the local, state, and national levels for the purpose of combating and eliminating poverty.
ACTIVITY: Human services, training and technical assistance, public education, and community organizing.
BUDGET: $4,800,000
EMPLOYEES: Full-time: 150; Part-time: 55; Volunteers: 100; Interns: 10

URBAN HOMESTEADING ASSISTANCE BOARD
120 Wall Street, 20th Floor
New York, NY 10005
Tel. 212/479-3300 or Fax 212/344-6457
Web site: *www.uhab.org*

PURPOSE: To assist low income neighborhood housing groups and tenant organizations in developing self-help housing solutions. Assists in developing sweat equity rehabilitation and homesteading projects in New York City.
ACTIVITY: Training and technical assistance, publications, community organizing, research and public education.
BUDGET: $1,000,000
EMPLOYEES: Full-time: 31; Part-time: 3; Volunteers: varies; Interns: varies

Medical and Health Care

Medical and health care nonprofits focus on a wide range of health issues, from mental health, cancer, and family planning to AIDS, minority health care, and the handicapped. Each major disease or medical problem area tends to have its own set of nonprofit organizations supporting research and education and providing technical assistance and direct services. Many of these groups lobby for changes in government health care policies.

During the past few years, numerous nonprofit organizations have formed throughout the country to deal with HIV/AIDS. Many of these groups are now well financed, having been successful in getting funding from foundations and federal, state, and local governments. Others continue to struggle for basic funding to support their services.

The organizations represented in this section primarily focus on health issues in the United States. Some of the largest organizations dealing with medical and health issues, especially those dealing with family planning, eye care, and medical relief, are international nonprofits. We identify and profile many of these international nonprofits in Chapter 9.

ACTION ON SMOKING AND HEALTH
2013 H Street NW
Washington, DC 20006-4205
Tel. 202/659-4310
Web site: *http://ash.org*

PURPOSE: To promote and take legal action for nonsmokers' rights.
ACTIVITY: Litigation, public education, publications, research.
BUDGET: $1,415,000
EMPLOYEES: Full-time: 10; Part-time: 1; Interns: 2

AIDS ACTION COUNCIL
1875 Connecticut Avenue NW, Suite 700
Washington, DC 20009
Tel. 202/986-1300 or Fax 202/986-1345
Web site: *www.aidsaction.org*

PURPOSE: To lobby the federal government on behalf of AIDS communities.
ACTIVITY: Lobbying, community organizing, media relations, publications.
BUDGET: $2,000,000
EMPLOYEES: Full-time: 21; Part-time: 3; Volunteers: varies; Interns: 2

AMERICAN FOUNDATION FOR AIDS RESEARCH
120 Wall Street
13th Floor
New York, NY 10005
Tel. 1-800-392-6327
Web site: *www.amfar.org*

PURPOSE: To raise funds to support research on HIV/AIDS as well as develop educational programs on preventing the spread of the disease.
ACTIVITY: Fund raising, education, awards, and publications.
BUDGET: $16,000,000
EMPLOYEES: 60

AMERICAN INDIAN HEALTH SERVICE OF CHICAGO
838 West Irving Park Road
Chicago, IL 60613-3011
Tel. 773/883-9100

PURPOSE: To increase financial and cultural accessibility to health and human services for American Indians.
ACTIVITY: Human services, community development, educational advocacy, research, publications, public education, and training and technical assistance.
BUDGET: $639,000
EMPLOYEES: Full-time: 14; Part-time: 5; Volunteers: 4; Interns: varies

AMERICAN LUNG ASSOCIATION
1740 Broadway
New York, NY 10019-4374
Tel. 212/315-8700
Web site: *www.lungusa.org*

PURPOSE: To fight lung disease and promote healthy lungs.
ACTIVITY: Research, lobbying, publications, human services, community organizing, direct action, public education/management, training and technical assistance, and professional education.
BUDGET: $52,083,000. However, each state, DC, Puerto Rico, and the Virgin Islands also has a lung association. Each is separately incorporated and does its own recruiting and hiring. Budgets range from less than $200,000 to over $2 million.
EMPLOYEES: 800. Staff size varies with each individual state lung association.

AMERICAN SOCIAL HEALTH ASSOCIATION
P.O. Box 13827
Research Triangle Park, NC 27709
Tel. 919/361-8400 or Fax 919/361-8425
Web site: *www.ashastd.org*
(Other office in Washington, DC)

PURPOSE: To stop sexually transmitted disease.
ACTIVITY: Public education; research, lobbying, publications, training and technical assistance.
BUDGET: $9,100,000
EMPLOYEES: Full-time: 250; Part-time: 206; Volunteers: 9; Interns: will accept applications.

BOSTON WOMEN'S HEALTH BOOK COLLECTIVE
240A Elm Street
Somerville, MA 02164
Tel. 617/625-0271 or Fax 617/625-0294
Web site: *www.bwhbc.org*

PURPOSE: To promote women's health education, advocacy and activism.
ACTIVITY: Public education, training and technical assistance, publications, research, community organizing, direct action, and litigation.
BUDGET: $724,000
EMPLOYEES: Full-time: 13; Part-time: 3; Volunteers: 5

CANCER CARE
1180 Avenue of the Americas
New York, NY 10036
Tel. 212/221-3300 or Fax 212/719-0263
Web site: *www.cancercare.org*

PURPOSE: To promote the development of social services to cancer patients and their families. Provides counseling and guidance in coping with the emotional and psychological challenges presented by cancer.
ACTIVITY: Public education, research, financial assistance, child care, transportation, and publications.
BUDGET: $724,000
EMPLOYEES: Full-time: 13; Part-time: 3; Volunteers: 5

CITIZENS FOR BETTER CARE
4750 Woodward Avenue, Suite 410
Detroit, MI 48201
Tel. 313/962-5968 or Fax 313/832-6387
(Other Michigan offices in Lansing, Grand Rapids, Saginaw,
Traverse City, and Iron Mountain)

PURPOSE: To help people with the selection of/or who have problems with
nursing homes, homes for the aged or other long-term health care services.
ACTIVITY: Handling consumer complaints and requests for information, developing issue papers, monitoring state and federal action, public education,
training and technical assistance, publications and lobbying.
BUDGET: $1,200,000
EMPLOYEES: Full-time: 30; Part-time: 5; Volunteers: 50; Interns: 3

ENVIRONMENTAL HEALTH COALITION
1717 Kettner Blvd., Suite 100
San Diego, CA 92101
Tel. 619/235-0281 or Fax 619/232-3670
Web site: *www.environmentalhealth.org*

PURPOSE: To prevent illness and environmental degradation resulting from
exposure to toxins in the home, workplace, and community.
ACTIVITY: Public education, training and technical assistance, research, community organizing, and direct action.
BUDGET: $300,000
EMPLOYEES: Full-time: 9; Part-time: 3; Volunteers: varies; Interns: varies

HEALTH CARE FOR ALL
30 Winter Street
Suite 1010
Boston, MA 02108
Tel. 617/350-7279 or Fax 617/350-0974
Web site: *www.ncfa.org*

PURPOSE: To create a health care system that is responsive to the needs of all
people, particularly the most vulnerable.
ACTIVITY: Community organizing, public education, human services, research,
publications, lobbying, direct action, and litigation.
BUDGET: $400,000
EMPLOYEES: Full-time: 8; Part-time: 2; Volunteers: 10; Interns: 6

HEALTH CRISIS NETWORK
5050 Biscayne Blvd.
Miami, FL 33134
Tel. 305/751-7775 or Fax 305/756-7880
Web site: *whitepartyweek.com/hcn/hcn.htm*

PURPOSE: To provide counseling and support services, public information and education in response to HIV spectrum illness for the greater Miami area.
ACTIVITY: Human services, public education, training and technical assistance.
BUDGET: $3,100,000
EMPLOYEES: Full-time: 54; Part-time: 20; Volunteers: 500; Interns: varies

LOS ANGELES REGIONAL FAMILY PLANNING COUNCIL, INC.
3600 Wilshire Boulevard
Suite 600
Los Angeles, CA 90010
Tel. 213/386-5614
Web site: *www.fpcai.org/larfhome.htm*

PURPOSE: To provide fiscal monitoring, quality assurance, training, data processing and other services to delegate agencies to increase the accessibility and availability of reproductive health services to all persons regardless of income.
ACTIVITY: Research, human services, public relations, public education, training and technical assistance.
BUDGET: $20,000,000
EMPLOYEES: Full-time: 46; Part-time: 2; Volunteers: 6; Interns: occasionally

NATIONAL ABORTION FEDERATION
1755 Massachusetts Ave., Suite 600
Washington, DC 20036--2123
Tel. 202/667-5881 or Fax 202/667-5590
Web site: *www.prochoice.org*

PURPOSE: To enhance the quality and accessibility of abortion care.
ACTIVITY: Public education, training and technical assistance, publications, human services, research, health care services-legal clearinghouse, and guidance on response to violence.
BUDGET: $1,578,000
EMPLOYEES: Full-time: 13; Part-time: 1; Interns: 2

NATIONAL ALLIANCE FOR THE MENTALLY ILL
200 N. Glebe Road, Suite 1015
Arlington, VA 22203-3728
Tel. 703/524-7600 or Fax 703/524-9094
Web site: *www.nami.org*

PURPOSE: To provide emotional support and information on the biological nature of serious mental illness through local family support groups, advocate for better treatment and community services, promote research on causes and treatments of serious mental illness, and seek to eliminate the stigma associated with these disorders.
ACTIVITY: An alliance of self-help/advocacy groups in all 50 states. Public education, training and technical assistance, human services, publications, lobbying, and direct action.
BUDGET: $4,400,000
EMPLOYEES: Full-time: 55; Part-time: 2; Volunteers: 30; Interns: varies

NATIONAL BLACK WOMEN'S HEALTH PROJECT
175 Trinity Avenue SW
Atlanta, GA 30303
Tel. 404/758-9590
(Other office in Washington, DC)

PURPOSE: To provide wellness education and services, self-help group development, and health information and advocacy in order to reduce the health care problems amongst black women and their families.
ACTIVITIES: 26 state groups and 150 local groups. Public education, community organizing and publications.
BUDGET: $1,600,000
EMPLOYEES: Full-time: 19; Part-time: 2: Volunteers: 10; Interns: varies

NATIONAL MINORITY AIDS COUNCIL
1931 13th Street NW
Washington, DC 20009-4432
Tel. 202/483-6622 or Fax 202/483-1127
Web site: *www.nmac.org*

PURPOSE: To develop and guide national public policy initiatives on HIV/AIDS infection in communities of color and serve as a clearinghouse for information on AIDS affecting minority communities.
ACTIVITY: Lobbying, publications, community organizing, public education, research, training and technical assistance, and conferences.
BUDGET: $12,000,000
EMPLOYEES: Full-time: 20; Part-time: 1; Interns: 1

NATIONAL NATIVE AMERICAN AIDS PREVENTION CENTER
134 Linden Street
Oakland, CA 94607
Tel. 510/444-2051 or Fax 510/444-1593
Web site: *www.nnaapc.org*
(Other offices in Minneapolis, MN and Oklahoma City, OK)

PURPOSE: To support community efforts in Native communities by providing education and information services and training/technical assistance as well as provide case management and client advocacy services to Native Americans with HIV infection.
ACTIVITY: Training and technical assistance, publications, case management.
BUDGET: $2,207,000.
Employees: Full-time: 16; Part-time: 2

NEW LEAF SERVICES
1853 Market Street
San Francisco, CA 94103
Tel. 415/626-7000

PURPOSE: To provide mental health and social services to the lesbian and gay community in a multicultural environment, with attention to youth, elders, the disabled, couples and families and substance abusers. Previously known as Operation Concern.
ACTIVITY: Human services, training, technical assistance, education.
BUDGET: $900,000
EMPLOYEES: Full-time: 26; Part-time: 16; Volunteers: 35; Interns: 13

PLANNED PARENTHOOD FEDERATION OF AMERICA, INC.
810 Seventh Avenue
New York, NY 10019
Tel. 212/541-7800 or Fax 212/245-1845
Web site: *www.plannedparenthood.org*

PURPOSE: To provide leadership in promoting voluntary fertility decisions, including contraception, abortion, sterilization, and infertility services.
ACTIVITY: Operates 900 centers delivering reproductive health services and educational programs. Human services, lobbying, litigation, public education, community organizing, research, training and technical assistance.
BUDGET: $685,200,000
EMPLOYEES: Full-time: 10,961; Part-time: 2; Interns: 1

PUBLIC CITIZEN HEALTH RESEARCH GROUP
1600 20th Street NW, Suite 700
Washington, DC 20009
Tel. 202/588-1000 or Fax 202/588-7796
Web site: *www.citizen.org/hrq*

PURPOSE: To promote the public's health by monitoring the work of the medical establishment, the drug industry and the health related regulatory agencies as well as writing and distributing publications that help give consumers more control over their health decisions.
ACTIVITY: Research, lobbying, publications, direct action and public education.
BUDGET: $600,000
EMPLOYEES: Full-time: 8; Part-time: varies; Volunteers: varies

SAN FRANCISCO AIDS FOUNDATION
P.O. Box 426182
San Francisco, CA 94142-6182
Tel. 415/487-3000 or Fax 415/487-3009
Web site: *www.stat.org*

PURPOSE: To provide direct services to people with AIDS and HIV by helping to educate the public to prevent transmission of HIV; helping individuals make informed choices about treatment options and other AIDS-related concerns; protecting the dignity and human rights of those affected by HIV; and initiating and supporting public policies to further these goals.
ACTIVITY: Lobbying, publications, human services, community organizing, direct action, public education, training and technical assistance.
BUDGET: $18,000,000
EMPLOYEES: Full-time: 105; Part-time: 2; Volunteers: 500; Interns: varies

WHITMAN-WALKER CLINIC, INC.
1407 S Street NW
Washington, DC 20009
Tel. 202/797-3500
Web site: *www.wwc.org*

PURPOSE: To provide or facilitate the delivery of high quality, comprehensive, integrated, and accessible health care services to diverse community. A nationally recognized HIV/AIDS Ambulatory Care Center, Research Center, and provider of Lesbian and Gay health care.
ACTIVITY: Education, training, and direct health care services.
BUDGET: $20,000,000
EMPLOYEES: Full-time: 250; Volunteers: 2000

Public Policy and Government Reform

Much of what nonprofit organizations do is aimed at influencing the content of government policy. Whether the issues are housing, education, health care, or environment, the methods and goals are often the same—lobby government decision-makers.

Numerous nonprofit organizations are organized specifically to influence government. Some of these groups, such as policy institutes and think tanks, conduct studies and present their findings to government officials. Others, like The Urban Institute, operate similarly to private contractors—receive contracts and grants to do government-sponsored research on important public policy issues.

Nonprofit organizations in this category range from very small operations to large public policy institutes. They represent both conservative and liberal groups. Common Cause, which has a great deal of public visibility, operates with an annual budget of $11 million and with a full-time staff of 100. Conservative think tanks, such as the CATO Institute ($11 million) and the American Enterprise Institute ($12 million) operate with relatively modest budgets and staffs. More liberal think tanks, such as The Brookings Institution ($22 million) and The Urban Institute ($21 million), are somewhat larger.

If you are passionately committed to particular public policy issues, or love to work with public policy issues, this group of nonprofit organizations may be an ideal "fit" for you.

AIDS ACTION COUNCIL
1875 Connecticut Avenue NW
Suite 700
Washington, DC 20009
Tel. 202/986-1300 or Fax 202/986-1345
Web site: *www.handsnet.org*

PURPOSE: To lobby the federal government to develop federal HIV/AIDS policies to increase AIDS research and improve treatment and prevention.
ACTIVITY: Lobbying, community organizing, media relations and publications.
BUDGET: $2,000,000
EMPLOYEES: Full-time: 21; Part-time: 3; Volunteers: varies; Interns: 2

AMERICAN ENTERPRISE INSTITUTE
1150 17th Street NW
Washington, DC 20036
Tel. 202/862-5800 or Fax 202/862-7178
Web site: *www.aei.org*

PURPOSE: To conduct public policy research on economics, government, and foreign and defense policy. Oriented toward an open economy and limited government.
ACTIVITY: Research, education, conferences, forums, seminars, and publications.
BUDGET: $12,000,000
EMPLOYEES: 125

THE ASPEN INSTITUTE
1333 New Hampshire Avenue NW, Suite 1070
Washington, DC 20036
Tel. 202/736-5800 or Fax 202/467-0790
Web site: *www.aspeninst.org*

PURPOSE: To enhance the quality of leadership through informed dialogue. Brings together men and women with diverse viewpoints and backgrounds from business, labor, government, the professions, the arts, and the nonprofit sector to exchange ideas and values on challenging issues facing society, organizations, and institutions. Operates popular executive seminars.
ACTIVITY: Education, conferences, forums, seminars, and publications.
BUDGET: $23,800,000
EMPLOYEES: 125

ARIZONA CENTER FOR LAW IN THE PUBLIC INTEREST
3208 E. Fort Lowell #106
Tucson, AZ 85716
Tel. 602/327/9547 or Fax 602/323-0642

PURPOSE: To provide an effective voice for individuals and groups that otherwise would be unable to obtain effective legal representation.
ACTIVITY: Research, lobbying, litigation, education, training and technical assistance.
BUDGET: $900,000
EMPLOYEES: Full-time: 21; Part-time: 1; Volunteers: 4; Interns: varies

BROOKINGS INSTITUTION
1775 Massachusetts Avenue NW
Washington, DC 20036
Tel. 202/797-6000 or Fax 202/797-6004
Web site: *www.brook.edu*

PURPOSE: To conduct nonpartisan research and provide education and publications in the fields of economics, government, and foreign policy.
ACTIVITY: Research, education, conferences, forums, seminars, publications.
BUDGET: $22,000,000
EMPLOYEES: 250

CATO INSTITUTE
1000 Massachusetts Avenue NW
Washington, DC 20001-5403
Tel. 202/842-0200 or Fax 202/842-3490
Web site: *www.cato.org*

PURPOSE: To conduct public policy research relating to limited government, individual liberty, and peace. A conservative/libertarian orientation.
ACTIVITY: Research, organizing, education, forums, seminars, publications.
BUDGET: $11,000,000
EMPLOYEES: 70

CENTER FOR POLICY ALTERNATIVES
1875 Connecticut Avenue NW, Suite 710
Washington, DC 20009
Tel. 202/387-6030 or Fax 202/986-2539
Web site: *www.cfpa.org*

PURPOSE: To serve as a policy resource organization specializing in innovation and reform by America's state governments.
ACTIVITY: Research, organizing, education, training and technical assistance.
BUDGET: $2,100,000
EMPLOYEES: Full-time: 25; Part-time: 3; Interns: varies

CITIZENS ACTION COALITION OF INDIANA
3951 N. Meridian St. #300
Indianapolis, IN 46208
Tel. 317/921-1120 or Fax 317/921-1143
Web site: *www.citiact.org*
(Other offices in South Bend, Ft. Wayne, and New Albany)

PURPOSE: To advocate in areas of energy policy, utility policy, health care policy, environmental policy and issues concerning small farmers.

ACTIVITY: Research, lobbying, community organizing, public education, litigation and publications.
BUDGET: $2,500,000
EMPLOYEES: Full-time: 85; Part-time: 30; Volunteers: 30; Interns: willing to accept applications

COMMON CAUSE
1250 Connecticut Avenue NW
Washington, DC 20036
Tel. 202/833-1200 or Fax 202/659-3716
Web site: *www.commoncause.org*

PURPOSE: To improve the way government operates as well as to make it more responsive and accountable to the public.
ACTIVITY: Lobbying and education.
BUDGET: $11,000,000
EMPLOYEES: Full-time: 100; Volunteers: 75; Interns: varies

DEMOCRATIC SOCIALISTS OF AMERICA
180 Varick Street, 12th Floor
New York, NY 10014
Tel. 212/727-8610 or Fax 212/727-8616
Web site: *www.dsausa.org/dsa*

PURPOSE: To attain a social order based on popular control of resources and production, economic planning, equitable distribution, feminism, racial equality and non-oppressive relationships.
ACTIVITY: Community organizing, publications, public education, research and direct action.
BUDGET: $590,000
EMPLOYEES: Full-time: 5; Interns: 3

FRIENDS COMMITTEE ON NATIONAL LEGISLATION
245 Second Street NE
Washington, DC 20002
Tel. 202/547-6000 or Fax 202/547-6019
Web site: *www.fcnl.org/pub/fcnl*

PURPOSE: To bring Quaker values to bear on public policy—especially in the areas of world peace, equity and justice for all, civil rights, environmental quality and economic justice.
ACTIVITY: Lobbying, research, education and publications.
BUDGET: $1,000,000
EMPLOYEES: Full-time: 18; Part-time: varies; Volunteers: varies; Interns: 4

THE FUND FOR PEACE
1701 K Street NW
11th Floor
Washington, DC 20006
Tel. 202/223-7940 or Fax 202/223-7947
Web site: *www.fundforpeace.org*

PURPOSE: To promote education, research, and public policy for resolving global problems that threaten human survival. Supports education and action for furthering peace, justice, and a secure world.
ACTIVITY: Research, education, and publications.
BUDGET: $3,000,000
EMPLOYEES: 40

HOOVER INSTITUTION ON WAR, REVOLUTION, AND PEACE
Stanford University
Stanford, CA 94305-6010
Tel. 415/723-0603 or Fax 415/723-1687
Web site: *www.hoover.org*

PURPOSE: To conduct interdisciplinary research in the social sciences and public policy on a variety of domestic and international issues that promote peace and freedom as well as safeguard the American System. A conservative "think tank" which is also known as the Hoover Institution.
ACTIVITY: Research, education, and publications.
BUDGET: $18,500,000
EMPLOYEES: 320

HUDSON INSTITUTE
5395 Emerson Way
Indianapolis, IN 46226
Tel. 317/545-1000 or Fax 317/545-9639
Web site: *www.hudson.org*

PURPOSE: To study public policy issues relating to national security, international and domestic economics, education and employment, energy and technology, and the future. A noted public policy "think tank".
ACTIVITY: Research, education, and publications.
BUDGET: $7,000,000
EMPLOYEES: 70

INSTITUTE FOR POLICY STUDIES
733 15th Street
Washington, DC 20005
Tel. 202/234-9382 or Fax 202/387-7915
Web site: *www.ips-dc.org*

PURPOSE: To provide research and public education on economics, politics, culture and social issues of democracy. Focuses on domestic policy, natural security, foreign policy, international economics, and human rights. International program centers on its Transnational Institute.
ACTIVITY: Research, public education and publications.
BUDGET: $1,400,000
EMPLOYEES: Full-time: 26; Volunteers: 2; Interns: 10

LEAGUE OF WOMEN VOTERS
1730 M Street NW
Washington, DC 20036
Tel. 202/854-4053 or Fax 212/854-8727
Web site: *www.lwv.org*

PURPOSE: To encourage the informed and active participation of citizens in government and influence public policy through education and advocacy.
ACTIVITY: Research, lobbying, litigation, publications, direct action, public education, training and technical assistance.
BUDGET: $3,550,000.
EMPLOYEES: 50; Part-time: varies; Volunteers: varies; Interns 2

NATIONAL CIVIC LEAGUE
1445 Market Street
Suite 300
Denver, CO 80202-1717
Tel. 303/571-4343 or Fax 303/571-440
Web site: *www.ncl.org*

PURPOSE: To work as a convener to communities interested in collaborative projects to improve the quality of life within their community.
ACTIVITY: Training and technical assistance, publications, community organizing and research.
BUDGET: $2,000,000
EMPLOYEES: Full-time: 21; Part-time: 1; Interns: 4

NATIONAL WOMEN'S POLITICAL CAUCUS
1275 K Street NW, Suite 750
Washington, DC 20005
Tel. 202/898-1100 or Tel. 202/785-3605

PURPOSE: To increase the number of women elected and appointed to political office.
ACTIVITY: Identifies, recruits, trains and supports pro-choice women to run for political office at all levels of government, regardless of party.
BUDGET: $1,500,000
EMPLOYEES: Full-time: 10; Volunteers: varies; Interns: varies

OMB WATCH
1742 Connecticut Avenue NW
Washington, DC 20009-1146
Tel. 202/634-8494 or Fax 202/234-8584
Web site: *www.ombwatch.org*

PURPOSE: To conduct research and support education and advocacy that monitors Executive Branch activities affecting nonprofit, public interest and community groups.
ACTIVITY: Research, publications, lobbying, training and technical assistance.
BUDGET: $750,000
EMPLOYEES: Full-time: 7; Part-time: varies; Interns: varies

PUBLIC CITIZEN'S CONGRESS WATCH
215 Pennsylvania Avenue SE
Washington, DC 20003
Tel. 202/546-4996 or Fax 202/547-7392
Web site: *www.citizen.org/congress*

PURPOSE: To represent the public through lobbying Congress, organizing, research and publications. Formerly known as Congress Watch.
ACTIVITY: Research, lobbying, community organizing and public education.
BUDGET: $800,000
EMPLOYEES: Full-time: 15 Part-time: 1; Volunteers: varies; Interns: varies

8

Top 623 Professional and Trade Associations

Trade and professional associations constitute two of the most important complexes of nonprofit organizations. Formed for a variety of reasons, most of these organizations primarily function to promote the interests of their members. Being nonprofit, cooperative, and voluntary organizations, most of these groups exchange ideas amongst members; examine common professional problems; establish professional standards; engage in technical assistance and community service; and provide mutual assistance. Some of these organizations also do research, provide training, conduct testing, issue certification and awards, offer career assistance, and serve as information clearinghouses for their members. Other associations perform these same functions, but they also are heavily involved in lobbying activities aimed at influencing the content of public policy. In contrast to the nonprofits identified in Chapter 8, professional and trade associations are less concerned with pursuing a passion than with representing the interests of its members.

Most major trade and professional associations are headquartered in and around Washington, DC (32%), New York City (13%), and Chicago (12%). Most others are found in and around Los Angeles, Cleveland, Philadelphia, Boston, Atlanta, Dallas, San Francisco, Detroit, Phoenix, and Denver.

The Organizations

Similar to the nonprofits in Chapter 7, the organizations identified in this chapter should be treated as a sampler. They by no means represent all associations—only examples of what you will likely encounter once you explore on your own the many thousands of associations found at the international, national, regional, state, and local levels. These groups represent every type of conceivable interest and affiliation, and then some!

While we only describe a few trade and professional associations, you'll discover thousands of other associations that represent numerous interest and activity categories. To get information on these and other associations, you'll need to conduct your own research using the many resources available in your local library, as we outlined in Chapter 5.

We've chosen to include only trade and professional associations because of their **linkage capabilities** vis-a-vis other types of public, private, and nonprofit organizations. From the perspective of job seekers, these associations provide important linkages—or serve as stepping-stones—to other organizations. Members of trade and professional associations represent over 90 percent of all businesses in the United States. Given their educational and public policy focuses, these organizations constantly interact with government, educational institutions, and other nonprofit organizations. If you work for one of these organizations, you will be

> **Associations provide important career linkages—or serve as stepping-stones—to other organizations.**

in a good position to make important contacts for future job and career moves into both the public and private sectors as well as into other areas of the nonprofit world.

Most associations are small, operated by 2 to 10 staff members with annual budgets ranging from $300,000 to $1 million. However, over 600 associations, or nearly 8 percent of the total, have annual budgets in excess of $5 million. These organizations have staffs of 50 or more individuals. For your quick reference, we identify the top 613 such associations—by name only—at the end of this chapter.

Therefore, the organizations identified in this chapter represent some of the largest and most politically active associations. These are well organized associations with large staffs and budgets. They offer a wide range of jobs and numerous opportunities for career advancement within and between these organizations.

Opportunities

Trade and professional associations offer excellent opportunities for individuals with a variety of skills. Since most associations are heavily involved in education, training, and lobbying activities, they need well educated individuals who have strong communication and organizational skills. They especially need people who can write, speak, plan, organize, maintain liaison, conduct meetings, and train. They operate large publication programs, publishing everything from newsletters and magazines to catalogs and books; conduct seminars and annual meetings; engage in research for members; and provide technical assistance. Associations with staffs of 100 or more, which usually have a $10+ million annual budget, will offer a large number of highly specialized career opportunities.

Resources

Your single best source of information on associations is the *Encyclopedia of Associations* (Gale Research). Published in four volumes, it includes descriptions of nearly 25,000 associations which are classified into 18 major categories:

1. Trade, business, and commercial
2. Environmental and agricultural
3. Legal, governmental, public administration, and military
4. Engineering, technological, and natural and social sciences
5. Educational
6. Cultural
7. Social welfare
8. Health and medical
9. Public affairs
10. Fraternal, nationality, and ethnic
11. Religious
12. Veterans', hereditary, and patriotic
13. Hobby and avocational
14. Athletic and sports

15. Labor unions, associations, and federations
16. Chambers of commerce and trade and tourism
17. Greek and non-Greek letter societies, associations, and federations
18. Fan clubs

These directories also are available in two other versions which cover over 50,000 regional, state, and local associations and nearly 13,000 international associations: *Encyclopedia of Associations: Regional, State, and Local Organizations* and *Encyclopedia of Associations: International Organizations.*

Two other useful resources for locating professional and trade associations are published by Columbia Books: *National Trade and Professional Associations* and *State and Regional Associations in the U.S.* These publication offer five useful indexes to associations—alphabetical, subject, geographic, budget, and executive. While not as detailed as the *Encyclopedia of Associations,* the indexes alone are worth your time and effort in examining these publications.

Armed with these resources, you should be able to uncover numerous associations that might have an ideal job for you. Once you identify an interesting association, be sure to follow our previous advice—call to get information on job opportunities and get a contact name and address.

The Associations

The following list of associations covers a large variety of organizations. Taken together, they offer thousands of job opportunities for enterprising job seekers. Examined separately, one or more of these associations may be an excellent "fit" for you.

Since most of these associations have Web sites, we strongly recommend visiting their sites before making phone calls or sending letters or faxes. In many cases, the Web site will include employment opportunities with the organization. Indeed, you'll find a wealth of information about the association which should help you decide whether or not the organization is right for you given your interests, skills, and abilities. If you're interested in pursuing job opportunities with some of these associations, make a few phone calls and follow-up with letters and resumes. You may soon discover you've uncovered an extremely rewarding job market!

ACADEMY OF MOTION PICTURE ARTS AND SCIENCES
8949 Wilshire Blvd.
Beverly Hills, CA 90211
Tel. 310/247-3000 or Fax 310/247-2600

PURPOSE: To promote the interests of motion picture producers, directors, writers, cinematographers, editors, actors, and craftsmen.
ACTIVITY: Education, awards.
BUDGET: N/A ($10,000,000+)
EMPLOYEES: 100

ADVERTISING COUNCIL
261 Madison Avenue, 11th Floor
New York, NY 10016-2303
Tel. 212/922-1500 or Fax 212/922-1676

PURPOSE: To conduct public service advertising campaigns in a variety of areas—drug abuse prevention, AIDS prevention, teen alcoholism, child abuse, crime prevention, forest fire prevention.
ACTIVITY: Research, education, public service awards.
BUDGET: $12,000,000
EMPLOYEES: 42

AIR LINE PILOTS ASSOCIATION INTERNATIONAL
P.O. Box 5524
Arlington, TX 76005
Tel. 972/988-3188 or Fax 972/606-5668

PURPOSE: To represent the labor interests of its 44,000 members. Serves as the collective bargaining agent.
ACTIVITY: Research, education, collective bargaining.
BUDGET: N/A ($100,000,000+)
EMPLOYEES: 350

AMERICAN ASSOCIATION OF AIRPORT EXECUTIVES
4212 King Street
Alexandria, VA 22302
Tel. 703/824-0500 or Fax 703/820-1395
Web site: *www.airportnet.org*

PURPOSE: Promote the interests of airport management personnel and representatives of companies serving the civil airport industry.
ACTIVITY: Education, research, testing.
BUDGET: $5,000,000
STAFF: 30

AMERICAN ASSOCIATION OF RETIRED PERSONS (AARP)
601 E Street NW
Washington, DC 20049
Tel. 202/434-2277 or Fax 202/434-2320
Web site: *www.aarp.org*

PURPOSE: To promote the interests of persons 50 years of age or older. Operates a large number of programs, from preretirement planning to group health insurance. Represents interests of its 32,000,000 members.
ACTIVITY: Education, research, community service, lobbying.
BUDGET: N/A ($250,000,000+)
STAFF: 1,200

AMERICAN AUTOMOBILE ASSOCIATION
1000 AAA Drive
Heathrow, FL 32746
Tel. 407/444-4240 or Fax 407/444-7380
Web site: *www.aaa.com*

PURPOSE: To sponsor public services relating to traffic, safety, better highways, energy conservation, and improved motoring conditions. A federation of 1000 automobile clubs with 40,000,000 members.
ACTIVITY: Research, education, membership services, lobbying.
BUDGET: N/A ($200,000,000+)
EMPLOYEES: N/A (2000+)

AMERICAN AUTOMOBILE MANUFACTURERS ASSOCIATION
1401 H Street NW, Suite 900
Washington, DC 20005
Tel. 202/326-5500 or Fax 202/326-5567
Web site: *www.aama.com*

PURPOSE: To monitor, analyze, and respond to federal and state legislative and regulatory initiatives affecting the automotive industry. Trade association sponsored by Chrysler, Ford, and General Motors.
ACTIVITY: Research, education, lobbying.
BUDGET: $30,000,000
EMPLOYEES: 100

AMERICAN BANKERS ASSOCIATION
1120 Connecticut Avenue NW
Washington, DC 20036
Tel. 202/663-5000 or Fax 202/663-7543
Web site: *www.aba.com*

PURPOSE: To promote the interests of its members—primarily commercial banks and trust companies representing 90% of the banking industry.
ACTIVITY: Education, research, testing.
BUDGET: $62,000,000
STAFF: 410

AMERICAN BAR ASSOCIATION
750 N. Lake Shore Dr.
Chicago, IL 60611
Tel. 312/988-5000 or Fax 312/988-5528
Web site: *www.abanet.org*

PURPOSE: To promote the interests of its 375,000 members who are attorneys in good standing with the bar of any state.
ACTIVITY: Education, research, public service, lobbying.
BUDGET: $65,000,000
STAFF: 800

AMERICAN CANCER SOCIETY
1599 Clifton Road NE
Atlanta, GA 30329
Tel. 404/320-3333 or Fax 404/329-7530
Web site: *www.cancer.org*

PURPOSE: To support education and research in cancer prevention, diagnosis, detection, and treatment. Includes 2.5 million volunteers.
ACTIVITY: Education, research, public service.
BUDGET: N/A ($30,000,000+)
STAFF: 390

AMERICAN CHEMICAL SOCIETY
1155 16th Street NW
Washington, DC 20036
Tel. 202/872-4600 or Fax 202/872-4615
Web site: *www.acs.org*

PURPOSE: To support the work and interests of chemists and chemical engineers. A scientific and educational society consisting of 151,000 members and 187 local societies.
ACTIVITY: Education, research, public service, career guidance.

BUDGET: $250,000,000
STAFF: 1,950

AMERICAN COMPENSATION ASSOCIATION
14040 N. Northsight Blvd.
Scottsdale, AZ 85260
Tel. 602/951-9191 or Fax 602/483-8352
Web site: *www.acaonline.org*

PURPOSE: To promote the interests of managerial, professional, and executive level administrative personnel in business, industry, and government who design, establish, execute, administer, or apply total compensation practices and policies in their organizations. Represents the interests and promotes professionalism amongst its 23,000 members.
ACTIVITY: Surveys, research, education, certification.
BUDGET: $15,000,000
EMPLOYEES: 100

AMERICAN COUNCIL OF LIFE INSURANCE
1001 Pennsylvania Avenue NW
Washington, DC 20004-2599
Tel. 202/624-2000 or Fax 202/724-2319
Web site: *www.acli.com*

PURPOSE: To promote the interests of legal reserve life insurance companies and to provide effective government relations. Consists of 538 member companies that represent 90 percent of the life insurance force in the United States.
ACTIVITY: Education, research, lobbying.
BUDGET: $39,500,000
STAFF: 184

AMERICAN FEDERATION OF LABOR AND CONGRESS OF INDUSTRIAL ORGANIZATIONS (AFL-CIO)
815 16th Street NW, Room 703
Washington, DC 20006
Tel. 202/637-5000 or Fax 202/637-5058
Web site: *www.aflcio.org*

PURPOSE: To represent the interests of members before employers and government. A federation of labor unions consisting of 13,300,000 members with 51 state groups and 620 local groups.
ACTIVITY: Education, research, lobbying.
BUDGET: N/A ($100,000,000+)
STAFF: 400

AMERICAN FEDERATION OF STATE, COUNTY, AND MUNICIPAL EMPLOYEES
1625 L Street NW
Washington, DC 20036
Tel. 202/452-4800
Web site: *www.afscme.org*

PURPOSE: To represent the interests of its 1.3 million members.
ACTIVITY: Education, research, organizing, lobbying.
BUDGET: N/A ($25,000,000+)
STAFF: 270

AMERICAN FEDERATION OF TEACHERS
555 New Jersey Avenue NW
Washington, DC 20001
Tel. 202/879-4400 or Fax 202/879-4545
Web site: *www.aft.org*

PURPOSE: To represent the labor interests of its 950,000 teachers and other educational employees through 2,500 chapters at the state and local levels.
ACTIVITY: Education, research, organizing, collective bargaining, lobbying.
BUDGET: $65,000,000
STAFF: N/A (400+)

AMERICAN GAS ASSOCIATION
1515 Wilson Blvd.
Arlington, VA 22209
Tel. 703/841-8400 or Fax 703/841-8406
Web site: *www.aga.com*

PURPOSE: To promote the interests of its 4,175 members—individuals (3,500), U.S. (250), and Canadian (11) distributors (utilities) and transporters (pipeline companies) of natural, manufactured, and liquefied gas.
ACTIVITY: Research, education, testing, public relations, lobbying.
BUDGET: $30,000,000
EMPLOYEES: 110

AMERICAN HOSPITAL ASSOCIATION
1 N. Franklin, Suite 27
Chicago, IL 60606
Tel. 312/422-3000 or Fax 312/422-4519
Web site: *www.aha.org*

PURPOSE: To promote improved health care services for its 54,500 members.
ACTIVITY:Research, education, community service, public relations, lobbying.

BUDGET: $79,000,000
EMPLOYEES: 884

AMERICAN HOTEL AND MOTEL ASSOCIATION
1201 New York Avenue NW, Suite 600
Washington, DC 20005-3931
Tel. 202/289-3100 or Fax 202/289-3199
Web site: *www.ahma.com*

PURPOSE: To promote the interests of this federation of 50 state and regional hotel associations with 12,000 members representing over 1.4 million rooms.
ACTIVITY: Education, research, publicity, lobbying.
BUDGET: $7,000,000
STAFF: 65

AMERICAN INSTITUTE OF CERTIFIED PUBLIC ACCOUNTANTS
1211 Avenue of the Americas
New York, NY 10036-8775
Tel. 212/596-6200 or Fax 212/596-6213
Web site: *www.aicpa.org*

PURPOSE: To establish auditing and reporting standards, influence the development of financial accounting, and preparing and grading the national Uniform CPA Examination for the state licensing bodies. Represents the interests of its 316,800 members.
ACTIVITY: Research, continuing education, surveillance.
BUDGET: N/A ($50,000,000+)
EMPLOYEES: 725

AMERICAN INSURANCE ASSOCIATION
1130 Connecticut Avenue NW, Suite 1000
Washington, DC 20036
Tel. 202/828-7100 or Fax 202/293-1219
Web site: *www.aiadc.org*

PURPOSE: To represent companies providing property and casualty insurance and suretyship. Serves as a clearinghouse of ideas, advice, and technical information for its 275 members.
ACTIVITY: Education, research, lobbying.
BUDGET: $25,000,000
STAFF: 140

AMERICAN LIBRARY ASSOCIATION
50 E. Huron Street
Chicago, IL 60611
Tel. 312/944-6780 or Fax 312/280-3255
Web site: *www.ala.org*

PURPOSE: To promote and improve library service and librarianship amongst its 56,800 members who are organized into 57 regional groups.
ACTIVITY: Education, research, standardization, career assistance, lobbying.
BUDGET: $32,000,000
STAFF: 275

AMERICAN MEDICAL ASSOCIATION
515 N. State Street
Chicago, IL 60610
Tel. 312/464-5000 or Fax 312/464-4184
Web site: *www.ama-assn.org*

PURPOSE: To improve medical education and practices and disseminate scientific information to its 297,000 members and the public.
ACTIVITY: Education, research, standardization, placement, lobbying.
BUDGET: N/A ($30,000,000+)
STAFF: N/A (300+)

AMERICAN PETROLEUM INSTITUTE
1220 L Street NW
Washington, DC 20005
Tel. 202/682-8000 or Fax 202/682-8029
Web site: *www.api.org*

PURPOSE: To represent the interests of its 300 members—corporations in the petroleum and allied industries.
ACTIVITY: Education, research, lobbying.
BUDGET: $56,000,000
STAFF: 400

AMERICAN POSTAL WORKERS UNION
1300 L Street NW
Washington, DC 20005
Tel. 202/842-4200 or Fax 202/842-4297
Web site: *www.apwu.org*

PURPOSE: To support the labor interests of its 320,000 postal workers.
ACTIVITY: Education, research, collective bargaining.
BUDGET: N/A ($17,000,000+)
STAFF: 200

AMERICAN PSYCHIATRIC ASSOCIATION
1400 K Street NW
Washington, DC 20005
Tel. 202/682-6000 or Fax 202/682-6114
Web site: *www.psycho.org*

PURPOSE: To further the study of the nature, treatment, and prevention of mental disorders and formulate programs to meet mental health needs. Develops programs for dealing with mental health needs. Represents the interests of its 40,000 members.
ACTIVITY: Education, research, program development.
BUDGET: $25,000,000
STAFF: 190

AMERICAN PUBLIC HEALTH ASSOCIATION
1015 15th Street NW
Washington, DC 20005
Tel. 202/789-5600 or Fax 202/789-5661
Web site: *www.apha.org*

PURPOSE: To protect and promote personal, mental, and environmental health. A professional organization of 31,500 physicians, nurses, educators, environmentalists, epidemiologists, social workers, optometrists, podiatrists, dentists, nutritionists, health planners.
ACTIVITY: Education, research, standards/procedures, job placement.
BUDGET: $9,000,000
STAFF: 65

AMERICAN SOCIETY FOR TRAINING AND DEVELOPMENT
1640 King Street
Alexandria, VA 22314
Tel. 703/683-8100 or Fax 703/683-8103
Web site: *www.astd.org*

PURPOSE: To promote effective practices amongst its 55,000 members who are engaged in the training and development of business, industry, education, and government employees.
ACTIVITY: Education, research, clearinghouse.
BUDGET: $15,000,000
STAFF: 120

AMERICAN SOCIETY OF ASSOCIATION EXECUTIVES
1575 I Street NW
Washington, DC 20005
Tel. 202/626-2723 or Fax 202/408-9633
Web site: *www.asaenet.org*

PURPOSE: To promote the interests of paid executives of national, state, and local trade, professional, and philanthropic associations. 23,700 members.
ACTIVITY: Education, training, lobbying, certification, career guidance.
BUDGET: $18,000,000
STAFF: 135

AMERICAN SOCIETY OF TRAVEL AGENTS
1101 King Street
Alexandria, VA 22314
Tel. 703/739-2782 or Fax 703/684-8319
Web site: *www.astanet.com*

PURPOSE: To promote travel and encourage the use of professional travel agents worldwide. Includes 28,600 members.
ACTIVITY: Education, training.
BUDGET: $13,000,000
STAFF: 95

AMERICAN TRUCKING ASSOCIATION
2200 Mill Road
Alexandria, VA 22314-4677
Tel. 703/838-1700 or Fax 703/684-5751
Web site: *www.trucking.org*

PURPOSE: To promote the interests of its 4,500 members—motor carriers, suppliers, trucking associations, national conferences of trucking companies.
ACTIVITY: Education, lobbying.
BUDGET: $52,000,000
STAFF: 298

AMERICAN WATER WORKS ASSOCIATION
6666 W. Quincy Avenue
Denver, CO 80235
Tel. 303/794-7711 or Fax 303/795-1440
Web site: *www.awwa.org*

PURPOSE: To develop standards and support research on waterworks design, construction, operation, and management for its 54,000 members—water utility managers, superintendents, engineers, chemists, bacteriologists, boards of health, manufacturers, officials, and consultants involved in water supply.

ACTIVITY: Education, training, career assistance.
BUDGET: $13,000,000
STAFF: 120

ASSOCIATION OF INTERNATIONAL AUTOMOBILE MANUFACTURERS
1001 19th Street North, Suite 1200
Arlington, VA 22209
Tel. 703/525-7788 or Fax 703/525-8817
Web site: *www.aiam.org*

PURPOSE: To act as a clearinghouse for information affecting the importation of automobiles and auto equipment into the U.S. and report proposed regulations by state or federal government to members.
ACTIVITY: Research, education, lobbying.
BUDGET: $5,000,000
STAFF: 22

ASSOCIATION FOR MANUFACTURING TECHNOLOGY
7901 Westpark Dr.
McLean, VA 22102
Tel. 703/893-2900 or Fax 703/893-1151
Web site: *www.mfgtech.org*

PURPOSE: To promote the interests of its 375 members—makers of power driven machines used in the process of transforming man-made materials into durable goods, including machine tools, assembly machines, inspection and testing machinery, robots, parts loaders, and plastics molding machines.
ACTIVITY: Research, education, marketing, lobbying.
BUDGET: $20,000,000
STAFF: 70

BUSINESS PRODUCTS INDUSTRY ASSOCIATION
301 N. Fairfax Street
Alexandria, VA 22314-2696
Tel. 703/549-9040 or Fax 703/683-7552
Web site: *www.bpia.org*

PURPOSE: To promote friendship and cooperation among its 200 members and enhance relationships with others in the industry. Formerly (1994) known as the National Office Products Association.
ACTIVITY: Research, education, lobbying.
BUDGET: $25,000,000
EMPLOYEES: N/A (175+)

CHAMBER OF COMMERCE OF THE U.S.A.
1615 H Street NW
Washington, DC 20062
Tel. 202/659-6000 or Fax 202/463-5836
Web site: *www.uschamber.org*

PURPOSE: To promote the interests of its 219,200 members, a federation of business organizations and companies whose membership includes chambers of commerce, trade and professional associations, and companies.
ACTIVITY: Research, education, community action, clearinghouse, lobbying.
BUDGET: $70,000,000
STAFF: 1,200

CHEMICAL MANUFACTURERS ASSOCIATION
1300 Wilson Blvd.
Arlington, VA 22209
Tel. 703/741-5000 or Fax 703/741-6083
Web site: *www.cmahq.com*

PURPOSE: To promote the interests of chemical manufacturers and promote public health and safety. 195 members.
ACTIVITY: Research, education, lobbying.
BUDGET: $41,000,000
STAFF: 300

COSMETIC, TOILETRY, AND FRAGRANCE ASSOCIATION
1101 17th Street NW, Suite 300
Washington, DC 20036
Tel. 202/331-1770 or Fax 202/331-1969
Web site: *www.ctfa.org*

PURPOSE: To promote the interests of manufacturers and distributors of finished cosmetics, fragrances, and personal care products; suppliers of raw materials and services. 525 members.
Activity: Education, public service, lobbying.
Budget: $8,000,000
Staff: 45

CREDIT UNION NATIONAL ASSOCIATION
P.O. Box 431
Madison, WI 53701
Tel. 608/231-4000
Web site: *www.cuna.org*

PURPOSE: To support more than 90% of all local credit unions (11,000) in the U.S. with a membership totaling more than 65 million people.

ACTIVITY: Membership services, research, education, lobbying.
BUDGET: $27,000,000
STAFF: 185

HEALTH INSURANCE ASSOCIATION OF AMERICA
555 13th Street NW, Suite 600E
Washington, DC 20004-1109
Tel. 202/824-1600 or Fax 202/824-1719
Web site: *www.hiaa.org*

PURPOSE: To support the interests of commercial health insurers in the states and in Washington, DC.
ACTIVITY: Research, education, lobbying.
BUDGET: $20,000,000
STAFF: 150

HELICOPTER ASSOCIATION INTERNATIONAL
1635 Prince Street
Alexandria, VA 22314-2818
Tel. 703/683-4646 or Fax 703/683-4745
Web site: *www.rotor.com*

PURPOSE: Promotes the interests of owners, operators, helicopter enthusiasts, and affiliated companies in the civil helicopter industry. 6,000 members.
ACTIVITY: Education, research.
BUDGET: $1,000,000
STAFF: 6

INFORMATION TECHNOLOGY ASSOCIATION OF AMERICA
1616 N. Fort Myer Drive
Suite 1300
Arlington, VA 22209-9998
Tel. 703/522-5055 or Fax 703/525-2279
Web site: *www.itaa.org*

PURPOSE: To promote the interests of companies offering computer software and services. Improve management methods, develop services, and set standards of performance.
ACTIVITY: Education, research, lobbying.
BUDGET: N/A ($3,000,000+)
EMPLOYEES: 35

INSTITUTE OF GAS TECHNOLOGY
1700 S. Mount Prospect Rd.
Des Plaines, IL 60018-1804
Tel. 847/768-0500 or Fax 847/768-0501
Web site: *www.igt.org*

PURPOSE: To promote the education and research interests of its sponsoring companies that are engaged in the production, processing, transmission, and distribution of natural gas and related fuels; oil and coal producers; engineering firms; and large energy consumers.
ACTIVITY: Education, research.
BUDGET: $30,000,000
EMPLOYEES: 300

INSTITUTE OF MANAGEMENT ACCOUNTANTS
10 Paragon Drive
Montvale, NJ 07645
Tel. 201/573-9000 or Fax 201/573-8185
Web site: *www.imanet.org*

PURPOSE: To conduct research on accounting methods and procedures and management uses of accounting. 80,000 members.
ACTIVITY: Research, education, certification, and technical assistance.
BUDGET: N/A ($10,000,000+)
EMPLOYEES: 99

INSTITUTE OF REAL ESTATE MANAGEMENT
430 N. Michigan Avenue
Chicago, IL 60611-4090
Tel. 312/329-6000 or Fax 312/410-7960
Web site: *www.irem.org*

PURPOSE: To promote the interests of its 10,460 members who are real property and asset managers.
ACTIVITY: Research, education, accreditation, career assistance.
BUDGET: $11,300,000
EMPLOYEES: 80

INSURANCE INSTITUTE OF AMERICA
720 Providence Road
Malvern, PA 19355-0716
Tel. 610/644-2100 or Fax 610/640-9576
Web site: *www.aicpu.org*

PURPOSE: To support 18 educational programs for property and liability insurance personnel.

ACTIVITY: Research, examination, certification, education.
BUDGET: $20,000,000
EMPLOYEES: 150

INTERNATIONAL COUNCIL OF SHOPPING CENTERS
665 5th Avenue
New York, NY 10022
Tel. 212/421-8181 or Fax 212/486-0849
Web site: *www.icsc.org*

PURPOSE: To promote professional standards of performance in the development, construction, financing, leasing, management, and operation of shopping centers for its 35,000 members.
ACTIVITY: Research, data gathering, education, training.
BUDGET: $25,000,000
EMPLOYEES: 100

INTERNATIONAL DAIRY FOODS ASSOCIATION
1250 H Street NW, Suite 900
Washington, DC 20005
Tel. 202/737-4332 or Fax 202/331-7820
Web site: *www.idfa.org*

PURPOSE: To provide services to three constituent groups—Milk Industry Foundation, National Cheese Institute, and International Ice Cream Association. Represents processors and manufacturers in this $65 billion a years dairy foods industry. Represents 800 members in 22 countries.
ACTIVITY: Research, education, lobbying.
BUDGET: N/A ($4,000,000+)
EMPLOYEES: 40

MOTION PICTURE ASSOCIATION OF AMERICA
1600 I Street NW
Washington, DC 20006
Tel. 202/293-1966 or Fax 202/296-7410
Web site: *www.mpaa.org*

PURPOSE: To promote the interests of its eight members—the principal producers and distributors of motion pictures in the U.S.
ACTIVITY: Education, lobbying.
BUDGET: N/A ($12,000,000+)
EMPLOYEES: 120

NATIONAL ASSOCIATION OF BROADCASTERS
1771 N Street NW
Washington, DC 20036
Tel. 202/429-5300 or Fax 202/429-5406
Web site: *www.nab.org*

PURPOSE: To support its 7,500 members who are primarily representatives of radio and television stations and networks.
ACTIVITY: Research, education, lobbying, career assistance.
BUDGET: $27,000,000
EMPLOYEES: 165

NATIONAL ASSOCIATION OF COUNTIES
440 1st Street NW, 8th Floor
Washington, DC 20001
Tel. 202/393-6226 or Fax 202/393-2630
Web site: *www.noco.org*

PURPOSE: To support the work of its members—1,750 elected and appointed county governing officials at the management or policy level.
ACTIVITY: Research, education, lobbying.
BUDGET: $10,000,000
EMPLOYEES: 70

NATIONAL ASSOCIATION OF MANUFACTURERS
1331 Pennsylvania Avenue NW, Suite 1500-N
Washington, DC 20004
Tel. 202/637-3000 or Fax 202/637-3182
Web site: *www.nam.org*

PURPOSE: To represent the interests of its 14,000 members who have a direct interest in or relationship to manufacturing.
ACTIVITY: Research, education, lobbying.
BUDGET: $15,000,000
EMPLOYEES: 180

NATIONAL ASSOCIATION OF REALTORS
430 N. Michigan Avenue
Chicago, IL 60611
Tel. 312/329-8200 or Fax 312/329-5962
Web site: *www.realtor.com*

PURPOSE: To promote education, professional standards, and modern techniques in specialized real estate work such as brokerage, appraisal, property management, land development, industrial real estate. 750,000 members.
ACTIVITY: Research, education, lobbying.

BUDGET: $40,000,000
EMPLOYEES: 350

NATIONAL ASSOCIATION OF SOCIAL WORKERS
750 First Street NE
Suite 700
Washington, DC 20002-4241
Tel. 202/408-8600 or Fax 202/336-8312
Web site: *www.naswdc.org*

PURPOSE: To create professional standards for social work practice; advocate public policies; and provide numerous membership services. 155,000 members.
ACTIVITY: Research, education, lobbying.
BUDGET: $18,000,000
EMPLOYEES: 120

NATIONAL AUTOMOBILE DEALERS ASSOCIATION
8400 Westpark Drive
McLean, VA 22102
Tel. 703/821-7000 or Fax 703/821-7075
Web site: *www.nada.org*

PURPOSE: To promote the interests of its members—19,500 franchised new car and truck dealers.
ACTIVITY: Membership services, lobbying.
BUDGET: $10,000,000
EMPLOYEES: 400

NATIONAL COUNCIL ON THE AGING
409 3rd Street SW, Suite 200
Washington, DC 20024
Tel. 202/479-1200 or Fax 202/479-0735
Web site: *www.ncoa.org*

PURPOSE: To promote the interests of older Americans, with a membership of 7,500 drawn from business, industry, organized labor, health professions, social workers, educators, government agencies.
ACTIVITY: Research, education, lobbying, community service.
BUDGET: N/A ($8,000,000+)
EMPLOYEES: 90

NATIONAL EDUCATION ASSOCIATION
1201 16th Street NW
Washington, DC 20036
Tel. 202/833-4000 or Fax 202/822-7767
Web site: *www.nea.org*

PURPOSE: To promote the professional interests of its 2,376,000 members—elementary and secondary school teachers, college and university professors, administrators, principals, and counselors.
ACTIVITY: Research, education, lobbying.
BUDGET: $200,600,000
EMPLOYEES: 600

NATIONAL FOOD PROCESSORS ASSOCIATION
101 I Street, NW
Washington, DC 20005
Tel. 202/639-5900 or Fax 202/639-5932
Web site: *www.nfpa-food.org*

PURPOSE: To promote the interests of commercial processors of food products, such as fruit, vegetables, meats, seafood, and canned, frozen, dehydrated, pickled, and other preserved food items. 500 members.
ACTIVITY: Research, education, lobbying.
BUDGET: $16,000,000
EMPLOYEES: 185

NATIONAL FUNERAL DIRECTORS ASSOCIATION
11121 W. Oklahoma Ave.
Milwaukee, WI 53227-4096
Tel. 414/541-2500 or Fax 414/541-1909
Web site: *www.nfda.org*

PURPOSE: To promote the interests of its members—state funeral directors' associations representing 15,000 members.
ACTIVITY: Education, home study, lobbying.
BUDGET: $9,100,000
EMPLOYEES: 44

NATIONAL MINING ASSOCIATION
1130 17th Street NW
Washington, DC 20036
Tel. 202/463-2625 or Fax 202/463-6152
Web site: *www.nma.org*

PURPOSE: To serve as a liaison between federal government agencies and its members—producers and sellers of coal, equipment suppliers, other energy

suppliers, consultants, utility companies, and coal transporters. Previously known as the National Coal Association. 150 members.
ACTIVITY: Research, education, lobbying, career assistance.
BUDGET: $7,000,000
EMPLOYEES: 55

NATIONAL RESTAURANT ASSOCIATION
1200 17th Street NW
Washington, DC 20036
Tel. 202/331-5900 or Fax 202/331-2429
Web site: *www.restaurant.org*

PURPOSE: To promote the interests of its 34,000 members—restaurants, cafeterias, clubs, drive-ins, caterers, institutional food services, and others.
ACTIVITY: Research, training, education, lobbying.
BUDGET: $24,908,000
EMPLOYEES: 150

NATIONAL SOCIETY OF PUBLIC ACCOUNTANTS
1010 N. Fairfax Street
Alexandria, VA 22314-1574
Tel. 703/549-6400 or Fax 703/549-2984
Web site: *www.nsa.org*

PURPOSE: To promote the interests of its 20,000 members who are independent practitioners.
ACTIVITY: Research, education, lobbying.
BUDGET: $3,750,000
EMPLOYEES: 29

PORTLAND CEMENT ASSOCIATION
5420 Old Orchard Road
Skokie, IL 60077-1083
Tel. 847/966-6200 or Fax 847/966-9781

PURPOSE: To improve and extend the uses of portland cement and concrete for the benefit of its 50 members—manufacturers and marketers in the U.S. and Canada.
ACTIVITY: Market promotion, research, education, lobbying.
BUDGET: $30,000,000
EMPLOYEES: 265

PROFESSIONAL SECRETARIES INTERNATIONAL
10502 NW Ambassador Dr.
Kansas City, MO 64195-0404
Tel. 816/891-6600 or Fax 816/891-9118
Web site: *www.gvi.net/psi*

PURPOSE: To monitor government activities affecting secretaries, sponsor audiovisual products, and offer group insurance. 40,000 members.
ACTIVITY: Research, education, lobbying.
BUDGET: $3,500,000
EMPLOYEES: 30

PROMOTIONAL PRODUCTS ASSOCIATION INTERNATIONAL
3125 Skyway Circle N.
Irving, TX 75038-3526
Tel. 972/252-0404 or Fax 972/258-3004
Web site: *www.ppa.org*

PURPOSE: To supply promotional products such as calendars, imprinted ad specialties, premiums, and executive gifts as well as develop industry contacts in 40 countries.
ACTIVITY: Education, training, distribution.
BUDGET: $10,000,000
EMPLOYEES: 55

THE RETIRED OFFICERS ASSOCIATION
201 N. Washington Street
Alexandria, VA 22314-2539
Tel. 703/549-2311 or Fax 703/838-8173
Web site: *www.troa.org*

PURPOSE: To promote the interests of retired commissioned or warrant officers in the Army, Navy, Air Force, Marine Corps, Coast Guard, NOAA, and Public Health Service. 400,000 members.
ACTIVITY: Education, membership services, lobbying.
BUDGET: $12,000,000
EMPLOYEES: 83

SECURITIES INDUSTRY ASSOCIATION
120 Broadway
New York, NY 10271
Tel. 212/608-1500 or Fax 212/608-1604
Web site: *www.sia.com*

PURPOSE: To promote the interests of its 761 members—investment bankers, securities underwriters, and dealers in stocks and bonds.

ACTIVITY: Education, membership services, lobbying.
BUDGET: N/A ($8,000,000+)
EMPLOYEES: 107

TOBACCO INSTITUTE
1875 I Street NW
Suite 800
Washington, DC 20006
Tel. 202/457-4800 or Fax 202/457-9350

PURPOSE: To promote the interests of its 11 members—manufacturers of cigarettes, smoking, and chewing tobacco, and snuff.
ACTIVITY: Education, training, lobbying.
BUDGET: N/A ($10,000,000+)
EMPLOYEES: 65

UNITED STATES CONFERENCE OF MAYORS
1620 I Street NW
Washington, DC 20006
Tel. 202/293-7330 or Fax 202/293-2352
Web site: *www.usmayors.org*

PURPOSE: To promote improved municipal government for its 1,050 members/mayors who represent cities with populations of over 30,000.
ACTIVITY: Education, technical assistance, lobbying.
BUDGET: $8,600,000
EMPLOYEES: 50

UNITED STATES MEAT EXPORT FEDERATION
1050 17th Street
Suite 2200
Denver, CO 80265-2073
Tel. 303/623-6328 or Fax 303/623-0297
Web site: *www.usmef.org*

PURPOSE: To promote the interests of its 183 members—meat producers, packers, purveyors, exporters, and processors; livestock breeding associations; and manufacturers of meat industry equipment.
ACTIVITY: Education, training, technical assistance.
BUDGET: $22,000,000
EMPLOYEES: 70

The $5+ Million Associations

The following associations report annual budgets in excess of $5 million. This usually translates into a staff size of more than 40 individuals per association, representing only 7% of all major associations. The majority of associations have annual budgets under $1 million and staffs of fewer than 10 people. Detailed information on each association is provided in both the *Encyclopedia of Associations* and the *National Trade and Professional Associations*, key directories found in the reference section of most public libraries. Many also have their own Web sites which may include job vacancy announcements. While these larger associations provide good job opportunities, do not neglect the under $5 million associations. They also offer numerous job opportunities. Associations highlighted in bold are exceptionally large, reporting more than $25 million in annual revenue, which translates into staffs of 200 or more. Associations followed with an asterisk (*) were already summarized.

Academy of General Dentistry
Academy of Motion Picture Arts and Sciences*
Actors' Equity Association
Aerospace Industries Association of America
Air and Waste Management Association
Air-Conditioning and Refrigeration Institute
Air Conditioning Contractors of America
Air Force Association
Air Line Pilots Association, International*
Aircraft Owners and Pilots Association
Alliance of American Insurers
Aluminum Association
Amalgamated Clothing and Textile Workers Union
Amalgamated Transit Union
American Academy of Dermatology
American Academy of Family Physicians
American Academy of Neurology
American Academy of Ophthalmology
American Academy of Orthopedic Surgeons
American Academy of Otolaryngology-Head and Neck Surgery
American Academy of Pediatrics
American Academy of Periodontology
American Academy of Physician Assistants
American Alliance for Health, Physical Education, Recreation and Dance
American Animal Hospital Association
American Arbitration Association
American Association for Cancer Research

American Association Clinical Chemistry
American Association for Respiratory Care
American Association for the Advancement of Science
American Association of Advertising Agencies
American Association of Blood Banks
American Association of Community Colleges
American Association of Critical-Care Nurses
American Association of Homes and Services for the Aging
American Association of Individual Investors
American Association of Motor Vehicle Administrators
American Association of Museums
American Association of Neurological Surgeons
American Association of Nurse Anesthetists
American Association of Oral and Maxillofacial Surgeons
American Association of Orthodontists
American Association of Petroleum Geologists
American Association of Retired Persons*
American Association of School Administrators
American Association of State Colleges and Universities
American Association of State Highway and Transportation Officials
American Astronomical Society
American Automobile Association*
American Automobile Manufacturers Association*
American Bankers Association*
American Bar Association*
American Booksellers Association
American Bureau of Shipping
American Cancer Society*
American Ceramic Society
American Chemical Society*
American Chiropractic Association
American College of Cardiology
American College of Chest Physicians
American College of Emergency Physicians
American College of Healthcare Executives
American College of Obstetricians and Gynecologists
American College of Physicians
American College of Radiology
American College of Surgeons
American Compensation Association*
American Concrete Institute
American Correctional Association
American Council of Life Insurance*
American Council on Education
American Counseling Association
American Crop Protection Association
American Defense Preparedness Association
American Dental Association

American Diabetes Association
American Dietetic Association
American Egg Board
American Electronics Association
American Farm Bureau Federation
American Federation of Labor and Congress of Industrial Organizations*
American Federation of Musicians of the United States and Canada
American Federation of State, County, and Municipal Employees*
American Federation of Teachers*
American Forest and Paper Association
American Gas Association*
American Geophysical Union
American Hardware Manufacturers Association
American Health Care Association
American Health Information Management Association
American Heart Association
American Horse Shows Association
American Hospital Association*
American Hotel and Motel Association*
American Industrial Hygiene Association
American Institute for Chartered Property Casualty Underwriters-Insurance Institute of America
American Institute of Aeronautics and Astronautics
American Institute of Architects
American Institute of Certified Public Accountants*
American Institute of Chemical Engineers
American Institute of Physics
American Insurance Association*
American Iron and Steel Institute
American Kennel Club
American Law Institute
American League of Professional Baseball Clubs
American Library Association*
American Lung Association
American Management Association
American Marketing Association
American Mathematical Society
American Meat Institute
American Medical Association*
American Meteorological Society
American Mining Congress
American National Standards Institute
American National Soda Ash Corporation
American Nuclear Society
American Nurses Association
American Occupational Therapy Association
American Optometric Association

American Osteopathic Association
American Payroll Association
American Petroleum Institute*
American Pharmaceutical Association
American Physical Society
American Physical Therapy Association
American Physiological Society
American Planning Association
American Plastics Council
American Podiatric Medical Association
American Postal Workers Union*
American Poultry U.S.A.
American Production and Inventory Control Association
American Psychiatric Association*
American Psychological Association
American Public Health Association*
American Public Power Association
American Public Transit Association
American Public Works Association
American Quarter Horse Association
American Radio Relay League
American Sheep Industry Association
American Society for Biochemistry and Molecular Biology
American Society for Engineering Education
American Society for Industrial Security
American Society for Microbiology
American Society for Quality
American Society for Testing and Materials
American Society for Training and Development*
American Society of Anesthesiologists
American Society of Association Executives*
American Society of Civil Engineers
American Society of Clinical Oncology
American Society of Clinical Pathologists
American Society of CLU and ChFC
American Society of Composers, Authors, and Publishers
American Society of Consultant Pharmacists
American Society of Health-System Pharmacists
American Society of Heating, Refrigeration and Air-Conditioning Engineers
American Society of Interior Designers
American Society of Internal Medicine
American Society of Landscape Architects
American Society of Mechanical Engineers
American Society of Plastic and Reconstructive Surgeons
American Society of Safety Engineers
American Society of Travel Agents*
American Soybean Association
American Speech-Language-Hearing Association

American Stock Exchange
American Trucking Association*
American Urological Association
American Veterinary Medical Association
American Water Works Association*
American Welding Society
American Wholesale Marketers Association
AMT—The Association for Manufacturing Technology
Appraisal Institute
ASM International
Associated Builders and Contractors
Associated Credit Bureaus
Associated General Contractors of America
Associated Surplus Dealers
Association for Computing Machinery
Association for Information and Image Management
Association for Investment Management and Research
Association for Manufacturing Technology
Association for Supervision and Curriculum Development
Association of American Medical Colleges
Association of American Publishers
Association of American Railroads
Association of Christian Schools International
Association of Flight Attendants
Association of International Automobile Manufacturers*
Association of Operating Room Nurses
Association of the United States Army
Association of Trial Lawyers of America
Association of Women's Health, Obstetric, and Neonatal Nurses
ATP Tour
Audit Bureaus of Circulations
Automotive Service Association
Bank Administration Institute
Bank Marketing Association
Blue Cross and Blue Shield Association
BPA International
Brotherhood of Maintenance of Way Employees
Building Officials and Code Administrators International
Building Owners and Managers Association International
Business Products Industry Association*
Business Technology Association
Career College Association
Catholic Health Association of the United States
Cellular Telecommunications Industry Association
Chamber of Commerce of the United States of America*
Chemical Manufacturers Association*
Child Welfare League of America
Chlorine Chemistry Council

Coffee, Sugar, and Cocoa Exchange
College of American Pathologists
Commercial-Investment Real Estate Institute
Communications Workers of America
Construction Specifications Institute
Copper Development Association
Cosmetic, Toiletry and Fragrance Association*
Cotton Council International
Council for Advancement and Support of Education
Council for Exceptional Children
Council for Tobacco Research-U.S.A.
Council of Better Business Bureaus
Council of Chief State School Officers
Council on Foundations
Credit Union National Association*
Cruise Lines International Association
Cystic Fibrosis Foundation
Direct Marketing Association
Directors Guild of America
Distilled Spirits Council of the U.S.
ECRI
Edison Electric Institute
EDUCOM
Electric Power Research Institute
Electronic Industries Association
Emergency Nurses Association
Employee Relocation Council
Endocrine Society, The
Engineered Wood Association
Environmental Industry Associations
Fabricators and Manufacturers Association International
Family Service America
Farm Credit Council
Federation of American Health Systems
Federation of American Societies for Experimental Biology
Federation of State Medical Boards of the U.S.
Financial Executives Institute
Florists' Transworld Delivery Association
Food Marketing Institute
Gas Research Institute
Gemological Institute of America
Geological Society of America
Glass Packaging Institute
Golf Course Superintendents Association of America
Government Finance Officers Association of the United States and Canada
Graphic Arts Technical Foundation
Grocery Manufacturers of America
Group Health Association of America

Health Industry Manufacturers Association
Health Insurance Association of America*
Healthcare Financial Management Association
Healthcare Forum, The
Healthcare Information and Management Systems Society
Hobby Industry Association of America
Holstein Association U.S.A.
Hotel Employees and Restaurant Employees International Union
IEEE Computer Society
Independent Bankers Association of America
Independent Cash Register Dealers Association
Independent Insurance Agents of America
Industrial Fabrics Association International
Institute for Interconnecting and Packaging Electronic Circuits
Institute for International Human Resources
Institute of Electrical and Electronics Engineers
Institute of Food Technologists
Institute of Gas Technology*
Institute of Industrial Engineers
Institute of Internal Auditors
Institute of Management Accountants*
Institute of Nuclear Power Operations
Institute of Paper Science and Technology
Institute of Real Estate Management*
Institute of Scrap Recycling Industries
Insurance Institute for Highway Safety
Insurance Institute of America*
International Transportation Society of America
International Arabian Horse Association
International Association of Bridge, Structural and Ornamental Iron
    Workers
International Association of Chiefs of Police
International Association of Fire Fighters
International Association of Machinists and Aerospace Workers
International Brotherhood of Boilermakers, Iron Shipbuilders,
    Blacksmiths, Forgers and Helpers
International Brotherhood of Electrical Workers
International Brotherhood of Painters and Allied Trades
International Brotherhood of Teamsters, AFL-CIO
International City/County Management Association
International Conference of Building Officials
International Copper Association
International Council of Shopping Centers*
International Dairy Foods Association
International Facility Management Association
International Foundation of Employee Benefit Plans
International Franchise Association
International Ladies Garment Workers' Union

International Lead Zinc Research Organization
International Longshoreman's Association
International Memory Institute
International Reading Association
International Society for Measurement and Control
International Union of Bricklayers and Allied Craftsmen
International Union of Electronic, Electrical, Salaried Machine, and
    Furniture Workers
International Union of Operating Engineers
**International Union, United Automobile, Aerospace and Agricultural
    Implement Workers of America**
Interstate Natural Gas Association of America
Investment Company Institute
IRSA—The Association of Quality Clubs
Laborers' International Union of North America
Ladies Professional Gulf Association
Landscape Nursery Council
Life Office Management Association
LIMRA International
Livestock Marketing Association
Magazine Publishers of America
Mastercard International
Medical Group Management Association
Meeting Professionals International
Million Dollar Round Table
Modern Language Association of America
Mortgage Bankers Association of America
Motion Picture Association of America
Motion Picture Export Association of America
Motor and Equipment Manufacturers Association
NACE International
NARD
National Academy of Sciences
National-American Wholesale Grocers' Association
National Association for Home Care
National Association for the Self-Employed
National Association for the Specialty Food Trade
National Association of Broadcast Employees and Technicians
National Association of Broadcasters*
National Association of Chain Drug Stores
National Association of College and University Business Officers
National Association of College Stores
National Association of Convenience Stores
National Association of Counties*
National Association of Federal Credit Unions
National Association of Home Builders of the U.S.
National Association of Independent Insurers
National Association of Independent Schools

National Association of Insurance Commissioners
National Association of Letter Carriers
National Association of Life Underwriters
National Association of Manufacturers*
National Association of Music Merchants
National Association of Printers and Lithographers
National Association of Professional Insurance Agents
National Association of Purchasing Management
National Association of Realtors*
National Association of Retired Federal Employees
National Association of Secondary School Principals
National Association of Securities Dealers
National Association of Social Workers*
National Association of State Boards of Accountancy
National Association of State Mental Health Program Directors
National Association of Wholesaler-Distributors
National Automobile Dealers Association
National Basketball Association
National Board of Boiler and Pressure Vessel Inspectors
National Business Aircraft Association
National Cable Television Association
National Cargo Bureau
National Cattlemen's Association
National Coal Association
National Collegiate Athletic Association
National Conference of Catholic Bishops
National Conference of State Legislatures
National Cooperative Business Association
National Cotton Council of America
National Council of Architectural Registration Boards
National Council of Juvenile and Family Court Judges
National Council of State Boards of Nursing
National Council of Teachers of Mathematics
National Council of the Churches of Christ in the U.S.A.
National Council of the Paper Industry for Air and Stream Improvement
National Council on Compensation Insurance
National Council on the Aging
National Court Reporters Association
National Decorating Products Association
National Education Association*
National Electrical Contractors Association
National Electrical Manufacturers Association
National Federation of Independent Business
National Fire Protection Association
National Food Processors Association*
National Football League
National Funeral Directors Association*
National Futures Association

National Governors' Association
National Ground Water Association
National Hockey League
National Industries for the Blind
National Institute of Building Sciences
National Insurance Crime Bureau
National Kidney Foundation
National Kitchen and Bath Association
National League for Nursing
National League of Cities
National Live Stock and Meat Board
National Marine Engineers Beneficial Association/National Maritime
    Union of America
National Marrow Donor Program
National Mining Association*
National Multiple Sclerosis Society
National Parks and Conservation Association
National Pork Producers Council
National Potato Promotion Board
National Recreation and Park Association
National Restaurant Association*
National Retail Federation
National Retail Hardware Association
National Rifle Association of America
National Roofing Contractors Association
National Rural Electric Cooperative Association
National Rural Letter Carriers' Association
National Rural Water Association
National Safety Council
National School Boards Association
National Shooting Sports Foundation
National Society of Professional Engineers
National Society to Prevent Blindness/Prevent Blindness America
National Soft Drink Association
National Spa and Pool Institute
National Sporting Goods Association
National Telephone Cooperative Association
National Tour Association
National Treasury Employees Union
National Wholesale Druggists' Association
NBFA: Association for Independent Marketers of Business Printing
    and Information Management Systems
New York Academy of Sciences
New York Cotton Exchange
New York Mercantile Exchange
New York Stock Exchange
Newspaper Association of America
Nonprescription Drug Manufacturers Association

Nuclear Energy Institute
Oil, Chemical, and Atomic Workers International Union
Oncology Nursing Society
Optical Society of America
Organization for the Protection and Advancement of Small Telephone
  Companies
Osborne Association
Pharmaceutical Research and Manufacturers of America
Photo Marketing Association-International
Portland Cement Association*
Practicing Law Institute
Preferred Hotels and Resorts Worldwide
Printing Industries of America
Produce Marketing Association
Professional Association of Diving Instructors
Professional Bowlers Association of America
Professional Photographers of America
Promotional Products Association International*
Public Relations Society of America
Public Securities Association
Radio Advertising Bureau
Radiological Society of North America
Recording Industry Association of America
Recreation Vehicle Industry Association
Residential Sales Council
Retail, Wholesale and Department Store Union
Retired Officers Association, The*
Risk and Insurance Management Society
Robert Morris Associates, the Association of Bank Loan and Credit Officers
Savings and Community Bankers of America
Screen Actors Guild
Securities Industry Association*
Semiconductor Equipment and Materials International
Service Employees International Union
Sheet Metal and Air Conditioning Contractors National Association
Sheet Metal Workers' International Association
Smokeless Tobacco Council
Social Science Research Council
Society for Human Resource Management
Society for Industrial and Applied Mathematics
Society for Neuroscience
Society of Actuaries
Society of American Florists
Society of Automotive Engineers
Society of Chartered Property and Casualty Underwriters
Society of Critical Care Medicine
Society of Exploration Geophysicists
Society of Manufacturing Engineers

Society of Nuclear Medicine
Society of Petroleum Engineers
Society of Plastics Engineers
Society of the Plastics Industry
Software Publishers Association
Southern Forest Products Association
Special Interest Group on Computer Graphics
SPIE—International Society for Optical Engineering
Sporting Goods Manufacturers Association
Synthetic Organic Chemical Manufacturers Association
Technical Association of the Pulp and Paper Industry
Telecommunications Industry Association
Television Bureau of Advertising
Telecator—The Personal Communications Industry Association
Tobacco Institute*
Transaction Processing Performance Council
Transport Workers Union of America
Transportation Communications International Union
Travel Industry Association of America
Treasury Management Association
U.S.A. Poultry and Egg Export Council
Union of American Hebrew Congregations
United Association of Journeymen and Apprentices of the Plumbing
    and Pipe Fitting Industry of U.S. and Canada
United Brotherhood of Carpenters and Joiners of America
United Dairy Industry Association
United Engineering Trustees
United Food and Commercial Workers International Union
United Mine Workers of America International Union
United Paperworkers International Union
United Rubber, Cork, Linoleum and Plastic Workers of America
United States Conference of Mayors*
United States Council for International Business
United States Energy Association
United States Golf Association
United States Meat Export Federation*
United States Pharmacopeial Convention
United States Soccer Federation
United States Telephone Association
United States Tennis Association
United States Trotting Association
United States Wheat Association
United Steelworkers of America
Universities Research Association
Urban Land Institute
Video Software Dealers Association
Water Environment Federation
Western Railroad Association

Western Wood Products Association
Wine Institute
Yellow Pages Publishers Association
Young Presidents' Organization

Serious job seekers join the American Society of Association Executives (see page 191 and their Web site: *www.asaenet.org*) as well as subscribe to *Association Trends* (see page 66 and their Web site: *www.associationtrends.com*). Consisting of nearly 24,000 members, ASAE is the key professional network for individuals interested in pursuing careers with associations. This association publishes a very useful annual membership directory and buyers' guide (*Who's Who in Association Management*, $160.00) as well as offers placement information and services.

9

Major Global Nonprofits

Most of the nonprofits identified in previous chapters operate within the United States. They primarily deal with domestic issues or they represent the interests of American trade and professional organizations. They tend to be national in scope or operate primarily at the state and local levels as community-based nonprofits. Few of these nonprofits venture outside the nation's borders.

A World of Rewarding Opportunities

If you are interested in pursuing global issues, if you get passionate about helping the poor and unfortunate in Third and Fourth World countries, or if you would love to work, travel, and live abroad, this may be the most important chapter for you. Here, we identify some of the major nonprofit organizations that tackle today's most pressing international problems, from disaster relief to feeding the poor and hungry. They save children, resettle refugees, help improve food production, educate the poor, provide needed medical assistance, and prevent blindness. Most of these organizations are charitable groups. Many of them, especially religious relief groups, are affiliated with other American nonprofit organizations.

217

The New Missionaries

Nonprofit organizations offer excellent international job opportunities for enterprising job seekers. These groups are disproportionately involved in social and economic development efforts in Third and Fourth World countries—the poor and the poorest of the poor.

Nonprofit organizations are the true missionaries in today's world. They feed the hungry; care for women and children; promote improved health care standards; provide needed medical assistance and education; improve sanitation; evacuate and resettle refugees; develop rural water and sanitation systems; promote family planning and pre-natal care; develop rural lending institutions and cooperatives; assist in marketing crops; and promote community development efforts. Feeling passionate and powerless about these issues, many people would love to work for the international nonprofits that specialize in these problem areas. These nonprofit organizations are the major catalysts for change in much of the developing world. They rely heavily on funding from government agencies, especially the United States Agency for International Development (USAID), and foundations as well as from their own innovative fundraising efforts.

> **Nonprofit organizations are the true missionaries in today's world.**

If you are interested in pursuing an international cause or making a difference in the lives of others, you should seriously consider working for an international nonprofit organization. While most of these organizations pay medium to low salaries, they do provide unique and extremely rewarding opportunities to get involved in solving international problems —opportunities that are largely absent with other types of organizations, except for perhaps the U.S. Peace Corps and specialized agencies of the United Nations.

The Organizations

Nonprofit international organizations are frequently referred to as Non-governmental Organizations (NGO's) or Private Voluntary Organizations (PVO's). These groups primarily promote a particular international issue or cause. In contrast to more than 1 million nonprofit organizations operating within the United States, international nonprofits are fewer in number and operate almost solely in the international arena. They span a broad spectrum of issues and causes:

foreign affairs	relief
education	human rights
energy	religion
economic development	rural development
population planning	cultural exchange
food	water resources
social welfare	housing
health	community development
children and youth	

Examples of different types of nonprofit organizations and their diverse missions abound throughout the international arena. Most of these organizations cluster around important health, agricultural, social welfare, and disaster issues that are inadequately dealt with in most poor countries: medical services, population planning, agricultural productivity, environment and resource management, community development, employment generation, refugee resettlement, and natural disaster relief. Nonprofit organizations such as the International Voluntary Service, Catholic Relief Service, and CARE provide similar development services as the U.S. Peace Corps. The Population Council's involvement in family planning and health issues affects all other development issues in Third World countries. The World Affairs Council functions to increase the awareness of Americans concerning international issues. The Council for International Exchange of Scholars (Fulbright-Hays) and Meridian House International focus on promoting educational and cultural exchanges.

The major nonprofit international organizations which hire international specialists for headquarter and field locations and have full-time staffs of at least 20 and an annual budget exceeding $5 million include:

- Africare
- Agricultural Cooperative Development International
- American Friends Service Committee
- American Institute for Free Labor Development
- American Jewish Joint Distribution Committee
- Association for Voluntary Sterilization
- Cooperative for American Relief Everywhere, Inc. (CARE)

- Catholic Medical Mission Board
- Catholic Relief Services
- Christian Children's Fund, Inc.
- Church World Service
- Direct Relief International
- Family Planning International Assistance
- Food for the Hungry
- Foster Parents Plan International
- Heifer Project International
- Holt International Children's Services
- The Institute of Cultural Affairs
- Interchurch Medical Assistance, Inc.
- International Eye Foundation
- International Executive Service Corps
- International Human Assistance Programs, Inc.
- International Planned Parenthood Federation
- International Rescue Committee
- Lutheran World Relief
- MAP International
- Mennonite Economic Development Associates, Inc.
- Overseas Education Fund
- Partnership for Productivity International
- Pathfinder Fund
- People to People Health Foundation, Inc.
- Population Council
- Salvation Army
- Save the Children Federation, Inc.
- United Methodist Committee on Relief
- Volunteers in Technical Assistance (VITA)
- World Concern
- World Relief
- World Vision International

Many of these nonprofit organizations, especially population planning groups but also religious-affiliated organizations, are major recipients of USAID contracts. They work closely with the USAID bureaucracy as well as with many private contracting firms and universities that are also major recipients of USAID funding. As such, they play an important role in the peripheral network of organizations involved in U.S. foreign policy efforts. Many other nonprofit organizations are not linked to the government in this manner. Organizations such as Oxfam America, a noted self-help development and disaster relief organization operating in Africa, Asia, Latin America, and the Caribbean, the Pearl S. Buck Foundation that works with Amerasian children, and numerous religious organizations doing development-related missionary work abroad have their own funding sources.

Most of these nonprofit organizations are headquartered in the United States—primarily Washington, DC, New York City, and a few other east coast cities—but have field operations in many countries throughout Latin America, Africa, Eastern Europe, and Asia. Most of the job opportunities will be in the field and thus require individuals with technical and linguistic skills along with some international experience.

Volunteer Opportunities

You will also find numerous volunteer groups operating in Third World countries. Many of these groups, such as Amigos de las Americas (5618 Star Lane, Houston, TX 77057, Tel. 800/231-7796, *www.amigoslink. org*) and Volunteers for Peace (43 Tiffany Road, Belmont, VT 05730, Tel. 802/259-2759, *www.vfp.org*), offer students and others opportunities to work on development projects in Third World countries. Many groups require you to pay for your own transportation, food, and housing—which are often minimal—but they do provide excellent opportunities to participate in international development projects without having to join the U.S. Peace Corps or some other type of organization. If you lack international experience and want to "test the waters" to see if this type of international lifestyle is for you, consider joining a volunteer group for three to six months that would put you in a work situation abroad. You will acquire valuable experience and learn a great deal about the Third World and the network of government agencies, nonprofit organizations, and contracting firms operating abroad—as well as yourself.

Useful Resources

When conducting research on international nonprofit organizations, you should examine several directories and Web sites that identify who's who in the international nonprofit arena. Start with these print directories:

- *Encyclopedia of Associations: International Organizations*
- *Encyclopedia of Associations: National Organizations*
- *Yearbook of International Organizations*
- *USAID Yellow Book*

The first three publications are found in the reference section of most major libraries. The fourth item, *USAID Yellow Book*, is literally a roadmap to nonprofit organizations funded by the federal government. It is produced by the United States Agency for International Development (USAID). Its official title is: *USAID's Contracts and Grants and Cooperative Agreements With Universities, Firms and Non-Profit Institutions.* It identifies most recipients of USAID funding. The good news is that you can access this directory online by going to USAID's Web site:

www.info.usaid.gov

If you go to the "Publication" section, click on to the *USAID Yellow Book* and you will receive instructions on how to download this valuable document. This same site also has a section called "Development Links" which functions as a major gateway to numerous nonprofit organizations. It includes links to more than 50 NGO and PVO sites as well as other government sites, embassies, international and regional organizations, and Internet sites in developing countries. Many of the NGO's, such as InterAction (*www.interaction.org/ia/sites.html*), also have numerous linkages to other NGOs and PVOs. If you follow these linkages, you will come into contact with numerous nonprofit organizations that operate in the international arena.

Several books on international jobs and careers identify and discuss numerous nonprofit organizations offering job opportunities:

- *American Jobs Abroad*
- *Careers in International Affairs*
- *Great Jobs Abroad*
- *Guide to Careers in World Affairs*
- *International Careers*
- *International Job Finder*
- *International Jobs*
- *International Jobs Directory*

- *Jobs Worldwide*
- *The Nonprofit's Job Finder*

Two directories focus specifically on nonprofit international organizations. These include:

➤ *InterAction Member Profiles:* Published by InterAction, 1717 Massachusetts Avenue NW, 8th Fl., Washington, DC 20036, Tel. 202/667-8227. Profiles 150 private humanitarian agencies that are members of the American Council for Voluntary International Action, one of the largest and most active groups of nonprofit organizations involved in all forms of development assistance, from health care and refugee aid to child care, environment management, human rights, disaster relief, and community development. $44.00 (includes shipping). Web site: *www.interaction.org*

➤ *Development Opportunities Catalog:* JustAct, Youth Action For Global Justice (formerly known as the Overseas Development Network): 333 Valencia Street, #101, San Francisco, CA 94103, Tel. 415/431-4204. A guide to internships, volunteer work, and employment opportunities with development organizations. Costs: Students: $7.00; Individuals: $10.00; Institutions: $15. JustAct also publishes several other useful international guides that focus on development work in both the U.S. and abroad. Visit their Web site for more information: *www.igc-apc.org/odn*

Several organizations provide clearinghouse, job listing, and placement services for individuals interested in working for nonprofit international organizations. Among these are:

➤ **InterAction: American Council For Voluntary International Action** (1717 Massachusetts Avenue NW, Suite 801, Washington, DC 20036, Tel. 202/667-8227): Consisting of a coalition of over 150 U.S. nonprofit humanitarian aid groups, InterAction provides information and advice on employment with nonprofit international organizations. Members of this organization are some of the largest and most active international nonprofit organizations. One of the best international networks providing useful information on organizations and employment opportunities. Visit their Web site for more information: *www.interaction.org*. Make sure you go into this site where you will find numerous useful linkages to other international nonprofits: *www.interaction.org/ia/sites.html*

➤ **PACT** (Private Agencies Collaborating Together, 1901 Pennsylvania Avenue NW, 5th Floor, Washington, DC 20006, Tel. 202/466-5666). Consortium of 19 nonprofit agencies working abroad. Web site: *www.pactworld.com*. This site includes some international job listings.

➤ **The International Service Agencies:** (66 Canal Center Plaza, Suite 310, Alexandria, VA 22314, Tel. 1-800-638-8079). A federation of 53 American service organizations involved in disaster relief as well as agricultural development, education, job training, medical care, and refugee assistance. Visit their Web site for more information: *www.charity.org*

➤ **Intercristo, The Career and Human Resources Specialists** (19303 Fremont Avenue North, Seattle, WA 98133, Tel. 800/251-7740 or 206/546-7330): This is a Christian placement network which focuses on job opportunities in mission and ministry organizations, many of which are overseas. Visit their Web site for more information: *www.jobleads.org*

➤ *Transitions Abroad:* Box 1300, Amherst, MA 01004, Tel. 1-800-293-0373). This resource-rich bimonthly magazine is especially useful for anyone interested in studying abroad, teaching English abroad, or working for nonprofit organizations abroad. The September/October issue is particularly useful since it includes an annual roundup of international employment resources. Subscriptions are $24.95 for one year (6 issues). Transitions Abroad also publishes two international books, *Work Abroad* and *Alternative Travel Directory*, and several specialty reports on working abroad. For more information, be sure to visit their Web site which also has numerous useful resources: *www.transabroad.com*

If you are in the field of international health, you are fortunate to have a career-aware professional organization to assist you in locating health organizations and job opportunities. The National Council for International Health (NCIH), which recently changed its name to the Global Health Council, promotes international health through numerous educational services and publishes the *International Health News, Directory of Health Agencies,* and *U.S. Based Agencies Involved in International Health.* It also publishes job listings: *Monthly Job Vacancy Bulletin.* For information on these publications and their job related services, contact:

> The Global Health Council
> (National Council for International Health)
> 1701 K Street NW, Suite 600
> Washington, DC 20036
> Tel. 202/833-5900 or Fax 202/833-2075
> Web site: *www.ncih.org* or *www.globalhealthcouncil.org*

If you are interested in international volunteer opportunities, including internships, you will find several useful directories and books to assist you in locating organizations whose missions most meet your interests and needs:

- *Alternative Travel Directory*
- *Alternatives to the Peace Corps: Gaining Third World Experience*
- *Career Opportunities in International Development in Washington, DC*
- *The Directory of International Internships*
- *Directory of Overseas Summer Jobs*
- *Directory of Volunteer Opportunities*
- *The Directory of Work and Study in Developing Countries*
- *The International Directory of Voluntary Work*
- *The International Directory of Youth Internships*
- *International Internships and Volunteer Programs*
- *Invest Yourself: The Catalogue of Volunteer Opportunities*
- *Jobs Abroad: Over 3,000 Vacancies of Interest to Christians*
- *U.S. Voluntary Organizations and World Affairs*
- *Volunteer! The Comprehensive Guide to Voluntary Service in the U.S. and Abroad*
- *Volunteer Vacations*

- *Volunteer Work*
- *Work Abroad*
- *Work, Study, Travel Abroad*
- *Work Your Way Around the World*
- *Working Holidays*

Other organizations can provide information on various types of international experiences, including sponsoring internships and volunteer experiences, that can be useful for developing international skills and experiences. A sample of the many such organizations available include:

➤ **World Learning:** Formerly known as The Experiment in International Living. This well established organization conducts numerous programs in international education, training, and technical assistance, including homestay programs where participants live with families abroad while learning about the local culture. It operates the School of International Training. Contact: World Learning, Kipling Road, Brattleboro, VT 05302-0676, Tel. 1-800-336-1616, 802/257-7751 or Fax 802/258-3500. Visit their Web site for more information: *www.worldlearning.com*

➤ **Association Internationale des Etudiants en Sciences Economiques et Commerciales (AIESEC).** This international management organization provides students with training opportunities in international business. Most positions are internships with businesses abroad for periods ranging from 2 to 18 months. Contact: Public Relations Director, AIESEC-U.S., Inc., 135 W. 50th Street, New York, NY 10020, Tel. 212/757-3774. Visit their Web site for more information: *www.aiesec.org*

➤ **International Association for the Exchange of Students for Technical Experience (IAESTE).** Provides students with technical backgrounds opportunities to work abroad for 2-3 month periods. Contact: IAESTE Trainee Program, c/o Association for International Practical Training (AIPT), Park View Boulevard, 10400 Little Patuxent Parkway, Suite 250, Columbia, MD 21044, Tel. 410/997-2200. Visit their Web sites for more information: *http://aipt.org/aipt.html* and *www.iaeste.org*

➤ **Volunteers for Peace, Inc.** Operates a program that places individuals in work camps at home and abroad (1200 short-term "peace corps" experiences in 70 countries). Much of the work involves construction, agricultural, and environmental programs. Contact: Volunteers for Peace, Inc., Tiffany Road, Belmont, VT 05730, Tel. 802/259-2759. Visit their Web site for more information: *www.vfp.org.*

Major job listing services that provide biweekly or monthly information on job vacancies with nonprofit organizations include:

➤ *Community Jobs: The Employment Newspaper For the Non-Profit Sector:* As mentioned in Chapter 5, this is a "must" resource for anyone looking for a job with nonprofits. Each monthly issue includes some listings for international nonprofit organizations. Individuals can subscribe by sending $29 for 3 issues or $39 for 6 issues to: Access: Networking in the Public Interest, 1001 Connecticut Avenue NW, Suite 838, Washington, DC 20036, Tel. 202/785-4233. Visit their Web site for more information: *www.communityjobs.org*

➤ *International Career Employment Opportunities:* Published weekly and includes more than 500 current openings in the U.S. and abroad, in foreign affairs, international trade and finance, international development and assistance, foreign languages, international program administration, international educational and exchange programs, including internships. Includes positions with the Federal government, U.S. corporations, nonprofits, and international institutions. Contact: International Careers, 1088 Middle River Road, Stanardsville, VA 22973, Tel. 1-800-291-4618 or Fax 804/985-6828. Subscriptions for individuals cost $26 for 6 issues; $46 for 12 issues; $86 for 24 issues; and $149 for 49 issues (1 year). Includes money back guarantee. They also operate a resume database. You can order online by visiting their Web site: *www.internationaljobs.org*

➤ *International Employment Hotline:* This is a monthly newspaper which includes over 300 job vacancies per issue. It's available in both hardcopy and email versions through the same publisher as the International Career Employment Opportunities: International Careers, 1088 Middle River Road, Stanardsville, VA 22973, Tel. 1-800-291-4618 or Fax 804/985-6828. Subscriptions for individuals cost $21 for 3 issues; $39 for 6 issues; and $69 for 12 issues (1 year). Accepts online orders: *www.internationaljobs.org*

➤ *International Employment Gazette:* One of the newest and most comprehensive bi-weekly publications listing more than 400 vacancies in each 64-page issue. Includes many jobs in construction and business but also with nonprofit organizations. Offers a custom-designed International Placement Network service for individuals. Contact: International Employment Gazette, 220 N. Main Street, Suite 100, Greenville, SC 29609, Tel. 1-800-882-9188 or fax 1-864-235-3369. $40 for 6 issues; $60 for 12 issues; $95 for 24 issues (1 year). Visit their Web site for placing online orders: *www.amsquare.com/america/gazette.html*

➤ *Career Network:* A monthly job listing bulletin published by the Global Health Council (formerly the National Council for International Health), 1701 K Street NW, Suite 600, Washington, DC 20006, Tel. 202/833-5900. Includes jobs for health care professionals only. One of the best networks and resources for finding international jobs in health care. Available in both paper an electronic (email) versions:

	Paper	Email
1 month		
member	$10.00	
nonmember	$20.00	
1 year		
member	$60.00	$25.00
nonmember	$120.00	$50.00

Visit their Web site (in transition from old to new) for more information: *www.ncih.org* or *www.globalhealthcouncil.com*

➤ *Monday Developments:* Published by InterAction, 1717 Massachusetts Avenue NW, Suite 801, Washington, DC 20036, Tel. 202/667-8227. Published biweekly (every other Monday). Single issue is $4.00. A one-year subscription costs $65.

If you are a **Returned Peace Corps Volunteer** (RPCV), you are in good luck. The Peace Corps takes care of its own. You will want to use the job services available through the Returned Volunteer Services office: Peace Corps, 1900 L Street NW, Suite 205, Washington, DC 20036, Tel. 202/606-7728 or Fax 202/293-7554, or visit the RPCV section on the agency's Web site: *www.peacecorps.gov*. It may well be worth your time and effort to visit this office. After all, Washington, DC is located in the heart of hundreds of organizations offering international job opportunities for those interested in pursuing jobs and careers with nonprofit organizations as well as with consulting firms and educational organizations relevant to the Peace Corps experience. Better still, many of these organizations are staffed by individuals who are part of the growing "old boy/girl network" of ex-Peace Corps volunteers who look favorably toward individuals with Peace Corps experience. At the same time, many nonprofit organizations, consulting firms, and educational organizations automatically contact this office when they have impending vacancies. Please do not contact this office unless you are a returned volunteer. This already over-worked office can only provide information and services to its former volunteers and staff members—both long-term and recently separated. If you left Peace Corps 20 years ago, you can still use this service. It has an excellent library of international resources as well as numerous job listings relevant to its volunteers. It also publishes a biweekly job listing bulletin called *HOTLINE: A Bulletin of Opportunities for Returned Peace Corps Volunteers*. This publication will be mailed free to all volunteers during the two-year period following their Close of Service. Thereafter, you can subscribe to it through the National Peace Corps Association (NPCA). Members of NPCA pay $30.00 a year; nonmembers are charged $50.00 a year. You may want to join the NPCA since it is a network of 16,000 former volunteers with 130 affiliated alumni groups—a good organization through which to conduct an active networking campaign. NPCA can be contacted through the same address as the Returned Volunteer Services office, or you can go directly into NPCA's Web site for information: *www.rpcv.org*

Job Search Strategies

Use the same strategies for landing a job with an international nonprofit organization as you would for any other nonprofit organization. The international job arena is a highly networked community: whom you know and your ubiquitous "connections" will serve you well in finding a job with an international nonprofit. You should do a great deal of networking, informational interviewing, and moving your face, name, and resume among key people associated with these organizations at both the staff and board levels. Success in landing such a job will take time, tenacity, and a positive attitude. Your best locations for literally "hitting the streets" and "pounding the pavement" for international nonprofit organ-izations will be Washington, DC and New York City.

Indeed, many international nonprofit organizations are headquartered in the United States, especially New York City and Washington, DC, but many of them maintain substantial field operations in developing countries. While most nonprofits hire through headquarters, many also hire directly in the field. If you are already in the field and neither have the time nor money to travel to Washington, DC or New York City to conduct an intensive job search, make sure you develop contacts with field representatives in your area. Nonprofit organizations tend to be very field oriented and thus many useful job contacts can be made at the field level. Your research on each organization will determine how, where, and with whom to best target your job search within each organization.

International Nonprofits

International nonprofits are modern-day missionaries who are less moti-vated by an evangelical zeal to save souls than by a commitment to humanity—help the very poor move into the mainstream of development. These organizations appeal to a certain type of person who still has a missionary zeal to improve the conditions of poor people throughout the world. They tend to be dedicated to certain human values and committed to helping others. Working conditions for employees of these organiza-tions can be difficult and pay is often low. But these organizations generate a sense of personal satisfaction that cannot always be matched by working for businesses, government, or private contracting firms.

While many of these groups are funded by individual and corporate contributions, most also receive contracts and grants from government agencies and foundations. Some of the more enterprising child survival groups, such as Save the Children Foundation, Foster Parents Plan, Children International, Childreach, and Christian Children's Fund, also operate individual "sponsorship" programs for generating income. You may frequently see their highly effective ads on television which use a variety of major media personalities to solicit for sponsors who pay anywhere from $12 to $22 a month to "sponsor" a child.

NGOs and PVOs are increasingly playing a major role in developing countries. Funding agencies view these groups as most capable of making a difference in developing countries. Their extensive field staffs, commitment to change, and adaptability make them favorite candidates for funding by government agencies and foundations. They continue to expand their operations in Third and Fourth World countries. Consequently, many of these organizations may experience significant growth during the coming decade.

The following international nonprofit organizations are some of the major players in international relief and development. Many are huge organizations with staffs in excess of 1,000 and with annual budgets exceeding $300 million. Some organizations may have 90 percent of their staffs assigned to field operations abroad whereas others may have less than 50 percent stationed abroad. Many of these organizations also operate large volunteer programs.

A few international nonprofits were included in Chapter 7: ACCION International, Bread for the World, Greenpeace. Oxfam America, World Resources Institute, World Wildlife Fund, Worldteach, and the Worldwatch Institute. Other groups, such as Planned Parenthood Federation of America, with an annual budget over $400 million and a staff of more than 10,000, have large international operations. You may want to review these international nonprofits along with the ones outlined in this chapter.

ADVENTIST DEVELOPMENT AND RELIEF AGENCY INTERNATIONAL
12501 Old Columbia Pike
Silver Spring, MD 20904
Tel. 301/680-6380 or Fax 301/680-6370
Web site: *www.adra.org*

PURPOSE: To provide technical assistance in the areas of education, agriculture, health care, nutrition, community development, social welfare, and disaster relief in Africa, Asia, Latin America, and the Pacific region. The development agency of the Seventh Day Adventist Church. Operates in 140 countries.
ACTIVITY: Education, training, technical assistance.
BUDGET: $85,000,000
EMPLOYEES: 92

AFRICARE
440 R Street NW
Washington, DC 20001
Tel. 202/462-3614 or Fax 202/387-1034
Web site: *www.africare.org*

PURPOSE: To provide assistance to Africa in the areas of water resources, agriculture and food production, education, construction, medical care, health services, and refugee assistance. 2,300 members.
ACTIVITY: Education, technical assistance.
BUDGET: $26,500,000
EMPLOYEES: 100

AMERICAN FRIENDS SERVICE COMMITTEE
1501 Cherry Street
Philadelphia, PA 19102
Tel. 215/241-7000 or Fax 215/241-7247
Web site: *www.afsc.org*

PURPOSE: To alleviate human suffering and promote global peace. Programs focus on integrated community development, agricultural production, cooperative organization, construction, public health services, peace education, and refugee assistance. Staff and volunteers operate in 22 countries of Africa, Latin America, the Middle East and Southeast Asia.
ACTIVITY: Education, technical assistance.
BUDGET: $27,700,000
EMPLOYEES: 356

AMERICAN JEWISH JOINT DISTRIBUTION COMMITTEE
711 Third Avenue, 10th Floor
New York, NY 10017-4014
Tel. 212/687-6200 or Fax 212/682-7262
Web site: *www.ajc.org*

PURPOSE: To maintain health, welfare, relief assistance, and rehabilitation programs for needy Jews in over 50 countries in Asia, Africa, Europe, the former Soviet Union, and Latin America. Operates sponsored programs in more than 85 countries.
ACTIVITY: Education, community services, technical assistance.
BUDGET: $186,600,000. Primarily funded by the United Jewish Appeal.
EMPLOYEES: N/A (400+)

AMERICAN RED CROSS
INTERNATIONAL SERVICES
8111 Gatehouse Road, 6th Floor
Falls Church, VA 22042
Tel. 703/206-7090
Web site: *www.redcross.org/intl/*

PURPOSE: To provide relief to disaster victims and refugees and extend assistance in the areas of health care, education, HIV/AIDS education, blood collection and processing, and capacity building. Collaborates with 170 International Federation of Red Cross and Red Crescent societies, the world's largest humanitarian network. This organization is a part of the larger American Red Cross effort which involves both domestic and international operations.
ACTIVITY: Education, technical assistance.
BUDGET: $1,500,000,000 (American Red Cross National Headquarters)
STAFF: 28,323 (American Red Cross National Headquarters)

AMERICARES FOUNDATION
161 Cherry Street
New Canaan, CT 06840
Tel. 203/966-6028 or Fax 203/972-0116
Web site: *www.americares.org*

PURPOSE: To provide international relief by soliciting donations of medicines, medical supplies, and other materials from American companies and delivering them to health and welfare professionals in the U.S. and 118 other countries. Responds to disasters caused by earthquakes, famines, floods, political upheavals, and wars.
ACTIVITY: Education, research, technical assistance, airlift/sealift.
BUDGET: $330,000,000
EMPLOYEES: N/A (1000+)

CARE
(COOPERATIVE FOR AMERICAN RELIEF
EVERYWHERE, INC.)
151 Ellis Street
Atlanta, GA 30303
Tel. 404/681-2552 or Fax 404/577-9418
Web site: *www.care.org*

PURPOSE: To provide international aid and development assistance by providing food, self-help development, disaster aid, and health care training overseas. Operates in 66 developing countries in Asia, Africa, Europe, and Latin America.
ACTIVITY: Emergency relief, technical assistance, education, research.

BUDGET: $454,000,000
EMPLOYEES: 9,000

CATHOLIC RELIEF SERVICES
209 W. Fayette Street
Baltimore, MD 21201
Tel. 410/625-2220 or Fax 410/685-1635
Web site: *www.devcap.org/crs*

PURPOSE: To conduct programs of disaster response, refugee relief and rehabilitation, social welfare services, and socio-economic development in 67 countries. The nonevangelical overseas relief and self-help development agency of the American Catholic community.
ACTIVITY: Disaster relief, education.
BUDGET: $246,000,000
EMPLOYEES: 1,600

CHILDREACH
155 Plan Way
Warwick, RI 02886
Tel. 401/738-5600 or Fax 401/738-5608
Web site: *www.childreach.org*

PURPOSE: To link caring people in the U.S. with children and their families in developing countries. Conducts one of the most active television and direct-mail campaigns to find "sponsors" for children. U.S. member of PLAN International.
ACTIVITY: Sponsorship, education, community development, technical assistance.
BUDGET: $33,759,000
EMPLOYEES: 86

CHRISTIAN CHILDREN'S FUND
2821 Emerywood Parkway
Richmond, VA 23294-3725
Tel. 804/756-2700 or Fax 804/756-2718
Web site: *www.christianchildrensfund.org*

PURPOSE: To provide assistance to needy children and their families in various countries by linking sponsors in the U.S. with children abroad. Operates in 32 countries, including the United States.
ACTIVITY: Sponsorship, education, community development, technical assistance.
BUDGET: $117,000,000
EMPLOYEES: 587

CHURCH WORLD SERVICE
475 Riverside Drive, Rm. 678
New York, NY 10115-0050
Tel. 212/870-2257
Web site: *http://ncccusa.org/cws/mainone.html*

PURPOSE: To provide worldwide development and emergency aid to the poor in more than 70 countries of Asia, Africa, Latin America, Middle East, and Eastern Europe. Responds to famines, floods, wars, and other emergencies. Cooperative agency of 34 Protestant, Anglican, and orthodox communions of the National Council of Churches of Christ in the U.S. (*http://ncccusa.org*)
ACTIVITY: Relief, technical assistance, reconstruction.
BUDGET: $41,900,000
EMPLOYEES: 130

FOOD FOR THE HUNGRY, INC.
7729 E. Greenway Road
Scottsdale, AZ 85260
Tel. 602/998-3100 or Fax 602/443-1420
Web site: *www.fh.org*

PURPOSE: To extend disaster relief and long-range self-help assistance. Provides information about world hunger, assist with direct relief, and offer developmental assistance in more than 25 countries of Asia, Africa, and Latin America. Conducts a child-sponsorship program that provides food, shelter, education, and training opportunities.
ACTIVITY: Relief, technical assistance, education.
BUDGET: $44,422,000
EMPLOYEES: N/A (300+)

HELEN KELLER INTERNATIONAL
90 Washington Street
15th Floor
New York, NY 10006
Tel. 212/943-0890 or Fax 212/943-1220
Web site: *www.hki.org*

PURPOSE: To assist governments and voluntary agencies in Asia, Africa, and the Americas in establishing services to prevent or cure eye diseases and blindness and to rehabilitate and educate visually disabled persons.
ACTIVITY: Education, research, technical assistance, rehabilitation.
BUDGET: $8,700,000
EMPLOYEES: 50

INSTITUTE OF INTERNATIONAL EDUCATION
809 United Nations Plaza
New York, NY 10017-3580
Tel. 212/883-8200 or Fax 212/984-5452
Web site: *www.iie.org*

PURPOSE: To develop better understanding between the people of the U.S. and those of other countries through educational exchange programs for students, scholars, artists, leaders, and specialists. Provides technical assistance in the area of educational development through the support of training and education efforts.
ACTIVITY: Exchange, education, research, technical assistance.
BUDGET: $91,825,000
EMPLOYEES: 350

INTERNATIONAL RESCUE COMMITTEE
122 E. 42nd Street
New York, NY 10165
Tel. 212/551-3000 or Fax 212/551-3180
Web site: *intrescom.org*

PURPOSE: To assist refugee victims of religious, political, and racial persecution, civil strife, famine, and war. Operates programs in Africa, Asia, Central America, Europe, North America, and the Middle East. Founded by Albert Einstein.
ACTIVITY: Relief, education.
BUDGET: $84,207,000
EMPLOYEES: 500

LUTHERAN WORLD RELIEF
390 Park Avenue South
New York, NY 10016
Tel. 212/532-6350 or Fax 212/213-6081
Web site: *www.lwr.org*

PURPOSE: To promote integrated community development projects which are usually operated through counterpart church-related agencies in the areas of disaster relief, refugee assistance, and social and economic development. Operates programs in Asia, Africa, the Middle East, and Latin America.
ACTIVITY: Education, research, technical assistance, relief.
BUDGET: $20,900,000
EMPLOYEES: N/A (300+)

MAP INTERNATIONAL
2200 Glynco Parkway, P.O. Box 215000
Brunswick, GA 31521-5000
Tel. 912/265-6010 or Fax 912/265-6170
Web site: *www.map.org*

PURPOSE: To help developing countries design, implement, and evaluate community development projects focusing on food production, water resources, health services, nutrition education, and disaster and emergency relief. Works with Christian mission organizations and churches in coordinating programs providing medical supplies, community health developing, emergency relief.
ACTIVITY: Education, community development, technical assistance, relief.
BUDGET: $148,200,000
EMPLOYEES: 200

MERCY CORPS INTERNATIONAL
3030 SW First Avenue
Portland, OR 97201
Tel. 1-800-292-3355 or Fax 503/796-6844
Web site: *www.mercycorps.org*

PURPOSE: To provide agricultural development assistance, primary health care, education, and emergency relief services. Motivates and educates the public about the plight of the poor and works for peace and justice. Provides assistance to 2.2 million people in 23 countries.
ACTIVITY: Education, training, community development, technical assistance.
BUDGET: $111,000,000
EMPLOYEES: N/A (600+)

PACT
(PRIVATE AGENCIES COLLABORATING TOGETHER)
1901 Pennsylvania Avenue NW, 5th Floor
Washington, DC 20006
Tel. 202/466-5666 or Fax 202/466-5669
Web site: *www.pactworld.org*

PURPOSE: To strengthen the community-focused nonprofit sector worldwide. Promotes participatory development approaches which promote social, economic, political, and environmental justice in the areas of microenterprise development, health care, AIDS treatment and prevention, child welfare, environmental protection, nonformal education, women's issues, human rights.
ACTIVITY: Education, training, technical assistance.
BUDGET: $20,000,000
EMPLOYEES: 40

PATHFINDER INTERNATIONAL
9 Galen Street, Suite 217
Watertown, MA 02172-4501
Tel. 617/924-7200 or Fax 617/294-3833
Web site: *www.pathfind.org*

PURPOSE: To promote population planning through innovative efforts to make fertility services more effective, less expensive, and more readily available to people in developing countries. Improves welfare of families and assists countries in implementing population policies.
ACTIVITY: Education, training, technical assistance.
BUDGET: $50,000,000
EMPLOYEES: 170

PLAN INTERNATIONAL
P.O. Box 7670
Warwick, RI 02887
Tel. 401/294-3693 or Fax 401/295-7062
Web site: *www.plan-international.org*

PURPOSE: To collect and disburse funds raised by 9 national groups, including Childreach (see entry above), for sponsoring children in developing nations of Africa, Asia, and Latin America. Uses funds for promoting self-sustaining communities through education of residents and technical assistance. One of the world's largest child-focused development organizations.
ACTIVITY: Education, training, technical assistance, sponsorship.
BUDGET: $200,000,000
EMPLOYEES: 4,800

POPULATION COUNCIL
1 Dag Hammarskjold Plaza
New York, NY 10017
Tel. 212/339-0500 or Fax 212/755-6052
Web site: *www.popcouncil.org*

PURPOSE: To assist decision makers and population professionals in developing countries to design, implement, and evaluate research and assistance programs. Conducts health and social science programs and research relevant to developing countries; conducts biomedical research to develop and improve contraceptive technology; provides advice and technical assistance to governments, international agencies, and organizations; disseminates information.
ACTIVITY: Education, research, training, technical assistance.
BUDGET: $50,000,000
EMPLOYEES: 430

SAVE THE CHILDREN FEDERATION, INC.
54 Wilton Road
Westport, CT 06880
Tel. 203/221-4000 or Fax 203/227-5667
Web site: *www.savethechildren.org*

PURPOSE: To assist children, families, and communities in achieving social and economic stability through community development and family self-help projects in health, education, natural resource management, economic opportunities, and emergency response. Operates in more than 40 countries, many being the poorest of the poor.
ACTIVITY: Education, research, technical assistance, relief.
BUDGET: $105,071,000
EMPLOYEES: 2,474

TECHNOSERVE
49 Day Street
Norwalk, CT 06854
Tel. 203/852-0377 or Fax 203/838-6717
Web site: *www.technoserve.org*

PURPOSE: To improve the economic and social well-being of low-income people in Latin America, Africa, and Eastern Europe. Provides agricultural and business training to help poor people build self-sustaining enterprises. Deals directly with more than 175 enterprises and institutions.
ACTIVITY: Research, technical assistance.
BUDGET: $8,000,000
EMPLOYEES: 225

U.S. COMMITTEE FOR UNICEF
333 E. 38th Street
New York, NY 10016
Tel. 212/686-5522 or Fax 212/779-1679
Web site: *www.unicefusa.org*

PURPOSE: To inform U.S. citizens of the U.S. programs of the United Nations Children's Fund and to provide opportunities for American citizens and groups to support its activities and appeals.
ACTIVITY: Education, public relations.
BUDGET: $60,408,000
EMPLOYEES: 150

VOLUNTEERS IN OVERSEAS COOPERATIVE ASSISTANCE
ACDI/VOCA
50 F Street NW, Suite 1075
Washington, DC 20001
Tel. 202/383-4961 or Fax 202/783-7204
Web site: *www.acdivoca.org*

PURPOSE: To recruit and assign volunteers on a short-term basis to provide technical assistance to cooperatives and agricultural producers in developing countries. Operates 23 offices in Africa, Asia, Latin America, and Eastern Europe.
ACTIVITY: Education, technical assistance.
BUDGET: $12,000,000
EMPLOYEES: 150

WINROCK INTERNATIONAL INSTITUTE FOR AGRICULTURAL DEVELOPMENT
38 Winrock Drive
Morrilton, AR 72110-9537
Tel. 501/727-5435 or Fax 501/727-5417
Web site: *www.winrock.org*

PURPOSE: To alleviate poverty and hunger worldwide through agricultural, rural development, and environmental resources management assistance. Develops farming systems.
ACTIVITY: Education, research, technical assistance.
BUDGET: $36,800,000
EMPLOYEES: 225

WORLD CONCERN
19303 Fremont Avenue N.
Seattle, WA 98133
Tel. 206/546-7201 or Fax 206/546-7269
Web site: *www.worldconcern.org*

PURPOSE: To empower refugees and poor people through relief and self-help development strategies. Improve health, assist families in attaining self-sufficiency, ensure basic education, prevent diseases, protect livestock, and improve the environment. Christian group. Operates in 85 countries.
ACTIVITY: Education, technical assistance, community development.
BUDGET: $21,000,000
EMPLOYEES: 45

WORLD RELIEF
P.O. Box WRC
Wheaton, IL 60189
Tel. 630/665-0235 or Fax 630/665-0129
Web site: *www.worldrelief.org*

PURPOSE: To provide emergency aid, development assistance, and refugee services in Asia, Africa, Latin America, and the U.S. Conducts programs of disaster relief; refugee relief and resettlement; community development programs, including public health, education, and economic assistance.
ACTIVITY: Education, technical assistance, community development.
BUDGET: $20,000,000
EMPLOYEES: 250

WORLD VISION
34834 Weyerhaeuser Way S.
Federal Way, WA 98001
Tel. 253/815-1000
Web site: *www.worldvision.org*

PURPOSE: To help establish agencies in 102 countries to meet emergency needs, carry out development activities, and provide needed assistance for over 14,000,000 people. Provides food, medicine, education, equipment, personnel, and literature for schools, hospitals, and communities. A Christian relief and development organization.
ACTIVITY: Education, technical assistance, community development.
BUDGET: $300,000,000
EMPLOYEES: 572

Index

FEATURED ORGANIZATIONS AND EMPLOYERS

The Authors

Ronald L. Krannich, Ph.D. and Caryl Rae Krannich, Ph.D., are two of America's leading career and travel writers who have authored more than 40 books. They currently operate Development Concepts Inc., a training, consulting, and publishing firm. A former Peace Corps Volunteer and Fulbright Scholar, Ron received his Ph.D. in Political Science from Northern Illinois University. Caryl received her Ph.D. in Speech Communication from Penn State University.

Ron and Caryl are former university professors, high school teachers, management trainers, and government consultants. As trainers and consultants, they have completed numerous projects on management, career development, local government, population planning, and rural development in the United States and abroad.

The Krannichs' career and business work encompasses nearly 30 books they have authored on a variety of subjects: key job search skills, public speaking, government jobs, international careers, nonprofit organizations, and career transitions. Their work represents one of today's most extensive and highly praised collections of career and business writing: *101 Dynamite Answers to Interview Questions, 101 Secrets of Highly Effective Speakers, 201 Dynamite Job Search Letters, The Best Jobs For the 21st Century, Change Your Job Change Your Life, The Complete Guide to International Jobs and Careers, Discover the Best Jobs For You, Dynamite Cover Letters, Dynamite Resumes, Dynamite*

Salary Negotiations, Get a Raise in 7 Days, Dynamite Tele-Search, The Educator's Guide to Alternative Jobs and Careers, From Air Force Blue to Corporate Gray, From Army Green to Corporate Gray, From Navy Blue to Corporate Gray, Resumes and Job Search Letters For Transitioning Military Personnel, High Impact Resumes and Letters, International Jobs Directory, Interview For Success, Find a Federal Job Fast, Jobs For People Who Love Travel, and *Dynamite Networking For Dynamite Jobs.* Their books are found in most major bookstores, libraries, and career centers as well as can be ordered directly from Impact's Web site: *www.impactpublications.com.* Many of their works are available interactively on CD-ROM (*The Ultimate Job Source*).

Ron and Caryl live a double career life. Authors of 13 travel books, the Krannichs continue to pursue their international interests through their innovative and highly acclaimed Impact Guides travel series (*"The Treasures and Pleasures....Best of the Best"*) which currently encompasses separate titles on Italy, France, China, Hong Kong, Thailand, Indonesia, Singapore, Malaysia, India, and Australia. When not found at their home and business in Virginia, they are probably somewhere in Europe, Asia, Africa, the Middle East, the South Pacific, or the Caribbean pursuing one of their major passions—researching and writing about quality arts and antiques.

The Krannichs reside in Northern Virginia. Frequent speakers and seminar leaders, they can be contacted through the publisher or by email: *krannich@impactpublications.com*

Career Resources

C ontact Impact Publications for a free annotated listing of career resources or visit their World Wide Web site for a complete listing of career resources: *www.impactpublications.com*. The following career resources, many of which were mentioned in Chapter 5, are available directly from Impact Publications. Complete the following form or list the titles, include postage (see formula at the end), enclose payment, and send your order to:

IMPACT PUBLICATIONS
9104-N Manassas Drive
Manassas Park, VA 20111-5211
1-800-361-1055 (orders only)
Tel. 703/361-7300 or Fax 703/335-9486
E-mail address: *nonprofit@impactpublications.com*

Orders from individuals must be prepaid by check, moneyorder, Visa, MasterCard, or American Express. We accept telephone and fax orders.

Qty.	TITLES	Price	TOTAL
	Key Nonprofit Books and Directories (From pages 57-62, 67)		
___	100 Best Nonprofits to Work For	16.95	___
___	Business Phone Book USA 1999	160.00	___
___	Community Jobs (6 month, 6-issue subscription)	39.00	___
___	Community Jobs (1 year, 12-issue subscription)	76.00	___
___	Directory of Executive Recruiters	44.95	___
___	Encyclopedia of Associations: National Organizations	490.00	___

____ Encyclopedia of Associations: Regional, State,
    and Local Organizations   570.00   ____
____ From Making a Profit To Making a Difference   16.95   ____
____ Good Works: A Guide to Careers in Social Change   24.00   ____
____ In Search of America's Best Nonprofits   25.00   ____
____ Invest Yourself: The Catalog of Volunteer Opportunities   8.00   ____
____ Jobs and Careers With Nonprofit Organizations   17.95   ____
____ National Job Hotline Directory   16.95   ____
____ National Trade and Professional Associations   129.00   ____
____ Nonprofits and Education Job Finder   16.95   ____
____ Research Centers Directory   548.00   ____

International and Travel Jobs (pages 222-223)

____ Back Door Guide to Short Term Job Adventures   19.95   ____
____ Careers in International Affairs   17.95   ____
____ Complete Guide to International Jobs & Careers   24.95   ____
____ Directory of Jobs and Careers Abroad   16.95   ____
____ Directory of Overseas Summer Jobs   16.95   ____
____ Directory of Work and Study in Developing Countries   16.95   ____
____ Getting Your Job in the Middle East   19.95   ____
____ Great Jobs Abroad   14.95   ____
____ Health Professionals Abroad   17.95   ____
____ International Directory of Voluntary Work   15.95   ____
____ International Jobs   16.00   ____
____ International Job Finder   16.95   ____
____ International Jobs Directory   19.95   ____
____ Jobs For People Who Love Travel   15.95   ____
____ Jobs in Paradise   14.95   ____
____ Jobs In Russia and the Newly Independent States   15.95   ____
____ Jobs Worldwide   17.95   ____
____ Work Abroad   15.95   ____
____ Work Your Way Around the World   17.95   ____

Government Jobs

____ Complete Guide to Public Employment   19.95   ____
____ Directory of Federal Jobs and Employers   21.95   ____
____ Federal Applications That Get Results   23.95   ____
____ Federal Resume Guidebook (with disk)   34.95   ____
____ Find a Federal Job Fast   15.95   ____
____ Government Job Finder   16.95   ____

Job Search Strategies and Tactics

____ Change Your Job, Change Your Life   17.95   ____
____ Complete Idiot's Guide to Getting the Job You Want   24.95   ____
____ Complete Job Finder's Guide to the 90's   13.95   ____
____ Five Secrets to Finding a Job   12.95   ____
____ How to Succeed Without a Career Path   13.95   ____

___ Me, Myself, and I, Inc	17.95	___
___ New Rites of Passage at $100,000+	29.95	___
___ The Pathfinder	14.00	___
___ What Color Is Your Parachute?	16.95	___
___ Who's Running Your Career	14.95	___

Best Jobs and Employers For the 21st Century

___ 50 Coolest Jobs in Sports	15.95	___
___ Adams Jobs Almanac 1998	15.95	___
___ American Almanac of Jobs and Salaries	20.00	___
___ Best Jobs For the 21st Century	19.95	___
___ Breaking and Entering: Jobs in Film Production	17.95	___
___ Great Jobs Ahead	11.95	___
___ Jobs 1998	15.00	___
___ The Top 100	19.95	___

Key Directories

___ American Salaries and Wages Survey	110.00	___
___ Careers Encyclopedia	39.95	___
___ Complete Guide to Occupational Exploration	39.95	___
___ Consultants & Consulting Organizations Directory	605.00	___
___ National Job Bank 1999	350.00	___
___ Occupational Outlook Handbook, 1998-99	22.95	___
___ O*NET Dictionary of Occupational Titles	49.95	___
___ Professional Careers Sourcebook	99.00	___

Electronic Job Search

___ CareerXroads 1999	22.95	___
___ Guide to Internet Job Search	14.95	___
___ How to Get Your Dream Job Using the Web	29.99	___
___ Job Searching Online For Dummies	24.95	___

$100,000+ Jobs

___ The $100,000 Club	25.00	___
___ 100 Winning Resumes For $100,000+ Jobs	24.95	___
___ 201 Winning Cover Letters For $100,000+ Jobs	24.95	___
___ 1500+ KeyWords For $100,000+ Jobs	14.95	___
___ New Rites of Passage at $100,000+	29.95	___
___ Six-Figure Consulting	17.95	___

Finding Great Jobs

___ 101 Ways to Power Up Your Job Search	12.95	___
___ 110 Biggest Mistakes Job Hunters Make	19.95	___
___ Careers For College Majors	32.95	___
___ College Grad Job Hunter	14.95	___

___ Get Ahead! Stay Ahead!	12.95	___
___ Get a Job You Love!	19.95	___
___ Great Jobs For Liberal Arts Majors	11.95	___
___ Knock 'Em Dead	12.95	___
___ New Relocating Spouse's Guide to Employment	14.95	___
___ No One Is Unemployable	29.95	___
___ Perfect Pitch	13.99	___
___ Professional's Job Finder	18.95	___
___ Strategic Job Jumping	20.00	___
___ Top Career Strategies For the Year 2000 & Beyond	12.00	___
___ What Do I Say Next?	20.00	___
___ What Employers Really Want	14.95	___

Assessment

___ Discover the Best Jobs For You	14.95	___
___ Discover What You're Best At	12.00	___
___ Do What You Are	16.95	___
___ Finding Your Perfect Work	16.95	___
___ I Could Do Anything If Only I Knew What It Was	19.95	___

Inspiration and Empowerment

___ 100 Ways to Motivate Yourself	15.99	___
___ Chicken Soup For the Soul Series	75.95	___
___ Doing Work You Love	14.95	___
___ Emotional Intelligence	13.95	___
___ Personal Job Power	12.95	___
___ Power of Purpose	20.00	___
___ Seven Habits of Highly Effective People	14.00	___
___ Your Signature Path	24.95	___

Resumes and Cover Letters

___ 101 Best Resumes	10.95	___
___ 101 Quick Tips For a Dynamite Resume	13.95	___
___ 201 Dynamite Job Search Letters	19.95	___
___ America's Top Resumes For America's Top Jobs	19.95	___
___ Asher's Bible of Executive Resumes	29.95	___
___ Complete Idiot's Guide to Writing the Perfect Resume	16.95	___
___ Cover Letters For Dummies	12.99	___
___ Cover Letters That Knock 'Em Dead	10.95	___
___ Dynamite Cover Letters	14.95	___
___ Dynamite Resumes	14.95	___
___ Heart and Soul Resumes	15.95	___
___ High Impact Resumes & Letters	19.95	___
___ Internet Resumes	14.95	___
___ Resume Catalog	15.95	___
___ Resume Shortcuts	14.95	___
___ Resumes For Dummies	12.99	___

___	Resumes That Knock 'Em Dead	14.95	___
___	Sure-Hire Resumes	14.95	___

Networking

___	Dynamite Networking For Dynamite Jobs	15.95	___
___	Dynamite Telesearch	12.95	___
___	How to Work a Room	11.99	___
___	Power Schmoozing	12.95	___
___	Power to Get In	24.95	___

Interview, Communication, Salary Negotiations

___	101 Dynamite Answers to Interview Questions	12.95	___
___	101 Dynamite Questions to Ask At Your Job Interview	14.95	___
___	101 Secrets of Highly Effective Speakers	14.95	___
___	111 Dynamite Ways to Ace Your Job Interview	13.95	___
___	Dynamite Salary Negotiations	15.95	___
___	Get a Raise in 7 Days	14.95	___
___	Interview For Success	15.95	___
___	Job Interview For Dummies	12.99	___

SUBTOTAL   ___

Virginia residents add 4½% sales tax   ___

POSTAGE/HANDLING ($5 for first
product and 8% of SUBTOTAL over $30)   <u>$5.00</u>

8% of SUBTOTAL over $30 ------------------------- ___

TOTAL ENCLOSED ----------------------- ___

NAME _____

ADDRESS _____

_____

❑ I enclose check/moneyorder for $ _____ made payable to
    IMPACT PUBLICATIONS.

❑ Please charge $ _____ to my credit card:
    ❑ Visa   ❑ MasterCard   ❑ American Express   ❑ Discover
    Card # _____
    Expiration date: _____/_____ Phone _____/_____
    Signature _____

Your One-Stop Online Superstore
Hundreds of Terrific Resources Conveniently Available On the World Wide Web 24-Hours a Day, 365 Days a Year!

Ever wanted to know what are the newest and best books, directories, newsletters, wall charts, training programs, videos, CD-ROMs, computer software, and kits available to help you land a job, negotiate a higher salary, or start your own business? What about finding a job in Asia or relocating to San Francisco? Are you curious about how to find a job 24-hours a day by using the Internet or what you'll be doing five years from now? Trying to keep up-to-date on the latest career resources but not able to find the latest catalogs, brochures, or newsletters on today's "best of the best" resources?

Welcome to the first virtual career bookstore on the Internet. Now you're only a "click" away with Impact Publication's electronic solution to the resource challenge. Impact Publications, one of the nation's leading publishers and distributors of career resources, offers the most comprehensive "Career Superstore and Warehouse" on the Internet. The bookstore is jam-packed with the latest job and career resources on:

- Alternative jobs and careers
- Self-assessment
- Career planning and job search
- Employers
- Relocation and cities
- Resumes
- Cover Letters
- Dress, image, and etiquette
- Education
- Recruitment
- Military
- Salaries
- Interviewing
- Nonprofits

- Empowerment
- Self-esteem
- Goal setting
- Executive recruiters
- Entrepreneurship
- Government
- Networking
- Electronic job search
- International jobs
- Travel
- Law
- Training and presentations
- Minorities
- Physically challenged

The bookstore also includes sections for ex-offenders and middle schools.

"This is more than just a bookstore offering lots of product," say Drs. Ron and Caryl Krannich, two of the nation's leading career experts and authors and developers of this on-line bookstore. *"We're an important resource center for libraries, corporations, government, educators, trainers, and career counselors who are constantly defining and redefining this dynamic field. Of the thousands of career resources we review each year, we only select the 'best of the best.'"*

Visit this rich site and you'll quickly discover just about everything you ever wanted to know about finding jobs, changing careers, and starting your own business—including many useful resources that are difficult to find in local bookstores and libraries. The site also includes tips for job search success and monthly specials. Its shopping cart and special search feature make this one of the most convenient Web sites to use. Impact's Internet address is:

www.impactpublications.com